Risk Management with Derivatives

Finance and Capital Markets series

Erik Banks
Asia Pacific Derivative Markets
Erik Banks
The Credit Risk of Complex Derivatives
Erik Banks
The Credit Risk of Financial Instruments
Erik Banks
Emerging Asian Fixed Income Markets
Nick Cavalla
OTC Markets in Derivative Instruments: strategic issues in asset/liability management
Kevin Connolly and George Phillips
Japanese Warrant Markets
Daniel Corrigan and Mark Pohlman
Bunds and Bund Futures
Charles Errington
Financial Engineering: a handbook for managing the risk-reward relationship
Andrew Inglis-Taylor
The Dictionary of Derivatives
Sandy McKenzie
Risk Management with Derivatives
Judith Mabry (ed)
International Securities Lending
Ron Paterson
Off Balance Sheet Finance
Trevor Pijper
Creative Accounting: the effectiveness of financial reporting in the UK
Zoe Shaw (ed)
International Securitisation: the scope, development and future outlook for asset-backed finance
Robert Tompkins
Bund Options
Robert Tompkins
Options Explained 2e
Jackie Whitley (ed)
The ALCO
Jackie Whitley
Foreign Exchange: function, limits and risk
Richard D. Willsher
Export Finance
Nicholas Wilson (ed)
ESOPs: their role in corporate finance and performance

Risk Management with Derivatives

Editor: **Sandy McKenzie**

MACMILLAN
Business

First published 1992 by
MACMILLAN PRESS LTD
Houndmills, Basingstoke, Hampshire RG21 6XS
and London
Companies and representatives
throughout the world

ISBN 0-333-55924-X

A catalogue record for this book is available from the British Library.

12 11 10 9 8 7 6 5 4
04 03 02 01 00 99 98 97 96

Printed in Great Britain by
Antony Rowe Ltd
Chippenham, Wiltshire

Contents

Acknowledgements

My thanks and appreciation to all at Unique Consultants.

To M. Desmond Fitzgerald and Janette Rutterford for their guidance, cynicism, friendship and many stimulating hours spent in watering holes throughout the world.

To Anna Kellock and Tracey Foxe for the special efforts they make on my behalf and despite the continuous ribald remarks I receive from them.

To my friend and former colleague Charles Beck of J. M. Finn & Co., for his permission to use the checklists in chapter four.

To all my co-authors for their contributions.

My sincere thanks.

Sandy McKenzie
August 1992

To
my sons
Mark Alexander James McKenzie
and
Luke Charles Patrick McKenzie
with love

Contributors

Daniel Corrigan is Associate Director responsible for the Repo desk at the US investment bank, Bear Stearns, in London. Prior to this he was Associate Director and Head of Government Bond Trading and Arbitrage for DG Investment Bank. He has also worked for CL-Alexanders Laing & Cruickshank Ltd., both in London and Tokyo as a Senior Bond Trader/Salesman. He has an MBA from the City University Business School. He has recently published books on the Bund and UK Gilt Markets.

Chris Currington is a partner in Arthur Andersen's Financial Markets Division and is a member of the Canadian and Scottish Institute of Chartered Accountants. Chris returned to Arthur Andersen in 1988, after spending 18 months as European Financial Controller for a major American investment bank. He has also been seconded to an international bank and to a major international trading and broking group. The majority of Chris' work is of an advisory nature, including treasury and risk management studies, business reviews and investigations. Chris has directed numerous reviews on the quality of management, financial dealing and treasury control environments for a number of major UK corporates and for a number of international banks based in London. He is a regular speaker at conferences on risk and treasury management and accounting for new financial products. Chris has also written a number of articles on these topics.

Martyn Holmes is Senior Risk Analyst with The London Clearing House Ltd, the central guarantor for London's futures and options markets. His responsibilities centre on the analysis of counterparty credit risk and default risk management within lerivative markets. He previously worked for the London Traded Options Market and ondon International Financial Futures Exchange.

)amian Kissane is Director, Private Placements at UBS Phillips & Drew, where responsible for development of risk management solutions and products for the st rate and currency problems of companies across Europe. He is also respon- or public and private placements of structured transactions covering debt, com- y and equity linked securities.

ıor to this he was Director, Capital Markets at Mitsubishi Finance International where he was responsible for the marketing of all derivative products in Europe. has extensive prior experience of the trading and hedging of securities, swaps and tions. He lectures throughout the world on all aspects of Corporate Finance and the apital Markets.

Sandy McKenzie is a consultant on derivative products to financial institutions and corporates throughout the world. He is a leading member of the Unique Consultants Ltd teaching faculty and also acts as an advisor on the control and methodology of derivatives trading.

Prior to becoming an independent consultant Sandy McKenzie worked as senior dealer in Financial Futures and Option markets, with responsibility for implementing trading, hedging and arbitrage strategies for many banking, corporate and government clients. He has traded both futures and options on all the world's leading markets. His current interests include the investment use of derivatives, optimal trading strategies and the vital importance of training in today's rapidly changing financial markets.

Chris Painter trained and worked as a banker in the City, specialising in corporate finance. A spell in ship financing and a chance meeting in the USA convinced him of the need for more imaginative use of computers throughout finance. Since then he has developed commercial systems in the derivatives area. In that capacity he has written and lectured on the use of artificial intelligence in risk management systems.

Patrick Thomas is an independent consultant specialising in the quantitative aspects of the securities markets. He is a Visiting Lecturer at the City University Business School and a consultant for the London International Financial Futures Exchange in addition to being involved in many assignments both at home and abroad. He has previously worked as a Senior Financial Analyst and also as a futures and options broker for a large international bank and as a manager in the Corporate Finance Department of an accountancy firm.

John Wisbey is Chairman of Lombard Risk Systems Ltd, and principal architect of the OBERON system used widely by banks and companies in over ten countries for their interest rate derivative product trading and risk management. Prior to developing OBERON he was head of option trading and then a director in the swap group at Kleinwort Benson Ltd in London. He has given lectures to bank traders and to corporate treasurers in several countries on the use of swaps and other derivatives for their risk management.

Introduction

Sandy McKenzie

Future generations will undoubtedly regard the years between 1989 and 1992 as being among the most significant of the twentieth century. If, in 1988, I had predicted that Germany would be reunified, apartheid abolished in South Africa, the breakup of the Warsaw Pact, the breakdown of the Soviet Union and communism, the invasion of Kuwait by Iraq and the subsequent Gulf War, and as I write, the bloody conflict in the Balkans, I suspect I would have been referred for psychiatric help.

In a world which is undergoing dramatic change the risks involved with the age-old business of commerce and finance become ever more marked. The vital need to have control over these business risks has become crucial in determining the success or otherwise of companies involved in the ever opening worldwide marketplace which we find today. Allied with the technological revolution in communications and media, the opening of previously closed doors has led to a diminishing and ever more competitive worldwide business environment. I strongly believe that in the last years of the twentieth century the line between success and failure will become increasingly thin. The ability to adapt to ever changing scenarios will be a crucial factor in determining the profitability of any type of business.

The development and growth of derivative products over the last fifteen years has not been a haphazard occurrence. As the potential rewards and risks of the global business community increase, the genuine need to use these derivatives becomes ever more apparent. Despite the popular misconception that new financial products are the brainchilds of the academic hierarchy of the United States of America, the truth of the matter is that the products which have proved successful have done so because there is a genuine need for these products to reduce the growing risks which are occurring in finance throughout the world.

I have been somewhat fortunate to have been involved with derivatives since I started my rather chequered career in finance. The ever increasing significance of derivatives in finance, and their growing acceptance throughout the world, has been a source of enjoyment to me over the years. As a consequence I regarded the invitation to edit a book on 'Risk Management with Derivatives' with some pleasure. My first reaction, I confess, was to be flattered that a humble practitioner such as myself should receive the invitation. Shortly afterwards, when my ego had received adequate massaging, I considered the task from a more rational viewpoint. One of the consequences of a plethora of new innovations is that it becomes very difficult for the potential user to evaluate the effects and consequences of the new instruments. There are a great number of books available on derivative products. Most of these look very impressive on the bookshelves of members of the board! Most are written by pure academics and perhaps do not convey the essential message that derivatives are there to make business life less traumatic rather than ever more complex and dangerous. As a result my aim with this book was to achieve a balance between theory and the practical applications of these products. In a sense my goal was to have well-thumbed copies of the book in everyday use. (Perhaps this will prompt institutions to order more copies, i.e. more royalties – I mistrust altruism in finance!)

The format I decided upon for the book thus consists of four main sections:

(a) Identifying Risk
(b) The Main Derivative Products
(c) Applications of Derivatives in Risk Management
(d) Establishing Systems and the Future.

My next task was to persuade people who I admired in their fields to write the relevant chapters. After somewhat complex negotiations, involving flattery, intimidation, statistics (i.e. lies, damn lies and statistics) and the age-old persuasive technique of getting someone so inebriated that they will agree to anything, I finally assembled a group of contributors to the book with whom I was delighted.

As always in introductions it is deemed necessary to comment on the individual chapters in the book.

Chris Currington's chapter on identifying and managing risk brings to light the problems of the user of derivative products. Once the initial risk of the participant has been fully comprehended it is then possible to use a derivative (or a combination of derivatives) to reduce the exposure accordingly. However, using derivatives brings another set of risks which must be understood if these products are to be used successfully. In the past it has often been the case that failure to discern these derivative risks (e.g. option sensitivities) has led to dissappointing risk management structures being used. It is entirely appropriate to establish a structured risk control framework to obviate these potential problems. Unless this framework applies to the gamut from senior management down to traders and back office personnel and systems then problems can occur.

It is self-evident that to use derivatives successfully it is essential to have a full understanding of the major products and their relationship with the underlying markets. Both Damian Kissane's chapter on Swaps and my chapter on Futures and Options can be taken in isolation from the remainder of the book and used for basic grounding on the relevant instruments.

My discourses on Futures and Options covers the origins of the markets, operations of exchanges, pricing of futures and options, option sensibilities and the basic uses of these products. It is imperative that the basics are comprehended before contemplating using these products.

Damian Kissane's chapter on swaps initially covers the basic structure and cash flows of both interest rate and currency swaps. I believe that the section regarding swaps as a combination of a floating rate note and bond position, or indeed as a series of FRAs, is vital to the risk manager as it illustrates the hegemony between the various financial products available. The use of swaps in asset and liability management, investment or borrowing arbitrage and tailored financial packages demonstrates the potential of swaps and also explains the huge growth in the global swap market over the last seven years. The chapter concludes with a discussion on the use of swaptions as an extension of the traditional swap market and the flexibility using swaptions can give the user.

The next section of the book concentrates on the practical applications of derivatives in risk management. Short-term interest rate management is discussed using FRAs, futures and options. Hedging interest rate risk for specific exposure dates and the attendant basis risk is dealt with using both futures and options. The case studies which follow are based on actual problems which the author has had to overcome and which in practice have proved to be extremely efficient methods of risk control. Although these case studies apply to a single exposure date, exactly the same methodology can be used to hedge a string of exposure dates, e.g. a two year borrowing requirement with three month rollovers. I am indebted to my friend Charles Beck of J. M. Finn & Co. for his permission to use a series of checklists on risks which financial derivatives can control. I believe that these checklists demonstrate the scope of derivatives in controlling risk and can also be used by the risk manager as an aid in identifying potential problem areas in which derivatives can be used to create acceptable financial profiles.

Paddy Thomas's chapter on equity portfolio management begins with a look at the key pricing relationships between the cash index, cash stocks, futures and options. Once established these relationships can be used effectively to construct the major themes of using derivatives in portfolio management. The classic techniques of hedging existing portfolios using futures and options are covered, followed by hedging anticipated portfolios. One use of derivatives which I believe will grow ever more important to the equity risk manager is their use in asset allocation procedures. Derivatives give the manager the ability to change the exposure of their portfolios, both in terms of domestic and global asset allocation, quickly and cheaply. Complementary to this, risk diversification within the portfolio can be accomplished without problems. Finally the chapter looks at synthetic funds, guaranteed funds and how yield enchancement can be achieved using derivatives. A portfolio manager who does not have the ability to use derivatives will find it ever harder to compete with rivals who are using derivatives.

Danny Corrigan's chapter on fixed interest uses of derivatives looks at cash and carry arbitrage and the pricing of bond futures. Emphasis is placed on the option adjusted basis and basis trading as the cash/futures relationship is crucial in bond hedging. My thanks to M. Desmond Fitzgerald of Unique Consultants for his permission to use the bond hedging case study which follows. The approach used in this case study is relevant to all major bond markets and is used extensively by bond marketmakers.

The final section looks at the procedures for establishing an effective risk management system and speculates on the future of risk management. John Wisbey takes a measured view on the criteria to be used when setting up risk management systems.

He then looks at the installation and potential pitfalls of these systems. It is essential to be aware of the possible weaknesses in any systems and how to establish controls. This chapter, combined with the chapter on Identifying Risk, should be carefully considered before any attempts to establish risk control systems are made. Martyn Holmes and Chris Painter look at potential developments in risk management and develop the theme of artificial intelligence systems.

In summary the use of derivatives is becoming ever more important to the risk manager. Successful risk control is facilitated by the appropriate use of derivative products. It is not coincidental that the world's leading financial institutions are the major users of derivatives. I hope this book proves to be readable, informative and useful and that it contributes to beneficial risk management techniques.

Sandy McKenzie
June 1992

PART 1

IDENTIFYING RISK

1: Identifying and Managing Risk

Chris Currington

The last ten years have seen substantial volatility in the foreign exchange and interest rate markets. Not surprisingly, a need has arisen for methods to manage the commercial risks arising from this volatility. Financial institutions have met this demand through developing new financial instruments.

These instruments, often called derivatives, were initially developed to cater for the needs of corporates and to enable financial institutions to manage their own risk profiles. The latter need was largely driven by capital adequacy constraints in that traditional risk management techniques required increasing credit risk (i.e. 'grossing up' the balance sheet) to manage price risk. Likewise, as capital utilisation is often measured in terms of a proportion of 'notional' principal, income from these instruments were attractive in that it could be earned without substantially increasing capital. The 'off balance sheet' nature of derivatives therefore appealed to financial institutions as they were attractive in terms of capital utilisation.

The growth in use of these instruments is likely to continue as they are now widely used by corporate treasurers and, in view of current volumes, their use has gone beyond that of providing a customer service and risk management to that of a trading nature.

In particular, the financial institutions now actively trade these instruments with a view to a profit. As the majority of these instruments are 'over the counter' (OTC), this active trading also maintains liquidity in the market place. In addition, financial institutions have clearly become intermediaries and this trend has been accelerated by innovations in the market place. These innovations enable the needs of investors and borrowers in different markets to be linked or arbitraged and they have also contributed to the growth of particular markets (e.g. bond and swap markets).

Accordingly, the financial instruments available to investors and borrowers have increased significantly and this has been accompanied by substantial competition amongst financial institutions to serve the needs of these investors and borrowers. As in all markets, increased competition has reduced returns and has therefore increased the risk-return profile.

The risk profile has not only been affected by increased competition, but also by the nature of the financial instruments themselves. In particular, whilst the new instruments are to some degree an extension of traditional risk management tools (i.e. parallel loans, forward foreign exchange contracts, etc.), their attributes differ fundamentally. Instruments such as futures, forward agreements, options, caps and swaps are complex from a legal, commercial and control perspective in that they have the ability to transform asset, liability and income streams. Accordingly, these instruments' risk profile is significantly higher than that of the more traditional instruments.

One example of this is the asymmetrical nature of certain of the instruments such as options and caps. Under these instruments, there is limited risk to the purchaser of the instrument whilst, in theory, there is unlimited exposure to the writer or the grantor of the instrument.

This can be illustrated by looking at the position of a writer of an interest rate cap. In simple terms, in exchange for a fixed premium, the writer agrees to compensate the buyer if interest rates exceed a set level (i.e. cap rate). Once interest rates exceed the cap rate, the writer has potential exposure to keep compensating the buyer over the term of the interest rate cap agreement.

A prudent approach to this exposure would be to hedge as interest rates approached the cap rate. This might be done by going short in an interest rate product (say for example, bonds). However, this 'hedge' can quickly turn into an exposure if interest rates suddenly fall. In particular, if the short bond position had not been removed in anticipation of a drop in rates, then the 'hedge' will represent a loss making position as there is no exposure under the cap which requires protection. In addition, no additional income will be earned from the cap to offset the loss on the bond position.

The above is a simple example of how the risk profile for derivatives is complex. Accordingly, a different approach must be adopted to identifying and managing the risks associated with derivative financial instruments.

This chapter discusses the risks and then sets out a risk control framework for managing them.

RISKS

The key risks for derivatives can be classified as follows:

- Market-price.
- Credit.
- Market liquidity.
- Settlement.
- Transaction and technology.

This section of the chapter sets out the nature of the above risks and how they relate to derivatives.

Market-price Risk

Market or price risk is the risk that the value of a financial instrument will decline as a result of changes in exchange or interest rates.

The concept of market-price risk is well understood and in addition to volatility, exposure to market-price risk may be increased through factors such as term structure, market liquidity and concentration to a particular type of position (i.e. non-diversification of a portfolio).

In addition, basis risk must also be considered. This is where the basis on which rates change for two instruments differ. For example, the impact of a 1 per cent change in LIBOR on the two 'legs' of a Futures–FRA hedge may not be the same.

This may be due to factors such as:

- The fact that futures are exchange based whilst FRAs are OTC.
- Different cashflow periods.

Basis risk must therefore be carefully considered when assessing whether 'hedged' positions are 'risk-free'. In particular, the initial interest rate differential or margin on a futures–FRA hedge position may not remain constant over time, and accordingly, must be reviewed periodically.

Understanding and evaluating basis risk is fundamental to controlling derivatives. This is often done through 'marking-to-market' both sides of the position as this enables one to determine if the initial 'spread' or margin has been maintained.

Equally important in evaluating and controlling exposure to market-price risk is sensitivity or 'what if' analysis. This technique evaluates how an exposure changes under certain assumptions regarding changes in market prices. It is in essence a volatility measure and is a fundamental tool in controlling derivatives such as options, caps and floors.

In summary, whilst market-price risk is a well understood concept, sophisticated techniques need to be applied to evaluate and control it for derivative products.

Credit risk

Credit risk is the risk that a counterparty to a financial transaction will fail to perform according to the terms and conditions of the contract, thus causing the other party to suffer a financial loss.

The wider use of derivative instruments has resulted in a broader range of participants whose creditworthiness is less well known. This necessitates a strict application of the 'know your customer' concept.

Credit risk is often thought of in bankruptcy or insolvency terms, but may also result from:

- Failure to understand custody and ownership issues.
- Concentration in particular instruments, positions and/or to particular counterparties.
- Technical issues which delay or render enforcement of contracts.

Failure to understand particular custody and ownership issues often stems from participants not being familiar with new instruments. This is a form of transaction risk which is discussed below.

The wide variety of globally tradeable derivative products used by the different operations of an international financial services organisation exposes each participant to a concentration risk. Concentrations of exposure are difficult to monitor because of the problems in establishing systems and measuring exposures that are compatible. In addition, measurement needs to occur on a 'real-time' basis.

The credit risk resulting from concentration is equally important as the exposure to a particular instrument, and both will need to be monitored. Unfortunately, most financial institutions currently do not have the systems to adequately measure, monitor and control world-wide exposures to any particular counterparty.

In addition to the above, a critical factor in understanding credit risk for derivatives is understanding the relationship with market-price risk.

A key feature of derivative instruments is that they enable participants to hedge, transfer or transform market-price risk whilst assuming a credit risk which is substantially smaller than the 'notional principal' underlying the transaction.

In addition, most derivative contract settlements are for 'difference' (i.e. the net gain/loss is paid or received), thus enabling the transfer of market-price risk to occur in a credit, capital and transaction cost efficient manner.

When considering credit risk in derivative instruments, some participants take the view that the exposure is really that of a market-price risk nature. In particular, as derivatives involve 'notional principals', the exposure is not for the full amount of the contract, but for the cost to replace the contract if the counterparty fails. This is often referred to as replacement risk.

Whilst the above is technically correct, it is not an appropriate approach to identifying risk as the first step should be assessing the creditworthiness of the counterparty. Counterparty risk should be evaluated upfront and this evaluation should consider the impact of market-price risk on the counterparty's ability to honour the contract.

Accordingly, credit risk for derivative instruments must be considered very differently than that of more traditional instruments and the relationship between credit and market-price risk can be illustrated by the UK Local Authority swap example.

In the late 1980s, UK Local Authorities wrote Swaps and other derivative contracts whereby they received fixed rate and paid floating rate interest streams. The volumes written were significant where the Local Authorities had assumed stable or falling UK interest rates.

The majority of the banks who acted as counterparties to the Local Authorities 'hedged' their positions by taking opposite positions with other banks.

UK interest rates then rose significantly and in 1990, the UK courts ruled that the Local Authorities were 'trading', and accordingly, had entered into transactions beyond their legal powers. As such, the contracts were ruled to be *ultra vires* (i.e. null and void). The counterparty banks then incurred significant losses in closing out their 'hedges' with other banks.

The above shows the relationship between credit and market-price risk. The latter must in aggregate sum to zero, whilst credit risk is related to the volume of contracts outstanding. In particular, derivative financial instruments are two-sided with respect to market-price risk (i.e. the gain on a long futures position should be equal to the loss on the equivalent short position) but are one-sided in terms of credit risk.

Whilst the market-price risk on certain derivative instruments is asymmetrical (i.e. the risk to the buyer of an option is limited, whilst the risk to the writer of that option is, in theory, unlimited), there is still risk to both parties.

This is not the case with credit risk as, assuming the premium is paid, the writer has no credit risk with the buyer whilst the buyer has credit risk with the writer. Accordingly, credit risk is one-sided once the contract is granted and events which affect the writer's ability to perform affect the buyer, whilst the reverse is not the case.

Clearly, the expansion of markets should not increase market-price risk as it should remain a 'zero-sum game'. However, the expansion of derivative markets does increase the overall credit risk in the market as the derivatives in essence spread market-price risk amongst a wider number of participants. As a result, whilst overall market-price risk and individual counterparty creditworthiness does not change, overall credit risk in the market does increase.

The above, in conjunction with the impact of increased competition on margins, reinforces the need for strong credit assessment and monitoring controls.

Market Liquidity

Market liquidity is the risk that a financial instrument cannot be sold quickly at a price which equates to their market value.

Liquidity will change over time and rapid changes will occur in highly volatile conditions. In some situations, liquidity will increase initially in times of volatility as participants enter the market to hedge or to make short-term profits. However, if volatility continues for a sustained period, liquidity is likely to decrease as hedges are obtained and because participants may take the view that the risks posed by higher volatility outweigh the potential returns.

Derivative instruments are relatively new and the liquidity of the market has yet to be fully tested. That said, some derivatives are exchange based and liquid markets in the major interest rate and currency products do exist. However, it must be recognised that many derivatives are OTC based and liquidity for these products can disappear quickly.

Clearly, sudden changes in liquidity risk will affect exposure to market-price risk. Also, a major deterioration in the creditworthiness of a significant participant may also affect market liquidity as that participant may become a 'forced seller' of a particular instrument or position.

Settlement Risk

Settlement or delivery risk is the risk that at a particular settlement or contract maturity point, the financial institution pays out funds before it is certain that it will receive the appropriate payment from the counterparty.

Examples for derivatives might include:

- Paying variation margin to an exchange and the corresponding margin from the customer not being received on time.
- A counterparty not making swap differential payments on time.

Settlement risk can also involve failing to deliver 'stock' (i.e. a commodity based OTC option where physical delivery is expected) to the correct location on the correct day.

Generally, settlement risk is temporary and is of an operational nature. Likewise, whilst settlement risk can give rise to market-price risk (adverse price movements in closing out a position arising from settlement errors), losses may be recoverable from the counterparty. However, this will not be the case for 'own account' settlement errors or in the case where settlement problem results from the counterparty defaulting on the transaction. In this situation, settlement risk becomes credit risk.

Settlement errors can arise from transaction volume backlogs, poor settlement controls and inadequate knowledge of contract terms and settlement procedures. As mentioned previously, the majority of derivative products are settled for 'difference'. However, the transactions can be complex (i.e. net present value based), involve different currencies and countries and in the case of futures and traded options, can involve daily settlements.

The rapid increase in derivative volumes has resulted in significant investments in communications, payment and transaction processing systems being made. These have been largely technology-led with the objective of improving control and reducing transaction costs.

This trend is likely to continue, especially given increased competition and the impact that settlement inefficiencies and errors can have on margins.

Transaction and Technology Risk

Transaction risk is the risk that a financial loss is incurred as a result of a transaction being being executed properly. Some types of settlement errors are a subset of transaction risk and the nature of the risks relating to each type of transaction will depend on:

- Quality of controls, systems and personnel (front and back office).
- Transaction volumes.
- Complexity of the particular instrument.

The majority of transaction errors will result from inexperienced personnel dealing with a high volume of complex instruments without the proper systems and controls. Errors are more likely to occur in a growth stage and managing transaction risk is really a question of:

- Proper management planning and supervision.
- Ensuring existing personnel and systems can cope with present and anticipated volumes.

In addition to the above, managing transaction risk requires risk management and processing systems which monitor transactions and exposures from transaction to value to settlement date.

Clearly, a substantial level of technological support is required to achieve the above in a cost-effective manner. Technology is also required to analyse derivative risk on a day-to-day basis and to perform the required sensitivity analysis. For certain instruments, such as options, existing risk management techniques (i.e. Delta hedging) can not be operated without substantial technological support. In other words, without the technology, the risk can not be managed.

The fundamental role of technology in successful derivative operations can not be over-emphasised. Technology is required to trade and to manage risk successfully and to be a low-cost transactor. In addition, at a more basic level, the failure of a computer system could lead to significant losses being incurred following a change in market prices.

In addition to market price, credit, liquidity, settlement and transaction/technology risks, there are a number of other factors to consider such as:

- Inadequate capitalisation.
- Regulatory considerations.
- Lack of appropriate senior management review and supervision.
- 'Overstretching' for profitability and market share.

The last two points above are often the fundamental cause of loss. In addition to managing the individual risks, senior management must have a clear understanding of the overall objectives and risk profiles acceptable to the firm and its shareholders and regulators. This is especially true in a highly competitive market place characterised by 'tight' margins which can be quickly erased through poor risk management.

To achieve the above, derivative operations need to be conducted within an overall control framework and such a framework is set out below.

RISK CONTROL FRAMEWORK

As mentioned above, the current market environment requires a greater awareness by management of the restrictions on activity, the requirements of the regulators and the need to balance profitability and risk exposure. It is the management of risk that determines profitability.

The pursuit of profit through increased risk taking in difficult and volatile markets has inevitably led to significant losses being taken by major participants. These losses have not only weakened financial positions but, just as importantly, have damaged reputations. These factors have forced many participants to recognise that unforeseen losses of this magnitude are unacceptable in monetary and reputation terms and they are now questioning whether their risk control is adequate.

This section of the chapter describes how trading and financial organisations can structure themselves to optimise control over trading risk and sets out some of the steps to success.

What is Risk Control?

Risk control is the process of:

- Identification, approval and communication of the risks appropriate to a firm's objectives, capital base and abilities;
- Operating a control and reporting system which ensures that actual and potential risks correspond to those approved by senior management; and
- Assessing and communicating actual and potential risks quickly and accurately to the appropriate people in the organisation.

Risk control is in essence an exercise in communication. Its overall objective is to ensure trading activities are planned, conducted, evaluated and reported in accordance with criteria set down by senior management who are accountable to the shareholders.

Risk cannot be controlled effectively if trading or operational personnel are insufficiently aware of senior management's risk perceptions or if lines of communication are blurred or too lengthy. Furthermore, no risk control system, however rigorous, can give absolute assurance that all operating risks and control weaknesses will be identified quickly enough. Similarly, an over-zealous approach to risk control will inhibit the ability to capitalise on opportunities which present themselves in volatile and changing markets.

Effective risk control requires an environment in which risks are managed within approved levels, allowing sufficient flexibility for traders to make the decisions with a view to profit. The most important features of such an environment are:

- The existence and communication of clear *corporate objectives* and strategies for both the firm as a whole and by individual business units.
- An appropriate level of *management control* through developing an acceptable attitude to risk taking and the establishment of relevant parameters within which each trading or operational unit can work.
- Ensuring that *dealing controls* exist and that day-to-day strategies and short-term risk positions are being taken, controlled and reported in accordance with agreed parameters.
- *Operational controls* that ensure trading results are processed efficiently and that these results, whether actual or potential, are communicated promptly and effec-

tively back to management and traders.

- *Technology* which is sufficiently planned and integrated to ensure that trading results are captured, analysed and reported accurately and promptly to all levels.
- *Organisational structures* which have been established to ensure that lines of communication can respond quickly to the 'real-time' demands of a trading environment.

Corporate Objectives

Many financial entities lack a clear statement of corporate objectives and, as such, lack a focus for their activities. A clear summary of objectives provides a cohesive force over a diverse range of products, activities and locations.

In order to develop such a statement of corporate objectives, most firms will need to undertake a strategic review of their activities. Such a review should include:

- A critical assessment of the strengths and weaknesses of each area of operation, including the quality of management.
- A detailed assessment of the existing and potential profitability of each activity identifying the reasons, commercial or otherwise, for participation.
- A detailed analysis of the existing or potential synergy between the organisation's different divisions and lines of business.
- An analysis of the desirable mix of activities in, and between, the firm's core and peripheral activities.

This process should not place undue emphasis on how the markets will behave in the future. The exercise should focus instead on developing operational plans for achieving objectives, these plans being consistent with risk control limits.

The process should result in an agreed review as to the acceptable degree of risk. Such a view should incorporate practical guidelines to assist trading and operational management in evaluating business opportunities and developing operational plans. These guidelines should indicate the safeguards required before any risk is accepted and should identify the manner in which risks are to be evaluated as well as the nature and extent of controls to be maintained over underlying exposures.

A well thought out set of corporate objectives and strategies, focusing on operational considerations, should provide clear and concise risk parameters and a structure which enables trading and risk consideration to be communicated and acted on quickly and decisively.

Management Control

Management control consists primarily of the establishment of formal plans and strategies for each major business area. This process incorporates the risk guidelines identified in the setting of corporate objectives and should be the responsibility of each business or operational manager. The plans and strategies should be compiled using a 'bottom-up' approach but with senior management co-ordination, review and approval. This will ensure consistency with overall group objectives and strategies and will reduce conflicts and inconsistencies between operating units.

Trading and operational management should establish detailed risk limits which reflect the agreed plan. These limits should cover all exposures and risks inherent in the operation's business activities and also incorporate the basis on which the authorised limits are delegated to various management levels. Management should then define the nature and timing of reports they require in order to manage the business and risks, and to ensure compliance with approved limits and to evaluate peformance. Trading is a dynamic activity, and it will therefore be necessary to change and update plans and limits; this should be acceptable with appropriate management approval.

It is essential that the individuals responsible for operational control are involved in the planning process as failure to include them will result in:

- Poorly designed and implemented procedures, systems and technology which do not adequately process and control transactions.
- Failure to accumulate, analyse and report meaningful information for management and traders promptly.

In many respects, management control is the most important feature of risk control since, if it is working effectively, it should identify and highlight potential significant losses before they arise, even if dealing and operational controls fail to operate effectively.

Dealing and Operational Control

Dealing controls ensure that transactions executed achieve the business objectives within defined risk parameters. Such controls include authorisation of transactions, approving counterparties and recording transactions, together with reporting day-to-day and short-term strategies and risk positions. Operational controls include accurate and timely processing, settlement and recording of transactions, together with the assessment and reporting of performance and actual and potential risks.

The content and timing of management and dealing reporting is of the utmost significance. Risk information must be accurate and timely and must be sufficiently tailored so that traders and management can take appropriate decisions and remedial action if necessary. Reports to dealers must either correspond to their perceptions of risk and performance, or must be reconciled with significant differences being explained.

Reports to management should preferably be limited to the main areas of existing or potential risk, positions and performance, together with details of all positions which are in excess of approved limits. Excessive risk data is not an effective management tool and may result in the underlying information being ignored or analysed incorrectly.

It is critically important that operational personnel be of sufficient calibre to assess the risks associated with trading and financial products. The risk characteristics of today's products are complex and risk characteristics can often change radically and in an unforeseen manner. Failure to detect and assess these complexities, particularly in new product areas, can obviously lead to loss. From an overall control standpoint, it is also essential that the individuals responsible for controlling dealing activities should have no responsibility for operational controls and the reporting process.

Technology

Most sophisticated trading environments are wholly dependent on computer technology and systems for transaction processing and reporting. Additionally, the complexity of new instruments results in substantial technical support being required in order to assess, evaluate and control risk.

Unfortunately, many organisations fail to plan their technology needs properly and thus fail to achieve the right degree of integration of their systems. This leads to systems which are decentralised, badly co-ordinated and often ineffective.

The importance of technology to success, especially in difficult market conditions, cannot be over-emphasised. Systems which are poorly planned or which fail to function as required pose significant business and control risks. In addition to the risks arising from systems failure, poorly planned and integrated systems can inhibit the risk control process in the following ways:

- The lack of a well defined systems strategy will result in piecemeal developments or short-term solutions without regard for long-term business plans or information requirements.
- Risk control information will be lacking in quality and frequency and will not meet the needs of all users. Accordingly, the information will fail to communicate the appropriate messages.
- Appropriate technology and systems will not be available or sufficiently flexible to meet the demands of changing markets and products. Operational personnel will therefore be unable to assess and report changes in risk quickly enough.
- Incompatible systems will emerge and the lack of integration will hinder the ability to accumulate, assess and report risk consistently between the trading desks, units and locations. Senior management will therefore be unable to take a consolidated or global view of risk.
- Operational personnel will waste substantial amounts of time attempting to extract meaningful risk information from the risk data provided by the systems. The completeness and quality of the information will suffer as a result.

A well thought-out systems plan focused on operational considerations together with the right level of integration will provide technology which is responsive to traders' and management's information needs.

Organisational Structure

An essential element in effective risk control is an appropriate organisation structure. Many organisational structures reflect historical development as well as the traditional independence of operating units. As a result, they do not reflect a firm's growth and change in its mix of activities. Accordingly, the systems of management information and control which support decision making and the monitoring of risk will not have kept pace with the change in environment.

As risk control is in essence an exercise in communication, a disjointed organisational structure can severely reduce the effectiveness of any risk control process. In particular, too much emphasis on the individual units or profit centres within a structure can pose the following problems:

- Groupwide objectives and risk parameters may not be communicated or understood, or may be ignored.
- Problems may be identified but communication to senior management outside the relevant unit may be too slow or even non-existent.
- Operational and financial control functions may lose their independence if they are too closely tied to particular trading operations.
- The effectiveness of the central financial control function may be reduced. This can result in a lack of uniform standards over the quality of processing, accounting policies, internal control and management information.
- The deterioration of financial and operational controls may go unnoticed until too late.

Any organisational structure which reduces communication between levels of management will impair the effectiveness of risk control. Accordingly, the establishment of such control will necessitate reviewing organisational structures to ensure they are appropriate.

PART 2

THE MAJOR DERIVATIVE PRODUCTS

2: Futures and Options

Sandy McKenzie

INTRODUCTION

From their first introduction in 1973 the growth of financial futures markets has been nothing short of spectacular. It appears that the majority of 'First World' countries now have a futures market or are planning the establishment of one. Many of these enterprises are doomed to failure or, at best, anonymity. To understand the nature of these markets and their success in global finance it is necessary to look at their origins and the role of the derivative product in relation to the underlying cash market. Indeed, without a strong and liquid cash market the role of the derivative is potentially only minimal and, in the worst case scenarios, can be positively dangerous.

ORIGINS OF FUTURES MARKETS

Despite the somewhat manic public image of financial futures pits with their boisterous traders and the cacophony of sound and vision which is reminiscent of the Grand Bazaar in Istanbul, these markets originated, purely, as a hedging medium and have been designed to fulfil this role. They should function as a method of reducing the risk which is inherent to the potential users of the underlying cash market. The use by hedgers in futures markets gives the liquidity to enable traders to participate in the markets and in their turn to enhance the liquidity of the markets. This interplay between hedgers and traders is vital to the success and efficiency of any futures market. In addition, the role of the arbitrageur in the markets must not be underestimated. Their function is to act as 'policemen' to the markets and to ensure that prices do not move out of line with fair levels or in relationship with one another. I have a mental image of arbitrageurs as vultures hovering over the world's financial markets, looking for prices which stray too far from the 'herd'. When this happens they will swoop and devour the profit available from this stray price.

The relatively recent rise to prominence of financial futures markets in Europe and the Far East has led to the erroneous impression that these markets are a new concept. However, this is far from the truth. The concept of fixing a price for delivery of a commodity at a date in the future goes back over two thousand years when the Egyptians were fixing prices for the wheat that they were growing. The first recognisable futures market was established in Japan in 1610 AD during the 1st Shogunate when a formalised rice futures market was traded.

However, it was in 1848 that we saw the introduction of the first truly significant exchange. This was, not surprisingly, the Chicago Board of Trade (CBT) which was formed as a market to which the major grain producers of the American Mid-West States could deliver their produce and receive the current free market price for the cash commodity. This ensured that the farmers would get a fair price, but forces of supply and demand meant that there was no guarantee that the fair price would prove economically viable for the producers. The farmers' need was for some form of certainty as to the price they would receive before they went through the long process of growing, harvesting and transporting their grain to the market place. Accordingly, the first grain futures contracts began trading on the Chicago Board of Trade in the early 1860s. This meant that the producers of the grain could fix a price for their produce for a delivery date in the future and, similarly, the consumers of the grain, e.g. flour merchants, bakeries etc. could fix the price for the raw materials needed for their businesses.

From that time commodity futures markets became established in many basic foodstuffs, e.g. sugar, cocoa, coffee etc. and in precious and strategic metals, e.g. gold, silver, copper, lead.

Let us consider a simple example of the use of these markets.

Alfredo Gomez owns a copper mine in Peru. He knows that in order to make a profit from his mine he must: (a) extract the copper ore from the mine, (b) refine the ore to get an acceptable level of purity of copper and (c) ship the refined copper to a part of the world where there is a demand for his raw material. Then, and only then, can he sell his copper to potential users of the metal.

His essential problems are that he will incur his costs before he ever sees any proceeds and that he has no assurances as to the price he will receive on delivery. Basically in the time it takes him to mine, refine and ship his copper he has a major exposure to the fluctuating price of the world cash copper market. If Alfredo could fix a price for his copper before he started the whole process he could ascertain the viability of going ahead with the project and also determine the profitability of the process.

Jim Sprockett runs a factory in the north-east of England which converts copper metal into copper pipes for use in plumbing. Jim has the possibility of a contract with Bimpeys the home-builders to supply all the copper pipes they need in the building of a huge housing estate currently under construction. He can determine his overheads and also knows how much Bimpeys will pay him for the pipes. His essential problem is the cost of his raw material over the lengthy period required for the house construction.

Alfredo's exposure is to a fall in world copper prices. Jim's exposure is to a rise in world copper prices. A logical solution is for them to get together and agree a price at which Alfredo will deliver his copper and Jim will take delivery of the copper at a date in the future. Of course, it is hardly likely that Alfredo in Peru has any contact with Jim in England. Accordingly they would come together through the medium of a futures exchange. A possible scenario is:

Alfredo	Jim
Copper mine – Peru	Factory – England
	$1650 per tonne – contract with Bimpey
Overall costs $1000 per tonne	$300 per tonne costs
Required profit $200 per tonne	$150 per tonne required profit
$1200 per tonne acceptable selling price	$1200 per tonne acceptable buying price

This deal would be arranged through an exchange such as the London Metal Exchange and would be for a future date acceptable to both parties.

OPERATIONS OF FUTURES EXCHANGES

The number of futures exchanges in the world is rapidly growing. At the time of publication there are over thirty exchanges, some more active than others. To fully understand how these exchanges can be used as a means of controlling risk it is important to consider how they work and the implications of their operation. Although each individual exchange has its own peculiarities they all operate on the same basic principles. Important areas to note are:

- The role of the exchange.
- The standardisation of contracts.
- The role of the clearing house.
- The margining of futures positions.

The Role of the Exchange

All futures contracts are traded on an organised exchange. The exchange will be a non-profitmaking organisation run for and on behalf of the members of that exchange. Typical members of an exchange would be: domestic banks, international banks, brokerage houses, stockbrokers, corporates, private individuals.

Membership of the exchange is normally taken in the form of market seats which are purchased by the market members and which can be traded to any interested party who has the approval of the exchange. Although the exchange is run for the participants in the market the actual administration is done by independent administrative officers of the exchange. This neutrality helps to guarantee the fair running of the exchange.

Standardised Contracts

One of the important characteristics of futures markets is the use of standardised contracts and this is a factor which differentiates these markets for the over-the-counter forward contracts which are available in many instruments. Each futures contract has a distinct set of specifications which will include the size of the contract, the delivery of the contract, a standardised quality of delivery against the contract, a specific quotation and minimum price movement for the contract.

A typical example of a futures contract is the three-month Eurodollar contract traded on the London International Financial Futures Exchange (LIFFE). A fungible contract is traded, albeit sparsely, on the Sydney Futures Exchange (SFE) and a similar, but non-fungible contract is traded on the Chicago Mercantile Exchange (CME) and the Singapore International Monetary Exchange (SIMEX).

Specifications of Three-month Eurodollar Futures Contract

Unit of trading	US $1 million
Standard	Cash settlement based on the Exchange Delivery Settlement Price (EDSP)
Delivery months	March, June, September, December.
Delivery day	Third Wednesday of the delivery month
Last trading day	11.00 am, second business day before the third Wednesday of the delivery month
Quotation	Indexed = 100 – LIBOR.
Minimum price movement	0.01% ($25)
Initial margin	$625 (subject to change)

The implications of these specifications for the Eurodollar contract will be discussed later.

The Role of the Clearing House

Every futures exchange operates a clearing house which plays a vital role in the smooth functioning of the market. This clearing house may be a separate entity to the exchange or may be a distinct part of the exchange itself.

Let us consider the implications for the two participants in a trade on the floor (or screen) of the market. The participants are ABC, a triple A rated international bank (I believe, at the time of writing that this rating still exists for banks) and Bert Higgins, a small local trader. In a direct situation it is improbable that ABC would consider a trade with an individual as it would incur a rather horrendous credit risk. Indeed, a triple A rated organisation would look very closely at any organisation with a lower credit rating than themselves. To facilitate the smooth trading process vital to the success of a futures market the clearing house effectively takes the counterparty role to both participants in the trade. In practice this means that all positions held on the market are with the clearing house rather than other market participants. Clearing houses normally have financial sureties from all their members and are also often backed by large financial institutions, e.g. in London the LIFFE market is backed by Barclays,

National Westminster, Lloyds, Midland and the TSB. Clearing houses are generally regarded as being the equivalent of a triple A rated organisation. By taking on the role of counterparty the clearing house is effectively removing credit risk from the players in the market. This, of course, means that it is the clearing house, itself, which is taking on the credit risk. The question to be asked is: How does the clearing house control its credit risk?

Margining on Futures Exchanges

Initial Margin

A potentially disastrous scenario could be envisaged if a clearing house took no account of its credit risk. In fact, the first step each clearing house takes in its credit control is to require a performance deposit from all participants in the market for each contract they trade. This performance deposit is called the initial margin requirement and is payable to the clearing house for each market position entered into by the market member. This deposit will accrue interest while being held by the clearing house and will be returned to the market member when they either close out their position or go to delivery of the contract. The actual amount of initial margin required will depend on the specific futures contract involved and the volatility of that market. Essentially what the clearing house is looking for is sufficient funds, up front, to cover the likely maximum movement of the market in any one day. As the volatility of the market increases then the likely maximum movement in a day also increases and if the trend is continued the initial margin requirement will be changed accordingly. The clearing house has to balance the amount so it is sufficient to cover market moves but as small as possible to encourage the use of the market. A somewhat extreme example of the change in initial margin requirement occurred at the time of the world's stock markets crash in October 1987. In London the LIFFE FT-SE 100 contact, in mid October had a cash value of around £57,000 and had an initial margin requirement of £1500. Was it really only four days later (people on ledges, people crying into their claret at all the best places!), the cash value of the index contract had dropped to around £42,000 but the initial margin requirement had increased to £7,500. This represents an increase from 2.63 per cent margin on the contract value to 17.85 per cent. Of course, as the index had dropped almost 20 per cent in one day on 'Black Monday' this move in margin requirement was not particularly surprising.

As the initial margin requirement only covers the potential market movement in one day for the clearing house it is essential that they have an additional margin for longer periods in the market.

Variation Margin and Marking to Market

The other main safeguard built into the system for the clearing house is one of daily resettlement of all open positions – marking to market. At the close of business every day a settlement price is announced by the exchange for each contract month tradeable. This settlement price is usually the last traded price but in a comparatively illiquid contract may well be the difference between the bid and offer prices at the close of business for the day. Each open position in the market is evaluated against this settlement price and daily profits are paid to the relevant holders of these profitable positions. More importantly, from the clearing house's point of view, all inter-day losses must be paid to the clearing house by the next day. This daily payment of profits and losses is known as variation margin.

Margining Example

Day 1 Bank DEF buys 10 December Eurodollars at 92.68. At close of business settlement price is 92.60. DEF has to deposit an initial margin with the clearing house of 10 × \$625 = \$6250.
Their open position is then marked to market against the settlement price of 92.60.
92.68 – 92.60 = 8 ticks loss per contract.
Variation margin payment to clearing house is 8 × 10 contracts × \$25 per tick = \$2000.
Total payment to clearing house is \$8250.

Day 2 DEF hold their position.
Settlement price 92.50.
Loss on day's trading is 92.60 – 92.50 = 10 ticks.
Variation margin loss on the day payable is 10 × 10 contracts × \$25 = \$2500

Day 3 DEF hold their position.
Settlement price 92.62.
Profit on day's trading is 92.62 – 92.50 = 12 ticks.
Variation margin profit receivable is 12 × 10 contracts × \$25 = \$3000.

Day 4 DEF close their position at 92.74.
Profit on day's trading is 92.74 – 92.62 = 12 ticks.
DEF receive 12 × 10 contracts × \$25 = \$3000 as a final payment on their trade and also receive back from the clearing house the initial margin they deposited of \$6250 (plus any interest on this initial margin). Thus a total amount of \$9250 is received by DEF from the clearing house.

It should be noted that the effect of variation margin on the profit and loss of a position in a futures market exaggerates the amounts involved. If a position is profitable variation margin will be received and can be invested to enhance the overall return. On the other hand a losing position must be financed leading to a greater loss than the straight futures hit. This interest leverage factor leads to a non-linearity for a futures position and in complex hedge structures should be taken into account.

FINANCIAL FUTURES

Definition

A financial future fixes the exchange rate, interest rate or stock index level at which a financial transaction will occur at a future date.

Currency Futures

The first financial futures contracts to be developed were those on the International Money Market (IMM) branch of the CME. With the advent of free floating foreign exchange rates in the early 1970s the opportunity was taken to regard a currency as a commodity and, accordingly, futures contracts were established as a means of controlling currency risk. The major currency futures contracts traded are: Deutschemark, Japanese Yen, Sterling and Swiss Franc. Although other currencies futures are available, in practice they are highly illiquid and should be used only in desperation. Indeed, the writer believes that the above contracts should be used only in Chicago as the success of currency futures elsewhere in the world has been negligible. The main reason for this is the extremely strong forward/forward market in foreign exchange which has obviated the need for these futures as hedging tools.

Delivery

By entering into a currency futures contract a trader is agreeing to exchange one currency for another at the agreed rate on the specific delivery date of the futures contract. One of these currencies will be US dollars. It is important to note that these are physical delivery contracts.

Short-term Interest Rate Futures

As the use of financial futures has grown widely in the last few years so the number of short-term interest rate futures has grown in unison. Almost all major financial futures exchanges now have a domestic short-term interest rate contract. Among the significant contracts available are: USA – Treasury bills, Eurodollar; UK – Short Sterling, Euromark, Euroyen, ECU deposits; France – Pibor, Euromark.

Definition

A short-term interest rate future fixes the effective borrowing or lending rates for funds at a specific date in the future.

Let us consider the implications of using the Eurodollar contract for a borrower in the cash market at a future date. The borrower has an exposure to rising interest rates between today and his actual borrowing date. As Eurodollar futures are quoted as 100 – interest rate (a futures price of 92.00 implies a borrowing rate of 8.00 per cent on the delivery date of the futures contract), to hedge his borrowing exposure the borrower would need to sell futures against his interest rate exposure.

Example

October 1992
Bank DEF have a borrowing requirement of $1 million on the futures delivery date of 15 December 1992 for three months. They are naturally concerned as to the adverse movement of the interest rate. They prudently decide to hedge this exposure. As the final settlement price of the futures contract is taken from the prevailing cash borrowing rate at delivery they know that they can lock into a borrowing rate for their exposure date using Eurodollar futures. The current December 1992 futures price is 91.60 implying a borrowing rate of 8.40 per cent (100 – 91.60) for 15 December. DEF sell one futures contract to hedge their borrowing exposure.

15 December	Cash LIBOR 3 months	= 9.15%
	Eurodollar delivery settlement price	= 90.85

They now have to borrow at a rate 75 basis points higher on the cash market (9.15% – 8.40%) but their profit on their futures contract of 75 basis points (91.60 – 90.85) exactly offsets this additional cost of borrowing.

Note: If interest rates had fallen by December the reduction in borrowing costs would be offset by a loss on their futures position. When futures are used to hedge cash market exposure they lock into a rate. If the cash market moves in favour of the hedger he will have a corresponding loss on the futures. If the cash market moves against his cash exposure he will be compensated by his futures position. It is also worth noting that if the hedger believes he can lock into today's three-month rate with futures he could well be in for a nasty shock! It is probably appropriate at this juncture to determine exactly what the futures price implies.

Pricing of Futures

Futures prices always have direct observable relationships with both spot prices and other prices generally available. To implement any meaningful hedging operation it is important to understand these relationships.

Basis
Basis is defined as the difference between the current spot price and the price available for a specific date in the future, i.e.

$$\text{Basis} = \text{cash price} - \text{futures price}$$

Example

Cash gold	\$400 per oz.
3-month gold	\$412 per oz.
3-month interest rate	10%

If we buy cash gold and simultaneously sell three-month gold via the futures would we make money?

Buy gold at a cost of \$400

Finance purchase	\$10	= (\$400 × 10% × 3/12)
Warehousing cost	\$2	= storage in valults at \$8 per oz. per annum
Total cost	\$412 per oz.	
Proceeds from future sale	\$412 per oz.	

This process is known as a 'cash and carry' and we can see that with these prices there is no potential for an arbitrage profit or loss. What would the situation be if the futures price was \$420 per ounce?

Total costs remain at \$412 per oz.

Proceeds are now \$420 per oz.

This represents a risk-free arbitrage profit of \$8 per oz. I suspect that if these prices were available there would be a stampede to borrow money, buy cash gold and see future gold. With arbitrageurs buying cash gold and selling future gold the prices would move accordingly until there was no arbitrage profit available. What would the situation be if futures gold was priced at \$404 per oz?

Total costs remain at \$412 per oz.

Proceeds of \$404 now provide an arbitrage loss of \$8 per oz.

Let us consider a 'reverse cash and carry'. In this instance we would sell cash gold for \$404 per oz., invest the proceeds at 10 per cent for three months and simultaneously buy futures gold for \$404 per ounce.

In this case we would lose \$4 per oz. on our purchase and sale of the gold but would be compensated by \$10 interest and not having our warehousing charge of \$2 per oz. Thus we obtain an arbitrage profit of \$8 per oz. by this manoeuvre. As before, as this operation was carried out the price of cash gold would be forced down and the futures prices forced up until no arbitrage potential was left.

This somewhat simplified example assumes that the arbitrageur has access to cash gold and can both borrow and lend at 10 per cent with equal facility. If this were the case we can see that the futures price of gold is dependent on two factors: the cash price and the 'cost of carry'. In practice it can often prove to be impossible to go short of the cash instrument and this will be discussed at length in a later chapter. As can be seen for a physical commodity such as gold there will be warehousing costs but for financial futures this does not apply.

Pricing a Eurodollar Future

When are futures relatively cheap or expensive relative to cash?

The three-month interest rate implied by the futures price should be equal to the equivalent three-month rate implied by the cash market. If this was not the case it would be possible to gain arbitrage profits by trading the cash against the futures, i.e. borrowing in the cash market and lending via the futures or lending in the cash market and borrowing via the futures.

Example
15 March

June Eurodollar future (delivery date 17 June) = 91.60

Cash rates: 3 months 8.00%–8.125%

6 months 8.25%–8.375%

What are the forward/forward lending and borrowing rates for 17 June implied by the current cash market rates?

A rate for lending three-month money on 17 June can be realised at a rate fixed on 15 March by simultaneously borrowing three-month and lending six-month money. This is equivalent to lending for three-months starting in three months time. To calculate:

Implied forward/forward lending rate where R is the rate:

$$1 + (R \times \text{days}/360) = \frac{[1 + (\text{6-mth lending rate} \times \text{days}/360)]}{[1 + (\text{3-mth borrowing rate} \times \text{days}/360)]}$$

$$1 + (R \times 92/360) = \frac{[1 + (0.0825 \times 184/360)]}{[1 + (0.08125 \times 92/360)]}$$

$$R = 8.20\%$$

A rate for borrowing three-month money on 17 June can be realised by simultaneously lending three-month and borrowing six-month money. Implied forward/forward borrowing rate where R is interest rate

$$1 + (R \times \text{days}/360) = \frac{[1 + (\text{6-mth borrowing rate} \times \text{days}/360)]}{[1 + (\text{3-mth lending rate} \times \text{days}/360)]}$$

$$1 + (R \times 92/360) = \frac{[1 + (0.08375 \times 184/360)]}{[1 + (0.08 \times 92/360)]}$$

$$R = 8.57\%$$

To prevent arbitrage the futures implied borrowing rate must lie above the forward/forward lending rate of 8.20 per cent. Hence the futures price must lie below (100 – 8.20%) 91.80.

Similarly, the futures implied lending rate must lie below the forward/forward borrowing rate of 8.75 per cent. Hence the futures price must lie above (100 – 8.57% – 0.125) or 91.31.

Note: The futures contract locks in to a borrowing rate. The lending rate achieved will be the usual bid/offer spread below this level. Thus the futures fair price channel is between 91.31 to 91.80. With the futures priced at 91.60 there are no arbitrage opportunities. However, if the arbitrageur was to be hit on the cash rates rather than him having to take the market rates the fair price channel would narrow considerably for him and in that case there may be chances for him to make a profitable deal.

Long-term Interest Rate Futures

Of all the financial futures contracts traded throughout the world it is almost always the domestic long bond contract which is the most successful. In fact, the only exception to this currently is in London where the German Bund contract has recently taken over from the UK gilt as the most actively traded contract. However, if government borrowing increases in the UK we can expect a rapid return to eminence of the gilt contract. The US Treasury bond contract is, in fact, the most successful futures contract ever introduced. This contract accounts for almost 50 per cent of the turnover on the CBT and until recently was the most active futures contract in the world. It is not surprising that the 'crown' has been taken over by the Japanese government bond in Tokyo. Bond futures contracts have a distinctive delivery system which it is essential to understand before we can successfully use these contracts to control risk.

US T-Bond Futures Contract

Contract Specifications

Unit of trading	US $100,000 par value of a notional US T-bond with an 8% coupon.
Standard	Any government bond with at least 15 years to maturity or if callable with at least 15 years to the first call date.

Months traded	March, June, September, December.
Last trading day	No trading in the last seven business days of the delivery month.
Delivery	Any business day in the delivery month (at the seller's choice).
Quotation	Per $100 face value.
Minimum price movement	1/32 of a full point ($31.25).
Exchange delivery settlement price	CBT delivery price two business days before delivery; bond values calculated using conversion factors; allowances are made for accrued interest on the delivered bond.

There is not currently a T-Bond which fulfils the standard deliverable bond specifications. Indeed, the reason that any bond of the required maturity can be delivered is to prevent market manipulation of a specific cash bond. There is a two-day delivery cycle which is instigated at the seller's discretion. A holder of a long futures position has to be aware that if the position is held into the delivery month they may have to take physical delivery of a bond. On the CBT the longest term holders of T-bond positions will be the first to be delivered but on LIFFE it is a purely random process as to the long holder to be delivered. It is prudent to ensure the differences in delivery procedure on different exchanges are noted! For the purposes of delivery the following delivery formula is used to calculated the invoice amount.

Invoice amount

$$= \text{futures settlement price} \times \text{conversion factor} \times \$1000 + \text{accrued interest}$$

The conversion factor is used to adjust the difference in value of deliverable bonds with different coupons and/or maturities to the notional bond of the futures contract. It is defined as the price per $1 nominal value at which each deliverable T-bond will yield 8 per cent given its current time to maturity.

The closer the coupon rate of a bond is to 8 per cent, the closer its conversion factor will be to 1. For bonds with coupon rates over 8 per cent the shorter the maturity the closer the conversion factor will be to 1. The opposite is true for bonds with coupon rates below 8 per cent. If there was a flat-term structure along the yield curve of 8 per cent all deliverable bonds would give the same relative value if delivered. However, as is likely, yields are not 8 per cent and there is not a flat-term structure a particular bond will be better to deliver than the others. In fact, most deliverable bonds will give different results. The bond which is best to deliver is called the 'cheapest to deliver' (CTD) and it follows that this is the bond that will actually be delivered. The CTD is defined as the bond which can be bought in the cash market and sold in the futures market with the maximum profit or smallest loss taking into account financing costs. Because of arbitrage the futures price and the price of the CTD will be closely linked. In fact it can be said that trading the bond future is equivalent to trading a future on the CTD.

Evaluating a Bond Cash and Carry

To evaluate a cash and carry using T-bonds the following procedure is followed:

Initial investment	Cash bond price quote + accrued interest
Total proceeds	Bond delivery formula + accrued interest
Coupon (if any)	Compounded value of coupon at delivery

Rate of return:

$$\frac{\text{Total proceeds} - \text{initial investment}}{\text{initial investment}} \times \text{annualising factor}$$

Example
6 June 1991

Cash bond: 7.25% 15/05/2016 Cash price 76–24
Conversion factor September 1991 delivery: 0.91958
September future price: 82–08 1st delivery date 02/09/1991

Initial investment Cash price = 76–24 × $1000 = $76,750.00
Accrued interest = $3,625 × 22/184 = $433.42
Total investment = $77,183.42

Proceeds for delivery on 2 September using the delivery formula:
82–08 × 0.91958 × $1,000 = $75,635.45
Accrued interest on 2 September = $3625 × 110/184 = $2167.12
Total proceeds = $77,802.57

$$\text{Rate of return} = \frac{\$77{,}802.57 - \$77{,}183.42}{\$77{,}183.42} \times \frac{360}{88} = 3.28\%$$

When doing this calculation it is important to note that both cash bonds and bond futures are quoted in 1/32nds and must be converted to decimals before using the delivery formula. The coupon on US bonds is paid semi-annually. Half the annual coupon is paid every six months on an actual over actual basis. The annualising factor used is normally on a 360-day basis to compare the cash and carry rate of return ('repo rate') with money market rates.

Stock Index Futures

Although stock index future contracts are a relatively recent innovation (the first contracts began trading in 1982) they have rapidly become well established and have begun to play an ever increasing role in the equity markets of the world. Indeed, it can be argued that they finally proved their worth during the 'crash' of October 1987.

Examples of liquid stock index contracts are:

USA	Standard and Poor's 500 (CME) Major Market Index (CBT) NYSE Composite Stock Index (NYFE)
UK	FT-SE 100 Index (LIFFE)
Germany	Dax index (DTB)
Hong Kong	Hang Seng Index (HKFE)
Japan	Nikkei-Dow Index (TSE)
France	CAC 40 Index (MATIF)

Definition

A stock index futures contract fixes the level at which the underlying index can be bought or sold at a specific date in the future.

Let us consider the most actively traded index future contract:

The CME Standard and Poor's 500 Index

Specifications	
Unit of trading	S&P 500 Index times $500 per index point e.g. 320 × $500 = $160,000.
Standard	Cash settlement based on the exchange delivery settlement price.
Months	March, June, September, December.
Last trading day	Third Thursday of the delivery month.
Delivery day	Third Friday of the delivery month.
Minimum price movement	0.05 of a full index point = ($500 × 0.05) = $25.

Note: The reason all stock index contracts are cash settlement is that it would be infeasible to deliver a parcel of 500 stocks in the correct ratio against the cash index.

A trader who purchased one December futures contract at a price of 302.00 and subsequently sold the contract at a price of 307.50 would make a profit of (307.50 – 302.00) × \$500 = \$2750.

Hedging Example

A fund manager is concerned about the short-term performance of the S&P 500 index and feels that she needs to control the risk on her current market exposure. As her concern is short term she feels the costs of selling a part of her portfolio are prohibitive and accordingly she elects to put on a full futures hedge. The portfolio she owns is well diversified and tracks the S&P 500 index very closely. (In practice it is highly unlikely that such a portfolio could be put together so it would be necessary to consider the portfolio beta prior to hedging.)

10 July 1991

Current portfolio value	:	\$15,000,000
Current level S&P 500	:	300.00
September S&P 500 future:		303.00

Her first step is to calculate the hedge ratio by using the formula:

$$\text{Hedge ratio} = \frac{\text{cash value of portfolio}}{\text{cash value of index}}$$

Accordingly she sells

$$\frac{\$15{,}000{,}000}{300 \times \$500} = 100 \text{ contracts}$$

Again, in practice, it is highly unlikely that the optimum number of contracts for the hedge would turn out as an exact number. The hedger would normally have to either round down or round up the number of contracts to be used.

What portfolio value has she locked in?

Number of contracts × futures price × \$500 = 100 × 303.00 × \$500 = \$15,150,000

20 September 1991

At delivery of the September futures contract

S&P 500 Index	290.00
S&P Futures Price	290.00

Her decision to fully hedge her portfolio has been vindicated as the index has dropped 3.3 per cent over the period of her hedge.

Value of cash portfolio	= \$15,000,000 × 290/300 = \$14,500,000
Futures profit	= 100 contracts × (303.00 + 290.00) × \$500 = \$650,000
Total position value	= \$14,500,000 + \$650,000 = \$15,150,000

This is exactly the value she anticipated locking into when she first established her hedge position. Again it is worth noting that if by 20 September the value of the S&P 500 Index had risen to 320.00 her overall position would have been:

Value of cash portfolio = $15,000,000 × 320/300 = $16,000,000
Futures loss = 100 contracts × (320.00 – 303.00) × $500 = $850,000
Total position value = $16,000,000 – $850,000 = $15,150,000

Hedging with futures means locking into a value. If the underlying cash market moves in favour of a cash position a loss will result on the futures hedge.

Pricing of Index Futures

To determine the fair price of an Index futures contract we can look at the problem from the arbitrageur's viewpoint. If we buy a cash stock portfolio with borrowed funds and simultaneously sell index futures there should be no arbitrage profit.

Let us look at a situation similar to that of our portfolio manager. In this instance she is going to borrow the $15 million at the current borrowing rate of 8 per cent and sell index futures to lock in the position. While she holds the cash stock position she will receive a dividend yield (currently at an annualised rate of 4 per cent) but will have to repay the principal plus interest on delivery of her position. Comparing her final position value against the loan repayment she has to make we find:

Final value = value locked in with futures + dividend yield
= $15,150,000 + (0.04 × 72/365 × $15 million)
= $15,268,356.16

Loan repayment = principal + interest
= $15,000,000 + (0.08 × 72/360 × $15 million)
= $15,240,000.00

This represents a potential arbitrage profit of $28,356.16. Although at first sight this appears to be a fairly attractive deal in fact there are several problems to consider:

(1) It may be difficult for the arbitrageur to match the future with an exactly similar cash portfolio. Both macro and micro economic factors would then have to be considered.
(2) The dividend stream for the index may not be continuous and level. A detailed study of exactly when and what dividends are expected during the period of the arbitrage must be undertaken.
(3) Cash settlement may cause uncertainties. To assume that a portfolio can be bought and sold at one time is naive.
(4) Transaction costs must be taken into account. Although these may be small in the case of the futures position, transaction costs in cash stocks can be considerable.

In conclusion, although cash-and-carry arbitrage will keep the futures price and the cash index closely in line there may often be occasions when the arbitrage bounds are exceeded without there being sufficient potential profit for the arbitrageur to act.

OPTIONS

One of the significant developments in finance during the 1980s was undoubtedly the rise to prominence of option and option related products. Indeed, the author progressed from dealing in commodity options in 1980, with a certain amount of success, without ever having heard of an option pricing model to offering an option on a 'caption' in 1990 (a caption is an option on a 'cap' which is itself a string of options on interest rates). Neither of these courses of action is recommended today on the grounds of insanity and the terminal loss of wealth which would undoubtedly ensue. Although over-the-counter options have been available for a considerable amount of time it was not until the introduction of formalised exchange traded options in the early 1970s that the true potential of these products began to be realised. The creation of the secondary market, which formalisation engenders, began the success story of options which was cemented by the, at the time, revolutionary option pricing model developed by Fischer Black and Myron Scholes first published in 1973. This essentially took some of the guesswork out of the task of pricing options. The Black–Scholes model was originally designed for pricing stock options and has since been modified to encompass options on currencies and interest rate products. As liquidity grew on option markets so new techniques began to be developed to cope with the ever more competitive field of option writing.

Definition

An option is the right to buy or sell a specific underlying asset at a specific price at (or before) a defined date in the future. The price paid for the option is called the premium.

Characteristics

There are two major types of options. A *call* option gives the buyer the right to receive a long position in the underlying asset. A *put* option gives the buyer the right to receive a short position in the underlying asset. The buyer of an option pays a premium to the seller. In return he acquires a right to receive a position if he so desires, whilst the seller of the option receives the premium in return for accepting an obligation to perform against the option if called upon to do so.

Three further distinctions can be made:

(1) Is the underlying asset the *cash* instrument or a *futures* (forward) position? In general an over-the-counter (OTC) option will have the cash instrument as the underlying whereas in many instances exchange-traded options will have a futures contract as the underlying. In the case of individual strock options, however, the underlying will be the cash stock.
(2) Can the option be exercised at any time or can it only be exercised on the expiry date? The former is called an 'American' style option and are normally exchange-traded options. The latter is called a 'European' style option and most OTC options are of this type.
(3) Is the premium *paid* up front by the buyer to the seller or is the option position *margined*? Traditionally all options had to have the premium paid but a relatively recent innovation is the margining of an options position where the option has an initial margin relative to the market exposure inherent in the option, is marked to market and the full premium is only paid at exercise or at expiry of the option.

One of each of these characteristics will be pertinent to any option. For example, a typical stock option would be Cash, American, Paid, whereas a Eurodollar option would be Future, American, Margined.

Example

Any option which is exchange-traded will have a set of contract specifications.

Eurodollar Option

Trading unit	One Eurodollar futures contract.
Exercise prices	At intervals of 0.25% (25 basis points), i.e. 90.25, 90.50, 90.75, 91.00
Price quotation	0.01% or $25.
Months traded	March, June, September, December.
Initial margin	Determined by risk factor.
Variation margin	Daily profits or losses.

15 October
Dec. 91.50 call option is priced at 40
Dec. futures contract currently 91.70

The buyer of this call acquires the right to receive a long December futures position at a price of 91.50. The cost of this right is the option premium of 40 ticks

× $25 = $1000. The seller (writer) of this option accepts an obligation to deliver a long December futures position to the buyer at a price of 91.50 if called upon to do so. In practice if the buyer exercised the option he would receive the long futures position at 91.50 and the seller would have to take the opposite market position, i.e. short the futures contract at 91.50. Profits an losses would then be realised by offsetting these futures positions by a closing sale or purchase of the futures. If at expiry the option had no intrinsic value (the exercise price was above the futures level) it would be abandoned as worthless and the seller would retain all the premium he received.

In the case of a 91.50 December put option priced at 10 the buyer would pay a premium of 10 × $25 = $250 for the right to receive a short futures contract at 91.50 if he so desired. The seller takes the obligation to deliver the short futures position and if exercised must take the opposing market position, i.e. long one future at 91.50.

It is essential to take note of the implications of buying and selling options. As can be seen from both Figure 2.1 and Figure 2.2 in both instances the buyer has a potential loss which is limited to the amount of premium he has paid for the option. His potential profit is only limited to the extent which the market might move in his favour. For the seller it is an entirely different ballgame. His potential profit is limited to the amount of premium he receives but his losses may be unlimited.

A well documented example of the dangers of writing options occurred during the

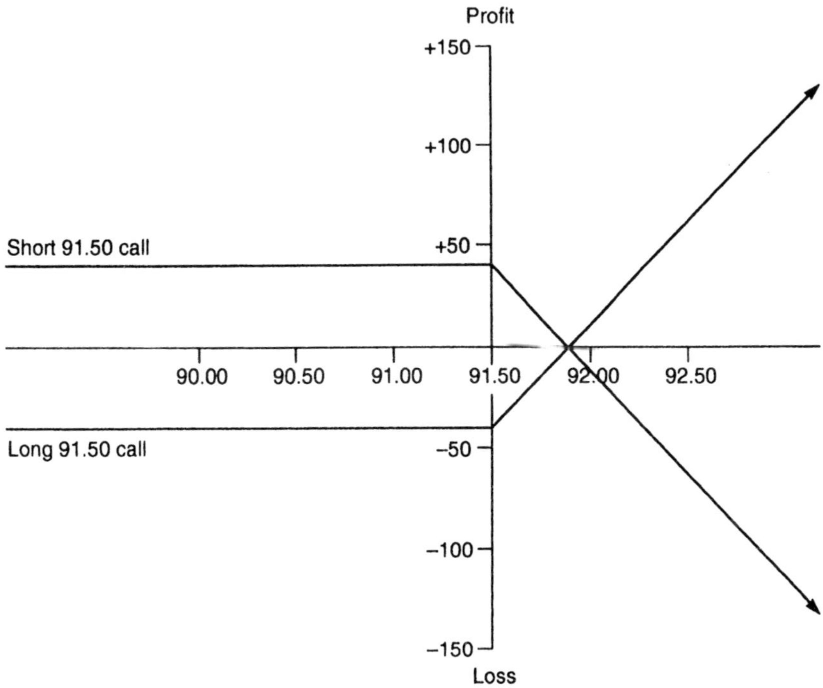

Figure 2.1

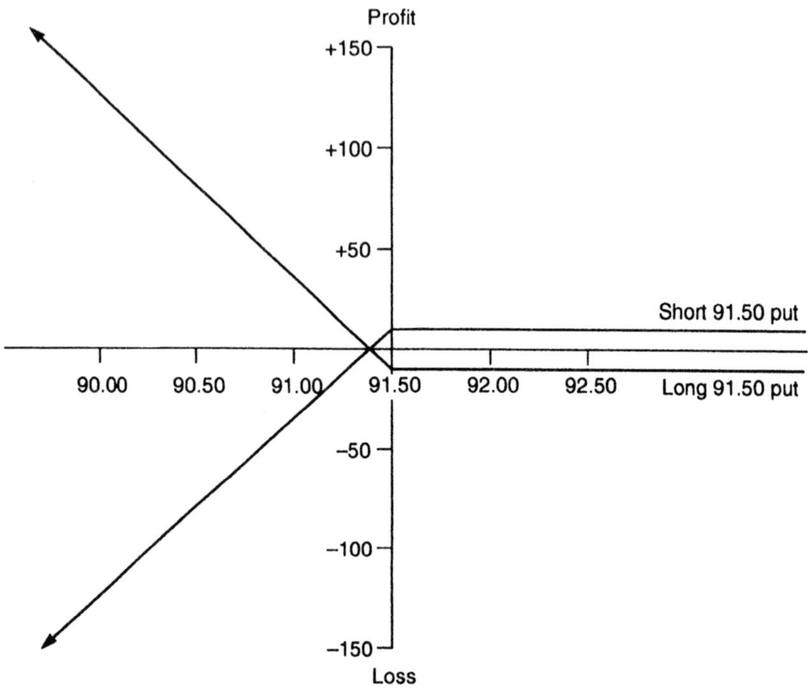

Figure 2.2

crash of 1987. A trainee accountant was allowed to sell put options on the FT-SE 100 index in London. For a few months before the crash the index steadily went up and accordingly the seller retained all of his premium. However on the day of the crash the put options he had sold lost him 3 million sterling. It is difficult to finance losses of that magnitude on a salary of 5000 sterling per annum.

Pricing of Options

Undoubtedly the most complex aspect of options is the pricing. It appears as if 50 per cent of professors of finance in the USA are currently doing research into option pricing. As ever more sophisticated pricing techniques are developed it becomes increasingly difficult for the non-mathematician to understand. However, an understanding of the basic elements within option pricing is essential for adequate comprehension of the potential uses of these instruments.

The two basic components of an option price are intrinsic value and time value. In our example of a eurodollar call option we had a 91.50 call with a price of 40. The underlying futures market was priced at 91.70. The intrinsic value of an option is defined as the amount that would be realised if the option was exercised immediately.

We can see that in this example the intrinsic value of the option is 20 ticks. Any value above intrinsic value is referred to as time value. For this option the time value would also be 20 ticks. For an option that is out-of-the-money the premium would consist entirely of time value. What factors determine intrinsic and time value? There are six factors which are relevant:

(1) The price of the underlying.
(2) The exercise price.
(3) The time to expiry of the option.
(4) The volatility of the underlying instrument.
(5) The risk-free interest rate till expiry.
(6) The dividend rate of the underlying stock or the interest rate on the underlying security (if applicable).

Factors 1 and 2 will determine the intrinsic value of the option or, if there is no intrinsic value, how far the option is from gaining any intrinsic value.

It can be intuitively seen that the longer an option has before expiry the more value that option will have (factor 3).

The more volatile the underlying instrument (factor 4) the greater the potential of the option to gain intrinsic value and thus the higher the option price.

Factor 5 assumes that the premium is paid upfront and the potential rewards are not received until expiry. The value of the premium must then be the discounted value of the premium at expiry. Remember the option is written on the future price of the underlying asset at expiry and this price is largely dependent on the cost-of-carry, i.e. the interest rate.

Factor 6 explores the potential gain from holding the underlying asset during the life of the option and its ramifications on the price of the underlying asset.

The time value of an option will always be at its highest when the option is at-the money and will decrease as the option moves either in-to or out-of-the-money.

It may be noted that the one factor that is not predetermined at the time of the transaction is the volatility of the underlying asset in the future. Indeed, because of this the single most important factor in option pricing is volatility.

Volatility

The higher the volatility the higher the option price, the lower the volatility the lower the option price. Without the benefit of a crystal ball how can we determine what volatility will be in the future?

Four common methods to 'guesstimate' volatility are:

(1) Analysis of historical futures price series where the resultant data is used to project what will happen in the future.

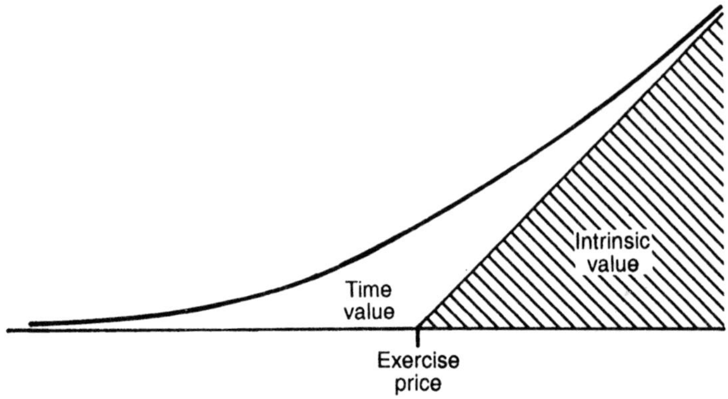

Figure 2.3

(2) Historical analysis of implicit volatility of near-to-the-money options. As these options are the most actively traded they are presumed to have the most accurate implied volatility figures.
(3) Analysis of implicit volatility in the current set of actual option prices. As the actual option prices are a market consensus as to the volatility implicit in those prices this is certainly the most commonly used method to estimate volatility. However if everyone used this method there would be little or no divergent opinion as to the volatility. A conservative method that perhaps assumes that the market is always correct.
(4) Direct judgemental assessment. The frivolous might call this a guess. Many experts in a particular field can use this method to great effect by utilising their knowledge and expertise about a specific set of option prices and their underlying instrument. This is not recommended for the beginner or the nervous.

Most formalised option valuation systems make certain assumptions:

(1) Markets trade continuously and do not gap, i.e. make large moves without trading.
(2) There is a risk-free borrowing and lending rate available for the period of the option.
(3) Transaction costs and taxation effects are ignored.

New research is attempting to eliminate these obvious anomalies from traditional option pricing but it is sensible to be aware of their effects.

There are many authoritative books on option pricing and to fully understand pricing one should explore these tomes, however as computer pricing systems, hopefully, take the pain out of pricing, this book will not concern itself with theory of such systems as Black–Scholes or the Binomial. However, as most pricing systems are based on the price of a call option we should next look at the relationship between call and put options.

Call/Put Parity

Trader ABC has the following portfolio position:

Long 1 Dec. call strike 92.00
Short 1 Dec. put strike 92.00

What will ABC's market position be at expiry?

If the market is below 92.00 the call option will be worthless and will be abandoned. The put option he sold will be exercised by the buyer and he will have to take the opposite position in the market, i.e. long 1 contract at 92.00.

If the market is above 92.00 at expiry ABC will exercise his call option and take a long futures position at 92.00. The put option he sold, being worthless, will be abandoned.

In both cases ABC's position at expiry will be long 1 Dec. contract at 92.00. In fact, his portfolio position is independent of the price of the underlying future contract price at expiry and is a synthetic equivalent of a long futures position at 92.00. This creation of a synthetic instrument places a constraint on the relationship between the call price and the put price. This constraint can be expressed by the formula:

Call price – put price = future price – exercise price

If this were not the case there would be an arbitrage opportunity between the actual future and the synthetic.

Example
December futures 92.10
December 92.00 Call premium 26
December 92.00 Put premium 20

Using the put/call parity formula

$$C - P = F - E$$

$$26 - 20 = 92.10 - 92.00$$

or

$$6 = 10 \quad ???$$

Obviously there is arbitrage potential in these prices. The trader would:

Buy Dec. 92.00 call for 26 basis points
Sell Dec. 92.00 put for 20 basis points

6 basis points net cash outlay

Sell December future at 92.10

At Expiry
The trader ends with a long futures contract at 92.00 against the futures contract he

sold at 92.10. A profit of 10 basis points. 10 basis points profit – 6 basis points outlay = overall profit of 4 basis points.

This strategy is known as a conversion.

Note: As the Eurodollar options are margined the premiums are only paid at exercise or expiry. If the options used are premium paid the financing cost of the options would have to be taken into account.

Example

December futures 92.10
December 92.00 Call premium 20
December 92.00 Put premium 6

Using the call/put parity formula

$$C - P = F - E$$
$$20 - 6 = 92.10 - 92.00$$
$$14 = 10 \quad ????$$

Again there is a discrepancy. In this instance the trader would:

Sell Dec. call at 20 basis points
Buy Dec. put at 6 basis points

14 basis points cash inflow

Buy Dec. future at 92.10

At Expiry

The trader ends up with a short futures position at 92.00 against his purchase at 92.10. A loss of 10 basis points. However, his net cash inflow from his options is 14 basis points giving an overall arbitrage profit of 4 basis points.

This strategy is known as a reversal.

We can see from these examples both the close relationship between similar call and put prices and the relationship between futures and option prices. The next step is to explore how the relationships between option prices and the factors which determine the option prices work and how we can use these relationships to control the risk of an options position.

The Greek Alphabet – Option Sensitivities

The five main option sensitivities are designated by letters of the Greek alphabet. They are:

Delta — The size of the change of an option price for a one unit change in the price of the underlying asset.

Gamma The size of the change of the delta of an option for a one unit change in the price of the underlying asset.
Kappa The size of the change in option price for a 1 per cent change in the volatility of the underlying asset (also known as Vega or Epsilon).
Theta The decrease in option value associated with a one period decrease in the time to expiry of the option.
Rho The change in option price associated with a 1 per cent change in the interest rate over the life of the option.

Delta

As we have seen from Call/Put parity a portfolio option position of long call and short put at the same exercise price is equivalent to a long futures position at that exercise price. The delta of that portfolio will be 100 per cent as the option prices will reflect any change in the price of the underlying. We also know that only one of these options will be exercised. What is the probability as to which option will be exercised? This obviously depends on the level of the underlying asset. The delta of an option can be thought of as the percentage chance of that option being exercised. In-the-money options will have a delta of over 50 per cent. The more deeply in-the-money the option the closer the delta will be to 100 per cent. Out-of-the-money options will have a delta below 50 per cent. The further out-of-the-money the option the closer the delta will be to 0 per cent. An at-the-money option would usually have a delta of 50 per cent. It is important to note that as the price of the underlying moves so will the deltas of options on that underlying asset. Deltas are accurate sensitivities only for small changes in the price of the underlying.

Application of the Delta Factor

All futures and options positions will have a delta factor.

Positive Deltas	**Negative Deltas**
Long Future (delta + 1)	Short Future (delta – 1)
Long Call	Short Call
Short Put	Long Put

Bank BCD has the following portfolio position:

Short 20 Futures
Long 40 Calls Delta 0.65
Short 25 Puts Delta 0.20
Long 100 Puts Delta 0.07

What is their overall market exposure?

			DELTA
Short 20 Futures		=	−20
Long 40 calls	(40 × 0.65)	=	+26
Short 25 puts	(25 × 0.20)	=	+5
Long 100 puts	(100 × −0.07)	=	−7
Overall position delta		=	+4

Although at first sight BCD's portfolio looks relatively complex, in fact their market exposure is equivalent to being long 4 futures contracts. The portfolio delta can be used as a measure of expressing market risk for small movements in the underlying asset. By selling 4 futures contracts BCD can neutralise their exposure to movements in the underlying. This is the principle behind many option margining systems. The initial margin requirement will be appropriate to the market risk in the overall position held by the market member.

How can we assess how the delta of an option will move?

Gamma

The delta of an option changes as the price of the underlying asset moves. The rate of change of the delta is measured by the gamma of an option. The gamma could be called the 'delta of the delta'. Large portfolio positions can have a delta very close to zero yet be highly sensitive to relatively small moves in the underlying asset. It is essential to be aware of how these movements can affect the overall portfolio exposure.

Vega/Kappa

The sensitivity of an option to changes in volatility will be at its greatest when the option is at-the-money where time value is at its peak. As the option moves either in-to-the-money or out-of-the-money its sensitivity to changes in volatility will gradually diminish. Being long of options can be regarded as being long of volatility, as if volatility rises so does the option price. Similarly, going short of options can be regarded as being short of volatility as if volatility falls the option prices will fall accordingly.

Theta

The decrease in value of an option with the passage of time is of significance both to the buyers and sellers of options. Being long of an option means being long of theta. Being short of options means being short of theta. As theta can only decrease the seller of an option always has the passage of time working in his favour. As with kappa, theta is at its greatest at-the-money as that is the point of the greatest time value.

Rho

Rho is only of significance in options which are long term. On shorter term options it would take massive interest rate moves to radically alter the option price. However, on long-term options such as caps changes in the interest rate are important and their impact cannot be ignored by the serious trader or hedger.

Trading with Options

Three factors have made option trading an attractive prospect for many people in finance.

(1) The high level of gearing involved gives the potential of large profits for a relatively small outlay.
(2) The ability to tailor the risk/reward profile of a trading position to the requirements of the individual trader.
(3) The ability to trade volatility without having to take a view on market direction.

A mistake which is often made by option buyers is to assume that because their losses are limited they can not lose a great deal of money trading options. It is, perhaps significant that there are always plenty of market professionals who are only too eager to write options on absolutely anything connected with finance. It could be argued that the fair price of an option is the amount that someone is prepared to pay for it. A mistake made by many is to assume that if an option does not cost much it therefore must be cheap. Remember an option bought for six basis points when its true value is three basis points is grossly overpriced. The professional runner of an options book will gladly write these options all day long.

Hedging with Options

Although hedging with options will be fully covered in later chapters it is probably appropriate to end this introductory chapter on futures and options with an example of a much used option hedge. This is the case of the holder of a long asset position who hedges his downside risk by buying a put option against his asset position.

Example

BCD bank has a long futures position in gold for September delivery. They purchased the future at a price of $360 per oz. and the market currently stands at $380 per oz. They feel that the gold price may well rise further but do not wish to throw away all the profit they have made to this juncture. The price of a September put option on gold with an exericse price of $380 is currently $10. They accordingly buy a September $380 put to hedge their downside risk.

As we can see from their profit and loss profile they have created for themselves a synthetic call option position. The minimum guaranteed profit they will achieve from this position is $10 per oz., but if the gold price continues to rise their futures position will make more profit for them. If the market falls from this level they can exercise their option and sell their gold at $380 per oz. If the gold price rises from this level their option will be worthless at expiry but the futures position will have benefited. Although in no circumstance is this more profitable than holding the straight position if the market goes up or selling the position if the market falls, it may well give the profit/loss profile which best suits their concept of risk against reward.

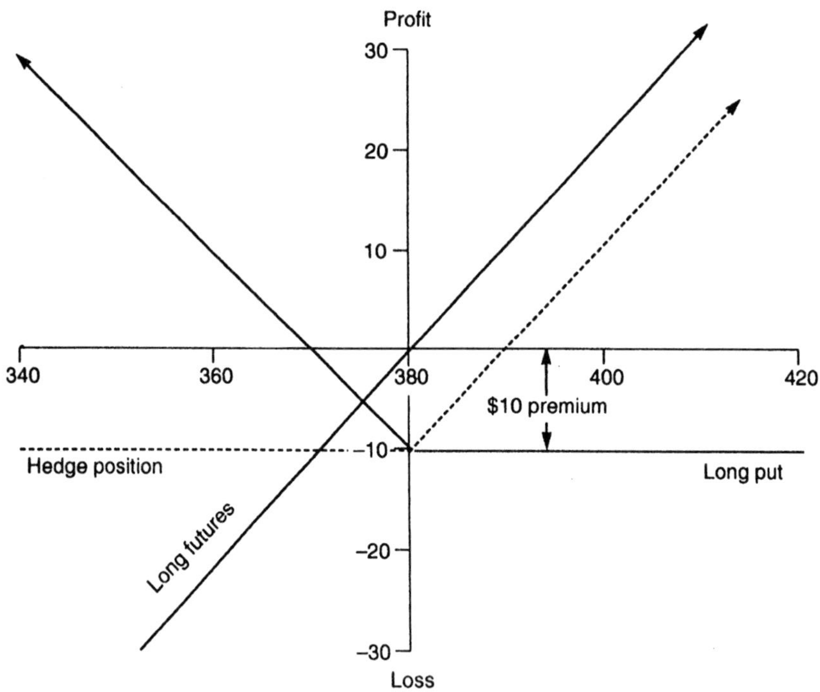

Figure 2.4

3: Swaps

J. Damian Kissane, U.B.S. Phillips and Drew

INTRODUCTION

The interest rate and currency swap market has become one of the world's largest financial markets since its inception at the end of the 1970s. An interest rate or currency swap is no more than a contract for the exchange of one series of cash flows for another series of cash flows on terms which are agreed at the beginning of the swap. Within this rather broad definition any series of cash flows can be exchanged:

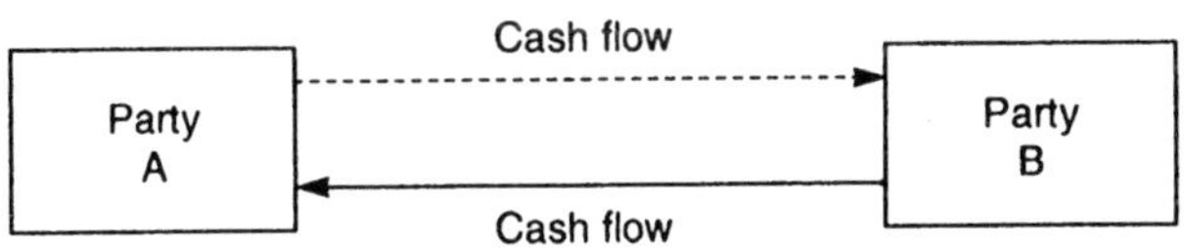

Figure 3.1 A Swap is an Exchange of Cash Flows

(1) A single or series of known cash flow payments for a series of also known 'fixed' payments. A 'fixed/fixed' swap, for example a payment of 10 per cent once a year versus receipt of two payments of say 5 per cent during the year.
(2) A single or series of known, i.e. fixed, payments for a series of payments which vary over time according to some agreed basis of calculation. A 'fixed/floating' swap. Example: a payment of 10 per cent every year versus receipt of a variable amount indexed to say short-term interest rates.
(3) A series of payments which vary over time according to some agreed calculation basis for an alternative series of payments which vary over time according to a different agreed schedule or different method of calculation. A 'floating/floating' or 'basis' swap.

The cash flow exchanged can be in the same currency 'interest rate swap', or in different currencies, 'currency swap' ('cross currency swap'). The cash flows can be paid according to any agreed schedule; monthly, quarterly, semi-annually, annual etc. Exchanges of individual cash flows need not occur on the same dates.

The cash flows can be a 'fixed' percentage or, alternatively, they can be a variable 'floating' percentage of the size or 'notional' amount of the swap, for example, they can be referenced to short-term floating interest rates. The notional amount or principal of the swap can also vary over time. It can increase in size, 'accreting' swap, decrease over time 'amortising' swap, or increase and decrease over time, a 'roller-coaster' swap.

In the most common type of interest rate swap one party, Party A, will commonly agree to pay/(receive) a fixed cash flow or a series of fixed cash flows calculated on an annual bond basis convention and made on agreed dates against receipt/(payment) of six-month Libor from Party B. 'Libor', the London interbank rate (written with a capital 'L'); the rate at which banks lend each other money in the London market for different maturities. Six-month Libor is recalculated every six months in advance and paid at the end of each six-month period based on an agreed fixed principal or 'notional' amount of the swap. A simple interest rate swap is shown in Figure 3.2.

Fixed rate payer	Party A
Floating rate payer	Party B
Notional amount	US$ 100.00
Fixed rate payer pays	7.00 per cent (Ann, 30/360)
Floating rate payer pays	6-month US$ Libor
Maturity	1 Year
Start date	Wednesday, 11 September 1991

The swap is described diagrammatically by the swap box diagram in Figure 3.2 below which sets out the direction of the movement of the cash flows. Floating cash flows are shown as dashed lines and fixed cash flows as full lines. The drawing of 'swap boxes' to describe transactions is common market practice as swaps can involve large numbers of counterparts and different cash flows.

The interest payments of the swap are set out below. In this example the principal or notional amount of the swap is US$100.00. The six-month US dollar Libor amount calculated by reference to the notional amount will vary over time with the level of interest rates. Note how the swap has a start or 'effective' date from which interest is calculated to accrue, here Wednesday, 11 September 1991. More importantly note how there is no exchange of the notional amounts of the interest rate swap, just the interest rate cash flows.

Start date	Fixed Payment Company A pays to Company B	Floating Payment Company B pays to Company A
Wednesday, 11 September 1991	0	0
Wednesday, 11 March 1992	0	6-month US$ Libor
Friday, 11 September 1992	US$ 7.00	6-month US$ Libor

Diagrammatically:

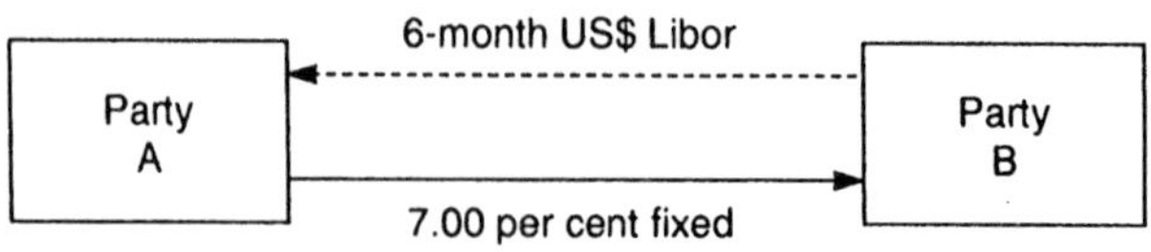

Figure 3.2 Simple Swap Outline.

The Libor or 'money market' rate for any particular Bank is the rate agreed in advance at which it is prepared to lend money to other banks for any given maturity on any given day calculated over a year assumed to have 360 days, not the calendar year of 365 days. A notable exception to this year of 360 days is sterling where Libor, money market, rates are calculated over a year assumed to have 365 days. The swap market is sufficiently developed to use daily published Libor rates for each currency which can be found on information services like Reuters, page 'ISDA' (International Swap Dealers Association) and Telerate, pages 3750 and 3745 published by the British Bankers' Association. These rates are updated daily at 11.00 hrs London time. The Reuters and Telerate pages display the average of the Libor rates quoted by a number of banks in the London market, excluding the extremes, at which they are prepared to lend each other money for periods from one month up to twelve months on any given day in London in different currencies.

Convention

The convention we will use throughout this text when expressing terms is:

Interest Rate (payment period, day count convention)

Thus an annual rate of 10.00 per cent calculated by reference to Libor payable in US dollars for a twelve-month advance would be expressed as:

10.00 per cent (Ann, A/360)

– 10.00 per cent per annum, payable annually, i.e. once a year calculated over a 360-day year. Effective annual rate 10.1389 per cent per annum. 'A' for actual number of days.

An annual rate of 10.00 per cent Libor payable in Sterling for a twelve-month advance would be expressed as:

10.00 per cent (Ann, A/365)

– 10.00 per cent per annum, payable annually, i.e. once a year calculated over a 365-day year. Effective annual rate 10.00 per cent per annum in a non-leap year.

If the payments were twice a year by reference to the number of days in that half year period the rate would be 10.00 per cent (s/a, A/360); quarterly (q, A/360); monthly (m, A/360) etc. The term 'money market' is often used to replace the convention above. Thus 10.00 per cent (s/a, A/360) may also be expressed as 10.00 per cent semi-annual, money-market.

The swap market usually makes the variable rate payments not on an annual basis but on a semi-annual basis, i.e. twice a year and linked to the six-month Libor prevailing for each interest period. Thus a simple interest rate swap would more typically look like that shown in Figure 3.3.

The six-month Libor rate is calculated two days in advance of each six-month period, thus on Monday, 9 September 1991 the six-month Libor rate would be agreed for the period Wednesday, 11 September 1991 to Wednesday, 11 March 1992; on

Start date	**Fixed Payment** Company A pays to Company B	**Floating Payment** Company B pays to Company A
Wednesday, 11 September 1991	0.00	0.00
Wednesday, 11 March 1992	0.00	6-month Libor
Friday, 11 September 1992	US$ 10.00	6-month Libor

Figure 3.3 Swap Interest Payments: 6-month Libor Payments not Known

Monday, 9 March 1992 the second six-month Libor rate would be agreed for the period Wednesday, 11 March 1992 to Friday, 11 September 1992. Thus if six-month Libor was 10.00 per cent on both dates, i.e. 10.00 per cent (s/a, A/360), (10.00 per cent payable semi-annually, i.e. twice a year calculated over a 360-day year), the actual cash flows on each interest payment date would be:

Wednesday, 11 March 1992:

$$\text{US\$ } 100.00 \times \frac{10}{100} \times \frac{\text{No of days (11/3/92–11/9/91)}}{360},$$

$$\text{US\$ } 100.00 \times \frac{10}{100} \times \frac{182}{360},$$

$$= \underline{\text{US\$ } 5.06}$$

and on Friday, 11 September 1992:

$$\text{US\$ } 100.00 \times \frac{10}{100} \times \frac{\text{No of days (11/9/92–11/3/92)}}{360},$$

$$\text{US\$ } 100.00 \times \frac{10}{100} \times \frac{184}{360},$$

$$= \underline{\text{US\$ } 5.11}$$

(Note that 1992 is a leap year with 366 days)

Start date	**Fixed Payment** Company A pays to Company B	**Floating Payment** Company B pays to Company A
Wednesday, 11 September 1991	0.00	0.00
Wednesday, 11 March 1991	0.00	5.06
Friday, 11 September 1992	10.00	5.11
Total	**10.00**	**10.17**

Figure 3.4 Swap Cash Flows with 6-month Libor known

The swap would then look as shown in Figure 3.4.

The reader will appreciate that the value of a single fixed payment of 10 per cent is less than the value of the two floating rate payments of 10.00 per cent (s/a, A/360), calculated due under the swap and paid at six-monthly intervals. In order to compare cash flows we need to be able to express annual cash flows on an equivalent quarterly, semi-annual basis etc.

Convert Annual Bond Rate to Equivalent Semi-Annual Bond Rate

10.00 per cent (Ann, 30/360) to Semi-Annual Bond (s/a, 30/360)

Formula: where R = 10.00 per cent (Ann, 30/360)

$$\left[\left(1+\frac{R}{100}\right)^{0.5}-1\right]\times 200$$

Calculation:

$$\left[\left(1+\frac{10}{100}\right)^{0.5}-1\right]\times 200$$

= 9.7617 per cent (s/a, 30/360)

General formula: where R = 10.00 per cent annual and N is the number of payments per annum.

$$\left[\left(1+\frac{R}{100}\right)^{(1/N)}-1\right]\times N\times 100$$

Convert Semi-Annual Bond Rate to Equivalent Annual Bond Rate

10.00 per cent (s/a, 30/360) to Annual Bond equivalent (Ann, 30/360).

Formula: where R = 10.00 per cent.

$$\left[\left(1+\frac{R}{200}\right)^{2}-1\right]\times 100$$

Calculation: where R = 10.00 per cent.

$$\left[\left(1+\frac{10}{200}\right)^{2}+1\right]\times 100$$

= 10.25 per cent (Ann, 30/360)

General formula: where $R = 10.00$ per cent and N is the number of payments per annum.

$$\left[\left(1+\frac{R}{(N\times 100)}\right)^N - 1\right]\times 100$$

INTEREST RATE SWAP AS A LONG/(SHORT) POSITION IN A BOND AND AN EQUIVALENT SHORT/(LONG) POSITION IN A FLOATING RATE NOTE

A simple interest rate swap to receive fixed/(pay) fixed versus payment/(receipt) of floating can be considered as a long/(short) position in a fixed rate bond with an equivalent short/(long) position in a floating rate note. A floating rate note is a bond which pays interest linked to a variable index, for example, six-month Libor. It can be alternatively considered as a variable rate loan.

Fixed rate payer	Party A, bond issuer
Floating rate payer	Party B, FRN issuer
Floating rate receiver	Party A, FRN investor
Fixed rate receiver	Party B, bond investor
Notional amount	US$ 100.00
Fixed rate payer pays	7.00 per cent
Floating rate payer pays	6-month US$ Libor
Maturity	3 years
Issue (start) date	Friday, 13 September 1991
Initial Libor setting	8.00 per cent

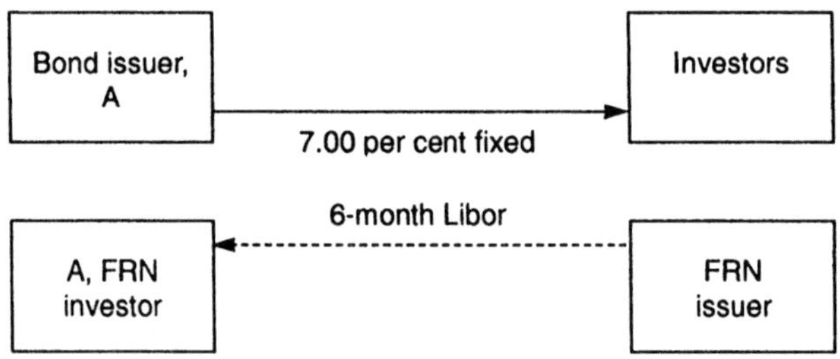

The interest rate swap transaction described above is:

Fixed rate payer	Party A
Floating rate payer	Party B
Notional amount	US$ 100.00
Fixed rate payer pays	10.00 per cent
Floating rate payer pays	6-month US$ Libor
Maturity	3 Years
Start date	Friday, 13 September 1991
Initial Libor setting	8.00 per cent

Date	**Bond** Fixed	**FRN** Floating	**Swap** Fixed	**Swap** Floating
13 September 1991	(100.00)	+100.00		
13 March 1992		(4.044)		(4.044)
13 September 1992	+7.00	(6-month Libor)	+7.00	(6-month Libor)
13 March 1993		(6-month Libor)		(6-month Libor)
13 September 1993	+7.00	(6-month Libor)	+7.00	(6-month Libor)
13 March 1994		(6-month Libor)		(6-month Libor)
13 September 1994	+7.00	(6-month Libor)	+7.00	(6-month Libor)
13 September 1994	+100.00	(100.00)		

Figure 3.5 Bond and FRN Outline

Notice how the interest rate swap has no exchanges of principal at the beginning or end of the swap because the principal amount of the bond and floating rate note offset one another. If we can view swaps as offsetting positions in bonds and floating rate notes we can develop a methodology for valuing swaps using the same techniques.

CURRENCY SWAP AS A LONG/(SHORT) POSITION IN A BOND AND AN EQUIVALENT SHORT/(LONG) POSITION IN A FLOATING RATE NOTE/BOND IN A DIFFERENT CURRENCY

A currency swap can be viewed as a long/(short) position in a fixed rate bond in one currency with an equivalent short/(long) position in a floating rate note or bond in a different currency.

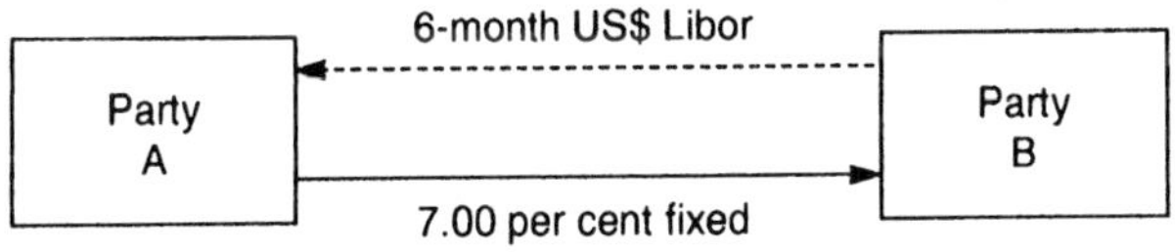

Swiss Franc fixed rate payer	Bond Issuer
US$ floating rate payer	FRN issuer
Notional amount	Swiss Francs 100.00

Fixed rate payer pays	7.00 per cent in Swiss Francs
Floating rate payer pays	6-month US$ Libor, on the Spot US$. Equivalent of the Notional Swiss Franc amount at the start date
Maturity	3 years
Issue (start) date	Friday, 13 September 1991
Initial US$ Libor setting	8.00 per cent
Spot exchange rate at start of swap	US$/CHF 1.5200

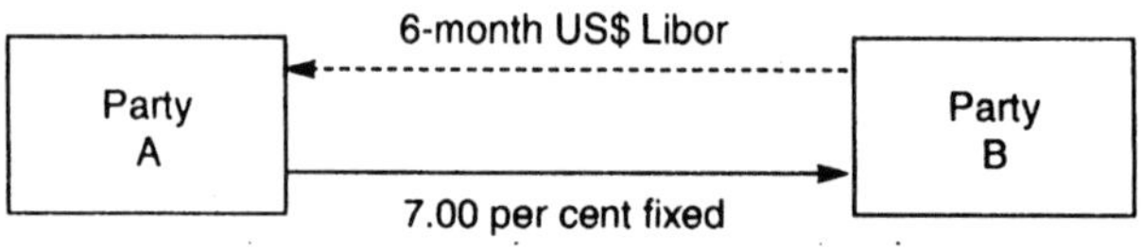

Figure 3.6 Interest Rate Swap as a Series of Forward Rate Agreements

Date	**CHF bond**	**US$ FRN**	**CHF/US$ Swap**	**CHF/US$ Swap**
	Fixed	Floating	Fixed	Floating
13 September 1991	(100.00)	+65.790	(100.00)	+65.790
13 March 1992		(2.661)		(2.661)
13 September 1992	+7.00	(6-month Libor)	+7.00	(6-month Libor)
13 March 1993		(6-month Libor)		(6-month Libor)
13 September 1993	+7.00	(6-month Libor)	+7.00	(6-month Libor)
13 March 1994		(6-month Libor)		(6-month Libor)
13 September 1994	+7.00	(6-month Libor)	+7.00	(6-month Libor)
13 September 1994	+100.00	(65.790)	+100.00	(65.790)

Figure 3.7 Cross-currency Bond and FRN Structure

The currency swap has an exchange of principal at the outset and at the maturity of the swap unlike the interest rate swap where there is no exchange of principal. The exchange rate is important because the present value of the two sides of the swap should be equivalent at the outset which is a function of the interest rates in each currency and the exchange rate. A currency swap like an interest rate swap can in principle be valued as two offsetting bond positions in different currencies whose present values are equivalent at the prevailing spot exchange rate.

INTEREST RATE SWAP AS A SERIES OF FORWARD RATE AGREEMENTS

Another way of looking at an interest rate swap is as a series of forward rate agreements ('FRAs') with end-period payments.

End-Period FRA

Customer agrees in advance to pay/(receive) the difference between a fixed rate of 7 per cent and 6-month Libor for a 6-month calculation period commencing 13 September 1991. All payments will be made on 13 March 1992.

$$\text{Payment on 13th March 1992} = (7.00 - \text{6-month Libor}) \frac{182}{360}$$

$$\text{Receive 13th March 1992} = (\text{6-month Libor} - 7.00) \frac{182}{360}$$

This is identical to a one-period swap. A series of end-period FRAs at 7.00 per cent would look identical to our Figure 3.3 example above of a simple interest rate swap to pay 7.00 per cent fixed versus receipt of six-month Libor. Interest rate swaps more typically have the fixed payments on an annual basis and the floating rate payments paid six monthly. We can also represent this structure with FRAs by compounding up the payments.

Example

Fixed rate payer	Company A
Floating rate payer	Company B
Notional amount	US$ 100.00
Fixed rate payer pays	7.00 per cent (Ann, 30/360)
Floating rate payer pays	6-months US$ Libor
Maturity	1 year
Start date	Wednesday, 11 September 1991

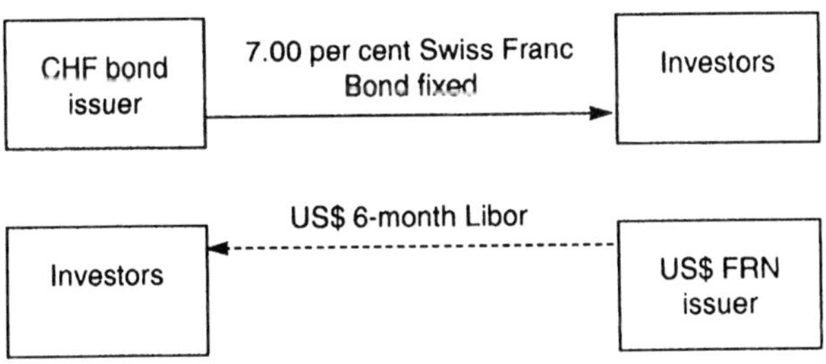

The cash flows of the swap would be set out thus:

Start date	Fixed Payment Company A pays to Company B	Floating Payment Company B pays to Company A
Wednesday, 11 September 1991	0	0
Wednesday, 11 March 1992	0	6-month US$ Libor
Friday, 11 September 1992	US$ 7.00	6-month US$ Libor

Payment: Friday, 11 September 1992

$$7 - \left\{100\left[\left(1 + R_1 \times \frac{182}{360}\right)\left(1 + R_2 \times \frac{184}{360}\right)\right] - 100\right\}$$

where R_1 = 6-month Libor due on 11 March 1992
R_2 = 6-month Libor due on 11 September 1992

Working through the numbers using six-month Libor rates of:
11 September 1991 to 11 March 1992 8.50 per cent
11 March 1992 to 11 September 1992 9.00 per cent

Date	Libor	Fixed	Floating
Wednesday, 11 March 1992	8.50 per cent		(4.297)*
Friday, 11 September 1992	9.00 per cent	7.00	$\left(9.0 \times \frac{184}{360}\right)$ or (4.60)

* Assume customer borrows 4.297 on Wednesday, 11 March 1992 at the then prevailing Libor rate, 9.00 per cent (s/a, A/360)

Net position on Friday, 11 September 1992 is:

$$+7 - \left[4.297\left(1 + 0.09 \times \frac{184}{360}\right)\right] - 4.600$$

$$= \underline{-2.0947}$$

CURRENCY SWAP AS A SERIES OF FORWARD FOREIGN EXCHANGE CONTRACTS AND FORWARD RATE AGREEMENTS

Currency swaps can be viewed as a series of spot, forward foreign exchange contracts and forward rate agreements ('FRAs'). Consider Company A who wishes to borrow US dollars but currently only has a sterling facility with its bank. It can create an effective US dollar loan through either (i) a currency swap or (ii) the combination of a series of forward foreign exchange contracts and FRAs to manage any residual interest rate risk created after the forward foreign exchange contracts.

Example

Company A borrows	Sterling 100.00
Fixed borrowing cost	10.75 per cent (Ann, A/365)
Maturity	2 years

Details of a currency swap:

Notional amount	Sterling 100.00
Party A pays fixed	10.75 per cent in Sterling (Ann, A/365)
Party A receives fixed	6.80 per cent in US dollars (Ann, 30/360)

Details of forward foreign exchange contracts and FRAs:

Spot exchange rate at start of swap	GBP–US$ 1.6800
One year forward rate	GBP–US$ 1.6107
Two year forward rate	GBP–US$ 1.5626
US$ FRA rate to lock in one year rate in one year's time	7.75 per cent (Ann, 30/360)

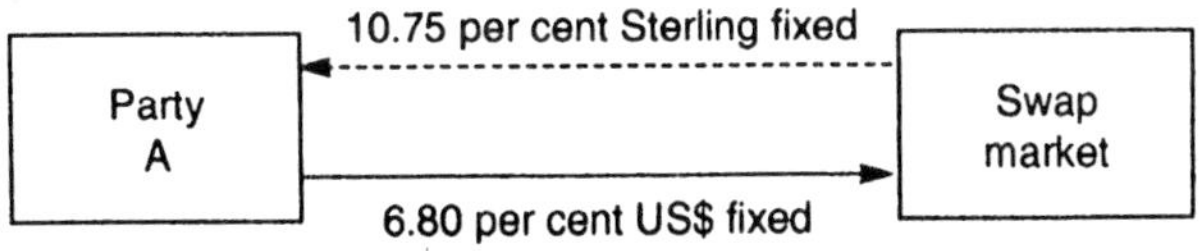

Figure 3.8 Currency Swaps are Equivalent to Foreign Exchange Contracts and FRAs

Alternative 1: Currency Swap

Date	**Borrow Fixed Sterling**	**Currency Swap to US$** Party A Receives	Pays
13 September 1991	+100.00	(100.00)	+168.00
13 September 1992	(10.75)	10.75	(11.42)*
13 September 1993	(10.75)	10.75	(11.42)
13 September 1993	(100.00)	100.00	(168.00)

* $168 \times \frac{6.80}{100.00} = 11.42$

Alternative 2: Spot and Forward Foreign Exchange Contracts and FRAs

As an alternative to the currency swap Party A borrows sterling fixed for two years from his bank and services the sterling interest liability by purchasing sterling forward against delivery of US dollars through the forward foreign exchange contract at the fixed rates for each of those dates in the future, thereby creating a US dollar liability at each point in time to service the sterling loan.

Date	**Borrow Sterling**	**Exchange Rates Spot and Forward**	**US$ Equivalent through the Forward Foreign Exchange Market**	**Currency Swap Cash Flows (from above)**	**Difference Between US$ Equivalent and Currency Swap Cash Flows**
13 September 1991	+100.00	1.6800	+168.00	+168.00	+0.00

13 September 1992	(10.75)	1.6107	(17.32)	(11.42)*	(5.90)
13 September 1993	(110.75)	1.5626	(173.06)	(179.42)	+6.36

The forward foreign exchange market does not create a series of even US dollar cash flows unlike the currency swap. In order to create identical US dollar cash flows, as with the currency swap, Party A needs to borrow US dollars 5.90 from the end of year 1 to the end of year 2, one year. We can fix the borrowing cost of the shortfall of US$ 5.90 at 13 September 1992 for one year using an FRA at a rate of 7.75 per cent which will realise a repayment of US$6.36 at the end of year 2 which corresponds to the cash flow surplus of the forward foreign exchange alternative. Thus a currency swap can be viewed as a package of forward contracts and forward rate agreements between payment dates. The currency swap is convenient because it is a single contract for that package.

USES OF SWAPS

Swaps effectively link the capital markets of all major currencies. They enable counterparts, as we have seen above, to exchange and make direct comparisons of cash flows, in the same or different currencies, most commonly fixed cash flows, versus floating or variable rate cash flows, reset on a regular basis against a benchmark such as six-month Libor. The uses of interest rate and currency derivatives, not just swaps but also forward rate agreements and options, can be broken down under three broad headings:

- Asset and liability management
- Investment or borrowing arbitrage
- Tailored financial packages (structured financings)

Liability and Asset Management

The most common uses of interest and currency rate swaps is for asset and liability management purposes by companies. A company 'Triple Apple', with a floating rate obligation, for example, from a loan upon which it is currently paying floating rate interest at Libor plus a margin can consider locking in the cost of that financing via an interest rate swap. Under the swap it pays fixed versus receipt of floating, matching its exact liability on the loan leaving it a net payer of a fixed interest rate. The company is then hedged against an increase in its exposure from further interest rate rises. A company concerned about rising interest rates will seek to reduce the adverse exposure from rises in interest rates by executing an interest rate swap to pay fixed versus receipt of floating to match its existing liabilities.

Example
Triple Apple has a three-year facility with its bank (Funding bank) to borrow at

six-month Libor plus 0.25 per cent also expressed as six-month Libor plus 25 (s/a, A/360), (0.25 per cent = 25 basis points) for three years. Triple Apple is concerned that interest rates are set to rise over the next few years and would like to fix the cost of its borrowing now for the following three years. The swap market is prepared to receive a fixed rate of 10.50 per cent (Ann, 30/360) versus payment of Libor plus 0.25 per cent (s/a, A/360).

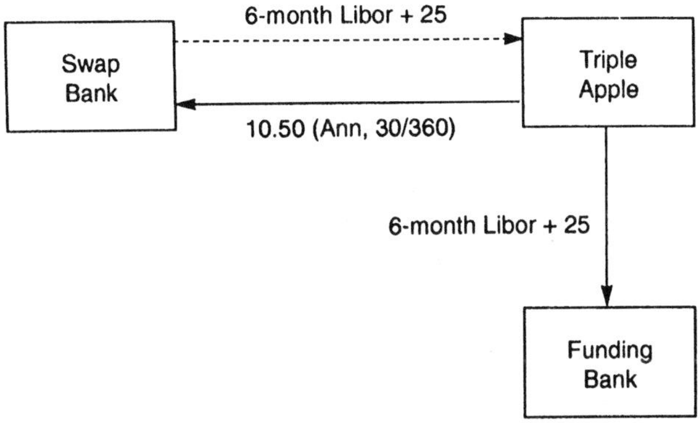

Figure 3.9 Triple Apple Swap to Pay Fixed versus Receipt of Libor

Triple Apple

	Pay (Ann, 30/360)	Receive (s/a, A/360)
Now	0.00	0.00
½ year	0.00	+4.55*
1 year	(10.50)	+6-month Libor + 25
1½ years	0.00	+6-month Libor + 25
2 years	(10.50)	+6-month Libor + 25
2½ years	0.00	+6-month Libor + 25
3 years	(10.50)	+6-month Libor + 25

Note: The payments in this example to Swap Bank are on an annual bond basis. Typically Triple Apple would wish to pay on a semi-annual money market basis, i.e. (s/a, A/360) to match the cost of its loan to Funding Bank exactly. In this case 10.50 per cent (Ann, 30/360) is equivalent to 10.0977 per cent (s/a, A/360).

*Note that the first six-month Libor payment will be known if the swap is a 'spot start' swap, i.e. if it starts immediately, two days hence. In this case 6-month Libor is 8.75 per cent and the first interest period is 182 days

Figure 3.10 Triple Apple's Swap Cash Flows

	Triple Apple (pays) Swap Bank (Ann, 30/360)	Triple Apple and Funding Bank (Ann, 30/360)	Triple Apple Receives from Swap Bank (s/a, A/360)	Triple Apple's Net Position (pays)/receives (Ann, 30/360)
Now		100.00		100.00
½ year	0.00	(4.55)	4.55	0.00
1 year	(10.50)	(6-month Libor + 25)	6-month Libor + 25	(10.50)
1½ years	0.00	(6-month Libor + 25)	6-month Libor + 25	0.00
2 years	(10.50)	(6-month Libor + 25)	6-month Libor + 25	(10.50)
2½ years	0.00	(6-month Libor + 25)	6-month Libor + 25	0.00
3 years	(10.50)	(6-month Libor + 25)	6-month Libor + 25	(10.50)
3 years		(100.0)		(100.00)

$$\text{US\$ } 100.00 \times \frac{9}{100} \times \frac{182}{360}$$

$$= \underline{\text{US\$ } 4.55}$$

Figure 3.11 Triple Apple's Net Position After Swap

In the above example Triple Apple locks in a cost of funds of 10.50 per cent (Ann, 30/360). The payments under the swap are shown in Figure 3.10.

Triple Apple's net position is having locked in a cost of the loan of 10.50 per cent (Ann, 30/360).

Asset Management

'Liquid Investments plc' currently invests short-term in money market instruments with maturities of not more than six months earning six-month Libor. Liquid is concerned about falling interest rates and wishes to protect itself as an investor from the adverse impact of a fall in interest rates. Through an asset swap it can lock in the prevailing higher twelve-month Libor. Liquid's solution is to enter into a one year interest rate swap in order to receive the fixed twelve-month swap rate versus payment of two separate payments of six-month Libor.

Example

Six-month Libor	8.75 per cent (s/a, A/360)
Twelve-month Libor	9.00 per cent (Ann, A/360)

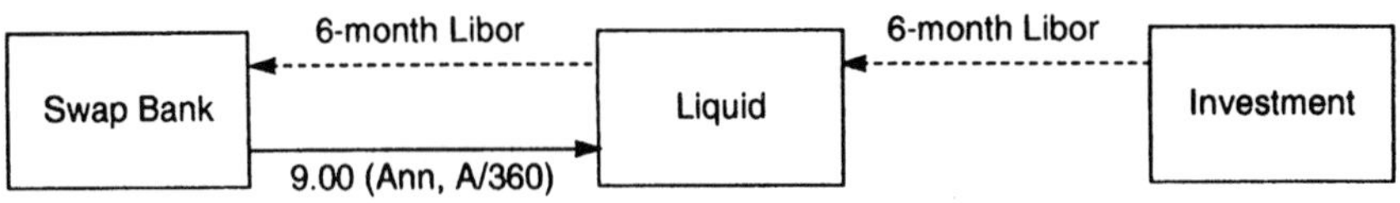

Figure 3.12 Asset Swap by Liquid Investments

In Figure 3.12 Liquid Investments locks in a return of 9.00 per cent (Ann, A/360) independent of the direction of interest rates. The payments under the swap are shown in Figure 3.13.

Liquid Investments

	Receives (Ann, A/360)	Pays (s/a, A/360)
Now	0.000	0.000
½ year	0.000	(4.400)*
1 year	9.125	(6-month Libor)

Figure 3.13a Liquid Investments Cash Flows from the Swap

*Note that the first six-month Libor payment will be known if the swap is a 'spot start' swap, i.e. it starts immediately, two days hence. In this case 6-month Libor is 8.75 per cent and the first interest period is 181 days.

$$\text{US\$ } 100.00 \times \frac{8.75}{100.00} \times \frac{181}{360}$$

$$= \underline{\text{US\$ } 4.40}$$

Liquid Investments Net position After the Swap

	Liquid (pays) Swap Bank (s/a, A/360)	**Liquid's Investment Return (s/a, A/360)**	**Liquid Receives from Swap Bank (Ann, A/360)**	**Liquid's Net Position (pays)/receives (Ann, A/360)**
Now		(100.00)		(100.000)
½ year	(4.40)	4.40	0.00	0.000
1 year	(6-month Libor)	6-month Libor	9.125	9.125*
1 year		100.00		100.000

Figure 3.13b Liquid Investments Net Position After the Swap

*Liquid's net position is having locked in an investment of 9.00 per cent (Ann, A/360)

$$\text{US\$ } 100.00 \times \frac{9}{100} \times \frac{365}{360}$$

INVESTMENT OR BORROWING ARBITRAGE

Investment or borrowing arbitrage is where assets or liabilities are restructured or 'repackaged' from one interest basis in a currency, for example a fixed basis, to another basis in the same currency, e.g. floating, or alternatively the same or different interest basis in a different currency. In all cases the liability or asset achieved should be attractive in that market relative to a comparable asset or liability otherwise available from accessing that market directly.

The most common example of borrowing arbitrage is that available to issuers in the Eurobond market who are able to issue fixed rate eurobonds and swap the liability of those bonds to floating rate liabilities at rates more attractive than could be obtained from Bank lines of credit or accessing the floating rate market direct.

BORROWING ARBITRAGE

Bond Issuer Arbitrage

The most common form of borrowing arbitrage is where an issuer of a fixed rate bond, for example a publicly issued and listed eurobond, exchanges the fixed rate liability on the bond for a floating rate liability usually linked to Libor via a swap.

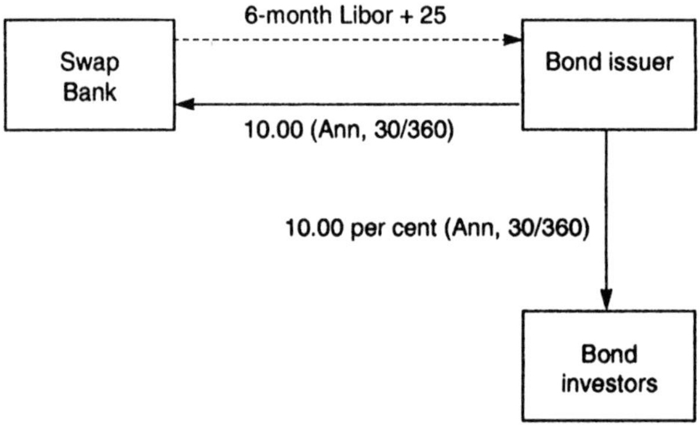

Figure 3.14 Bond Arbitrage Swap

As an example, the swap market is willing to pay an annual fixed rate of 10.00 per cent (30/360) to match the coupon on the bond and in return receive six-month Libor less 0.25 per cent per annum (A/360). The company if it were to access the floating rate market or to borrow floating would have to pay a margin above six-month Libor, e.g. 0.15 per cent. Thus a saving is created in the order of 0.40 per cent (s/a, A/360) in this example.

INVESTMENT ARBITRAGE

Investment Arbitrage (Variable Rate Assets)

In this situation the investor is generally a bank with a variable rate (Libor based) funding source. By paying away via a swap an unwanted fixed income stream received, for example from a fixed rate bond investment the investor secures a yield at a spread above Libor, akin to the margin on the bank loans with which it is familiar.

From the perspective of the investor, the Bank, this structure has a number of attractions. The disintermediation process which has occurred as short-term paper facilities have replaced syndicated bank credits has resulted in a shortage of traditional banking assets and a suppressing of spreads. The repackaged paper has served to replace much of this. For the smaller bank or branch the repackaged transaction is easier to administer than competitive tender panels every three to six months.

By far the greater volume of this paper is low coupon ex-warrant paper, either bank guaranteed or non-guaranteed. However, straight issues come to market with regular frequency priced purely as an asset swap. These generally represent a cost to the borrower which is a premium to the costs which could be achieved via a bank loan (fixed rate, or with a swap). However, for a company which is already highly leveraged, the much more relaxed Euromarket covenant structure and speed of execution after mandate, make this a more attractive approach. It may also provide the means by which the investor base can be diversified.

Note that in general the bond sale and accompanying swap are independent transactions. Thus the identity of the investor cannot be withheld from the swap counterpart. This also adds to the credit exposure of the investor. Also some investors have tax and/or accounting problems with certain structures.

The most common variation of this structure is the fixed rate bond package as a floating rate instrument.

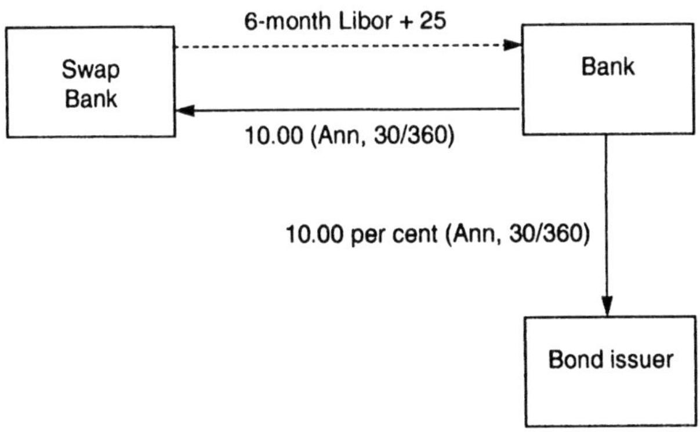

Figure 3.15 Investment Arbitrage Swap

The swap market is willing to receive an annual fixed rate of 10.00 per cent (30/360) matching the coupon on the bond and in return pay six-month Libor plus 0.25 per cent per annum (A/360). If the Bank were to lend the bond issuer funds directly it would expect to earn a margin above six-month Libor of say 0.15 per cent (s/a, A/360). The asset swap provides an improvement of 0.10 per cent (s/a, A/360) over the straight loan.

The one effect of repackaging from a trading perspective is to reduce the liquidity of an issue. This is particularly severe when an otherwise apparently unrepackagable issue has had a bad syndication, or the lead manager has used the technique to clear away some of his underwriting position.

TAILORED FINANCIAL PACKAGES

Tailored financial packages cover a wide range of complex swaps and options. At one extreme they may be swap structures specifically targeted to borrowers' unusual cash flow timings and schedules, at the other end they may include complex packages as outlined below of embedded options and swaps offered to investors publicly as complete structures. The examples below are of Nikkei linked structures which have been offered in the past to investors as public eurobond issues. The different types of structures come under two broad headings and are discussed below in the context of a financial package linked to the performance of the Nikkei 225 index:

- Future or forward linked structures
- Option linked structures

Future or forward linked structures require the investor to hold a forward position in the Nikkei 225 Index at a level fixed at the outset thereby creating an exposure to upward and downward movements of the Index. Option linked structures generally expose the investor to a one directional movement of the Index, i.e. up or down, although bi-directional structures are possible (straddles). The exposures created can be favourable or unfavourable. Option linked structures can be categorised as either high coupon or low coupon:

- High coupon – capital at risk structures. These structures offer a high coupon to the investor from the writing of a call (put) option on the Index but place the investor's capital at risk. The investor earns a high coupon but his principal redeemed at maturity is reduced if the index rises (falls) about the strike rate of the transaction.
- Low coupon – capital gain. These structures offer a low coupon where the investor effectively purchases a call (put) option on the Index. The investor's return is enhanced by a rise (fall) in the index about the strike rate set at the outset which can alter the coupon or the principal redeemed at maturity.

Beyond these two basic categories the variations are limitless. An investor who believed at the time of launch that the Nikkei 225 Index would fall over the next twelve months and required protection from that fall or wished to take advantage of that fall could invest in a high coupon – capital risk structure where he earns a high interest coupon but in return puts his capital to be repaid at maturity at risk.

High Coupon – Capital Risk Structure: One Year Call

Investor writes a call on the Nikkei 225 Index to the issuer in return for a higher coupon. If the Nikkei 225 rises from the strike rate set on the structure at the outset the principal redeemed at maturity is reduced.

Typical Issue Terms

Issuer:	European AA Rated Financial Institution
Principal:	Yen 2 billion
Coupon	
Annual (30/360):	16.50%
Issue price:	100.875%
Fees:	0.875%
Maturity:	One year from launch
Payment date:	One month from launch
Redemption formula:	In Yen at maturity

Maximum 100 per cent, Minimum Redemption Amount 10%, then

$$100 - \left[\frac{(\text{Nikkei at maturity} - \text{Nikkei at launch})}{\text{Nikkei at launch}} \times 100\right]$$

Nikkei at Maturity per cent of Current Level		Bond Redemption	Coupon	Total Repaid
		(Percentage of principal, 100 per cent)		
50	(14,490.23)	100	16.50	116.50
60	(17,388.27)	100	16.50	116.50
70	(20,286.32)	100	16.50	116.50
80	(23,184.36)	100	16.50	116.50
90	(26,082.41)	100	16.50	116.50
100	(28,980.45) Launch	100	16.50	116.50
110	(31,878.50)	90	16.50	106.50
115	(33,327.52)	85	16.50	101.50
120	(34,776.54)	80	16.50	96.50
130	(37,674.59)	70	16.50	86.50

Figure 3.16 Pay-off Table High Coupon – Capital Risk Structure

Typically in the above structure the investor's return would be enhanced further by additional gearing, e.g.

$$100 - \left\{\text{Gearing} \times \left[\frac{(\text{Launch Nikkei} - \text{Nikkei maturity})}{(\text{Nikkei at launch})}\right] \times 100\right\}$$

Gearing	Coupon
2×	27.000%
3×	36.625%

In a geared structure the investor effectively writes an option based on a larger principal amount than the issue size. At a gearing of 2×(3×), the investor writes an option based on a principal of Yen 4 billion (Yen 6 billion) to the issuer. The issue size remains at Yen 2 billion. The reader will recognise that in a structure where the investor's principal is at risk the most he can lose is his original investment, i.e. 100 per cent. At a gearing of 2×(3×), each one Yen rise in the Nikkei 225 Index, from Yen 28,980 to Yen 28,981, has the effect of reducing the investor's principal redeemed at maturity by two Yen (three yen).

Level at Launch Gearing	Level of Nikkei at Maturity	Principal Remaining
1×	28,980	0
2×	14,490	0
3×	9,860	0

The attraction of geared structures is that they offer the confident or aggressive investor even higher returns although they put more of the investor's capital at risk, i.e. they have higher exposure. They do not involve a higher market risk than the non-geared structures. The market risk in the above structures is that the Nikkei 225 Index at maturity will be below the strike rate at launch. '0' funds or 'money back' structures use swaps extensively to produce the desired financial package.

SWAPTIONS

Interest rate swaps are important money market tools for companies which actively monitor their exposure to interest rate movements in respect of both borrowings and investments. Swaps allow a company to hedge its exposure in order to maximise its interest earnings and minimise its interest expense. Swaptions, options on swaps or contingent interest rate swaps as they are variously known, are an extension of conventional swaps in which the writer of the swaption earns a premium in consideration for granting to the purchaser of the swaption the right, but not the obligation, to enter into an interest rate swap before or on a specified future date at a pre-agreed fixed interest rate versus payment of the floating rate, for example, six-month Libor.

Swaptions can be cross currency, i.e. where the fixed rate is in a different currency from the payment of the floating rate. They can involve an actual swap when exercised or be cash settled at the exercise date of the option period. Cash settlement has important implications for reducing the credit risk in the swaption if exercised.

Definition of a Swaption

A swaption is effectively an option on a swap where the fixed rate of interest and life of the swap are established at the outset but the decision to execute the swap is at the choice of one party, the swaption purchaser, who pays a premium for this privilege. The fixed rate of interest on the swaption is called the strike rate. At the end of the option period if the swap is not exercised all rights under the original agreement terminate.

The swap can be either to pay or to receive the fixed rate of interest in return for receiving or paying the prevailing floating rate of interest according to a benchmark agreed in advance. The swap writer cannot refuse to execute the swap if requested by the swap purchaser nor can he subsequently change the terms of the swap agreed at the outset.

Who should Enter into a Swaption

Swaptions are of interest to any institution which has a target interest rate on it assets or liabilities which is different from current levels and/or any institutions which has a view on the future direction of interest rates over the life of the option period.

The following discussion assumes that a company wishes to reduce the cost of its sterling borrowing to a level lower than that currently prevailing in the money markets. In order to do this the company would write a swaption with a strike rate below current interest rates. In this case the writer would be of the view that either:

(1) Rates will not fall below the strike rate on the swap during the option period so that the swap will not be exercised. In this case, the option premium will represent a clear profit to the writer and would serve to reduce his borrowing costs; or
(2) Rates may fall below the level of the strike rate during the option period so that the swap would be exercised against him, but he would be happy to have locked in the strike rate which represents a significant fall in rates from current levels. The effective rate which the writer will have locked in will be equivalent to the strike rate on the swap less the value of the premium he received discounted appropriately.

Outline of a Transaction involving Company 'XYZ' as Swaption Writer

In the example transaction below company XYZ writes an option where the purchaser of the option has the right but not the obligation to receive from XYZ a fixed rate of interest in return for payment of six-month Libor. XYZ would typically be a corporate in a net borrowing position.

XYZ PLC writes a swaption with the following details:

Amount	£10m or more in multiples of £5m to be agreed.
Strike level	Fixed Strike Rate of 9.875 per cent. Interest on the swap is payable annually at this rate against receipt of prevailing six-month sterling LIBOR fixed in advance payable twice yearly in arrears.
Swap counterparty	Corporate or financial institution of standing acceptable to XYZ PLC.
Option period	Up to and including 1 year.
Underlying swap	Maximum maturity of 10 years from date of writing of swap, should the option be exercised. From the end of option period the swap would be for 9 years.

Settlement	'Swap' settlement is execution of actual swap. Not 'cash' settlement on exercise date.
Indicative premium	£77,600 per £10 millions, payable in advance for a swap with a maximum life of 10 years.

(The strike rate in this example is currently 0.45 per cent below the market 10 year swap rate of pay fixed 10.33 per cent versus receipt of six-month Libor.)

Components of the Swaption Premium

The premium earned by the swap writer is dependent upon the current level of interest rates for the maturity of the swap and option (the shape of the yield curve), the strike rate of the swap, the length of the option and swap periods and the volatility of the underlying interest rate for the period of the swap.

The relationship between swap premium and these components in the above example is that the swap premium rises as:

(1) the strike level gets closer to the current 10-year swap rate,
(2) the swap period gets longer,
(3) the option period gets longer,
(4) the volatility of interest rates for the swap and option periods rises.

Table 3.1 gives indicative premiums for different points between the 10-year swap rate and the strike level on the swaption where the swap writer will pay the fixed rate of interest annually and receive the floating rate semi-annually. In the example above the strike level selected is below the current level of interest rates for the swap period.

Table 3.1

Absolute Difference Between Current Swap rate and Strike Level (Percentage Points)	Option Period (Years)	Period of Swap (Years)	Indicative Premium (£ Per £10 Million)
0.25%	1	10	100,000
0.50%	1	10	72,000
0.70%	1	10	51,000
1.00%	1	10	32,000
1.50%	1	10	14,000
0.25%	2	10	148,000
0.50%	2	10	114,000
0.70%	2	10	90,000
1.00%	2	10	63,000
1.50%	2	10	32,000

Operation of the Swaption

Considering the swap transaction above, the swap will be exercised at the onset if the 10-year swap rate falls below 9.875 per cent per annum. Ten-year comparable rates are 10.33 per cent today.

The swap can be exercised partially or in whole at any time during the option period.

XYZ PLC will earn a premium for writing the swaption which can be regarded as further reducing the effective rate at which the swap is exercised. If the swap is exercised at the end of the option period the benefit of the initial indicative premium is 12.5 basis points per annum on the transaction discussed above. This reduces the effective rate from 9.875 per cent to 9.75 per cent on an annual basis, equivalent of 9.52 per cent on a semi-annual basis.

Because it is an option, the swaption always has an element of time value prior to maturity. If it is exercised prior to its maturity date this time value is lost and therefore a swap writer could expect that it will not be exercised before this date. However, there are a number of instances where the swap might be exercised prior to maturity, for example, if the 10-year swap rate was below the strike rate on the swap and the holder of the swap believed that interest rates were about to rise. If he thought that rates would not subsequently fall to recoup the decline in value of his option then he may choose to exercise the swap. If the swap is exercised it will always be at the rate which was agreed at the time when the swap was written. In so far as this represents a target rate for the writer then this rate should be attractive. The writer should therefore not be influenced by the manner in which the swap is exercised. A further possibility is that the option purchaser is unable to sell the swaption at a price which is above its intrinsic or exercise value, for example, where XYZ's credit quality has deteriorated.

It is also possible in the above example that the swap will be exercised in an amount which varies from the total amount of the swap.

The swap writer should be indifferent as to what percentage of the swap is exercised because he will earn premium on the full amount of the swap at the outset and because if the swap is not exercised when it is economic to do so the option purchaser's loss will be directly matched by a further gain to the writer of the swap.

Illustrating this with an example, on a total swap of £25 million, if the 10-year swap rate fell by 1.00 per cent to 9.332 per cent and only 90 per cent of the swap written was exercised, XYZ could realise an additional profit of £83,720 below the target borrowing cost of 9.52 per cent on a semi-annual basis by locking in to a 10-year swap at 9.33 per cent on the 10 per cent not exercised.

Interest Rate Scenarios

In order to show the effects of the swaption we have set out below four different interest rate scenarios based around a market swap rate of 10.33 per cent for 10 years. XYZ wishes to reduce its overall cost of funding. If XYZ believes that over the swaption life:

(1) *Ten-year swap rates will remain at or around 10.33 per cent level.* In this case the swap will not be exercised since the option purchaser can earn a more attractive rate than 9.875 per cent (the strike rate) in the market. If the option purchaser does exercise the swaption it will be at an unfavourable off market interest rate and XYZ will have earned the option premium, which reduces the effective cost of any swap by a further 0.13 per cent per annum.
(2) *Ten-year swap rates fall slightly over the next year to approximately 10.00 per cent level.* Again the option will not be exercised leaving XYZ, the option writer, in a position to enter into a swap at its expiry at an effective cost 0.13 per cent below the then market rate. If XYZ believes that rates are about to rise during the life of the swaption XYZ could enter into a separate swap at a level which XYZ considers to be the low point. XYZ's exposure to a subsequent fall in interest rates to below 9.875 per cent when the option would be exercised, could be hedged at that time to prevent XYZ ending up with double the amount of fixed rate payment obligations than was intended.
(3) *XYZ believes 10-year swap rates will rise above 10.33 per cent.* XYZ should enter into both the swaption and a simple interest rate swap, since the up front payment on the swaption will serve to reduce the effective fixed rate of this straight swap by 0.13 per cent per annum.
(4) *No clear view on interest rates.* The swaption may also be attractive to XYZ if he is uncertain as to the direction of the movement in interest rates, but XYZ is happy to secure fixed rate sterling at 9.52 per cent on a semi-annual basis in any event. In this case, if rates fall below 9.875 per cent, the option will be exercised, giving XYZ a swap rate which meets its current target; if rates rise, XYZ will always be in a position to lock into fixed rate funding at 0.13 per cent below the prevailing rates.

Swaptions for Investors

Swaptions can also be used as an investment management tool to swap into or out of fixed rate or floating rate funds according to an investor's view of interest rates. An example of a transaction would be where the investor with a floating rate income would be prepared to allow a counterparty, the swaption purchaser, to take the floating rate income and pay a fixed rate of say 12 per cent to the investor. The investor would receive a premium for writing this option which would be of particular interest to him if he thought that interest rates over the swap life would not rise above 12 per cent plus the annuity of the premium he receives.

Conclusion

The value of swaptions lies in their ability to hedge unanticipated interest rate or cash movements or where the financial manager has a view on the direction of interest rates or clearly defined targets for funding or investment levels. As such, swaptions are an additional tool to add to interest rate and currency swaps, and caps, and floors as methods of profitably managing financial risks.

PART 3

USING DERIVATIVES

4: Short-term Interest Rate Risk Management

Sandy McKenzie

INTRODUCTION

The three main derivative instruments we will consider are:

(1) Forward Rate Agreements (FRAs).
(2) Futures.
(3) Options.

These can be regarded as the basic tools of short-term interest rate risk management. Many of the new 'exotic' products available are simply combinations of these instruments. A sophisticated market operator can create his own 'exotics', often at a lower cost than the finished product which is for sale. The important point to note about FRAs, futures and options is that, in practice, they have all proved effective in achieving the controls the risk manager desires.

FORWARD RATE AGREEMENTS

A forward rate agreement (FRA) is an over-the-counter equivalent to a short-term interest rate futures contract. It consists of an agreement between two counterparties (of whom at least one is usually a bank) to pay or receive the difference between a fixed interest cost and an actual interest cost at the time a loan is made. In fact, an interest rate swap is simply a combination of several FRAs, one for each rollover date in the swap.

Example

24 August 1991.
A 3-month FRA borrowing agreement of 2,000,000 Swiss Francs on 1 December 1991 at 8 per cent.

If the 3-month rate on 1 December is over 8 per cent the lender pays the borrower the differential between the rate and 8 per cent.

If the 3-month rate on 1 December is under 8 per cent the borrower pays the lender the differential between the rate and 8 per cent.

The amount to be paid is:

$$\frac{\text{SF } 2{,}000{,}000\ [(R - 0.08)\ 90/360]}{[1 + (R \times 90/360)]}$$

where R is the 3-month cash borrowing rate on 1 December.

Note: The amount paid is discounted as it is paid before the loan period, not afterwards.

If the 3-month rate on 1 December was 9 per cent the lender would pay to the borrower:

$$\frac{\text{SF } 2{,}000{,}000 \times [(0.09 - 0.08) \times 90/360]}{1 + (0.09 \times 90/360)}$$

$$= \text{SF } 4{,}889.98$$

This discounted value of the extra interest payable on the borrowing can now be invested for 3 months at 8.875 per cent, the cash 3-month lending rate.

$$\text{SF } 4889.98\ [1 + (0.08875 \times 90/360)] = \text{SF } 4998.48$$

Therefore the effective interest rate on the borrowing is:

$$\frac{[\text{SF } 2{,}000{,}000\ (0.09 \times 90/360)] - \text{SF } 4998.48}{\text{SF } 2{,}000{,}000} \times \frac{360}{90}$$

$$= 8 \text{ per cent}$$

This is almost exactly the rate agreed for the period. In reality, a small difference occurred due to the bid/ spread on the cash market rate.

The Pros and Cons of FRAs

The two major advantages FRAs have over futures contracts are the made-to-measure dates and amounts involved which can make FRAs very user-friendly. FRAs are not marked-to-market. This means that if the FRA is losing money this loss does not have to be financed as with a futures position. However, if the hedge is making money then it is advantageous to have a futures hedge rather than an FRA as profits are received and can be utilised.

The main drawbacks of FRAs are:

(1) Cost.
(2) Lack of price visibility.
(3) Lack of standardisation.
(4) Credit risk.

FRAs in major currencies are usually priced off the more liquid futures contracts available. The rate which will be given will be one which can be hedged using the futures markets and still give a reasonable profit.

Whereas futures prices are always known and available, the price of an FRA with non-standard dates and amounts can be difficult to determine. The fair market level of an FRA can be said to be the highest level to which a counterparty will agree.

If a hedge to be lifted prior to the borrowing date it may be difficult to achieve a fair· price to reverse the FRA.

Although credit status is not as important for short maturities as for longer maturities it must be taken into consideration in any over-the-counter deals (BCCI being a recent example of bad credit exposure).

FUTURES

The ideal scenario for a hedger of short-term interest rate exposure is that:

(1) His exposure dates coincide with the delivery dates of the relevant futures contract.
(2) The duration of his exposure is the same as the duration of the futures contract.
(3) The amount he has to hedge can be achieved with an exact number of futures contracts.

Although it is unlikely that his exposure will fulfil the above requirements, it is significant that many borrowers and lenders now try to manipulate their market exposure to equate to these conditions.

The basic hedge ratio formula used is:

$$\text{Number of contracts} = \text{ratio of face values} \times \text{ratio of maturities}$$

However this basic formula assumes that their exposure period rate and the futures rate correlate perfectly. To refine this somewhat naive assumption it is wise to determine the historical correlation between these rates and apply this regression coefficient to the hedge ratio formula. Thus:

Number of contracts

$$= \frac{\text{Face value exposure}}{\text{Face value contract}} \times \frac{\text{Duration exposure}}{\text{Duration contract}} \times \text{Regression coefficient}$$

Hedging a Futures Delivery Day Exposure

Example

To hedge a 6-month exposure of DM 20 million starting on the futures delivery day in December 1991 with a regression coefficient between the 6-month rates and the 3-month rate of the Euromark contract of 0.97; a straightforward hedge would consist of:

$$\frac{\text{DM 20 million}}{\text{DM 1 million}} \times \frac{\text{6-months}}{\text{3-months}} \times 0.97 = 38.80 \text{ contracts}$$

The number of contracts used would probably be rounded up to 39 and the rate achieved should equate to the futures price plus or minus the rounding error.

Interpolated Hedging

Let us now consider a more usual situation. In this instance the exposure is not for a futures delivery date.

10 July 1991
Bank ZAB has a borrowing requirement of $10 million for three months on 20 November 1991.
Eurodollar futures prices are:

September 1991	93.40
December 1991	93.10
March 1991	92.80

The regression coefficient is 1.

ZAB will hedge their exposure to rising rates between 10 July and 18 November, when they will fix their 3-month borrowing rate for 20 November and lift their hedge.

Anticipated Rate
The rate at which they would hope to borrow can be determined by a linear interpolation between the September and December futures prices.

$$\begin{array}{ccccc} & \text{63 days} & & \text{28 days} & \\ \text{16 Sept.} & \longrightarrow & \text{18 Nov.} & \longrightarrow & \text{16 Dec.} \\ 6.60\% & & & & 6.90\% \end{array}$$

To calculate

$$(6.60\% \times 28/91 \text{ days}) + (6.90\% \times 63/91 \text{ days}) = 6.81\%$$

Hedge Ratio

Number of contracts

$$= \frac{\$\ 10 \text{ million}}{\$\ 1 \text{ million}} \times \frac{\text{92 days}}{\text{91 days}} \times 1 = 10.1 \text{ contracts}$$

To determine which contracts to use to equate to the exposure date a similar interpolation is used.

September contracts = 10.1 × 28/91 days = 3.1 or 3 contracts

December contracts = 10.1 × 63/91 days = 6.99 or 7 contracts

Thus the initial interpolated hedge would be:

Sell 3 September 1991 Eurodollar futures

Sell 7 December 1991 Eurodollar futures

Hedging Basis Risk

Although the best forecast for the basis level between the cash and futures prices at a specific date in the future can be made by a straight line interpolation between the current cash and futures levels, in practice, the basis will not converge to zero following exactly this straight line.

Changes in short-term interest rates and any arbitrage boundary violations can lead to significant changes in the basis level. In situations where there are large movements in short-term interest rates (i.e., when there is the greatest need to hedge an interest rate exposure) the change in basis from interpolated levels can be as much as 40 basis points. This movement in basis can seriously affect the interest rate level achieved by a hedge. Nevertheless, do not despair! These changes in rates also cause changes in

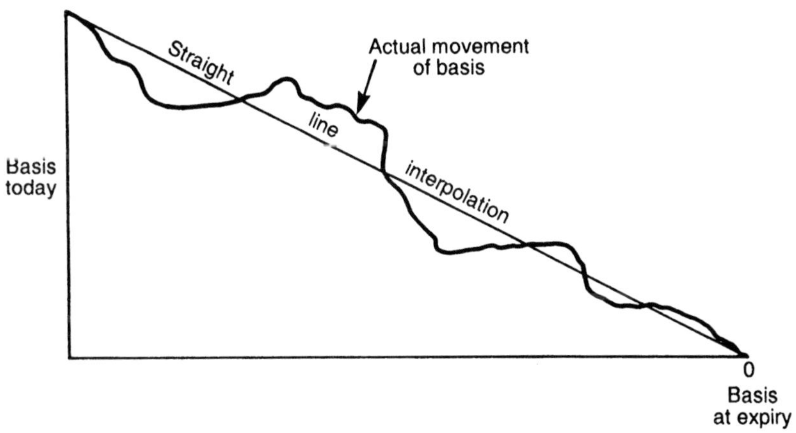

Figure 4.1

the spread differentials between different futures deliveries. These changes in spread levels can be used to minimise the effects of the potentially detrimental changes from anticipated basis levels.

The interpolated hedge for ZAB bank has no basis risk until the September futures contracts expire. At this point ZAB have to adjust their hedge by rolling their September positions to the next delivery date, December. The interpolated hedge now becomes a spot hedge consisting of being short 10 December futures. All spot hedges have basis risk.

The basis risk of ZAB is the period from 18 November until the last trading day of the December contract. Adverse moves in the basis by 18 November can lead to higher borrowing costs. However, if we regard the last trading day of the December contract as a potential yield curve pivot point we can see that the expected basis of nine basis points (December futures level – anticipated rate) on 18 November is only two basis points. This would mean a higher borrowing cost of seven basis points. However this yield curve shift has meant the December/March spread has moved 23 basis points. If the appropriate ratio of straddles are used to protect against this unwelcome basis change

$$\frac{7 \text{ basis points}}{23 \text{ basis points}} \times 10 \text{ contracts} = 3 \text{ spreads}$$

These spreads will offset adverse moves in the basis for the exposure date.

Alternatively

A ratio of the number of days of basis risk against the number of days between the December and March delivery dates

$$\frac{28 \text{ days}}{91 \text{ days}} \times 10 \text{ contracts} = 3 \text{ spreads}$$

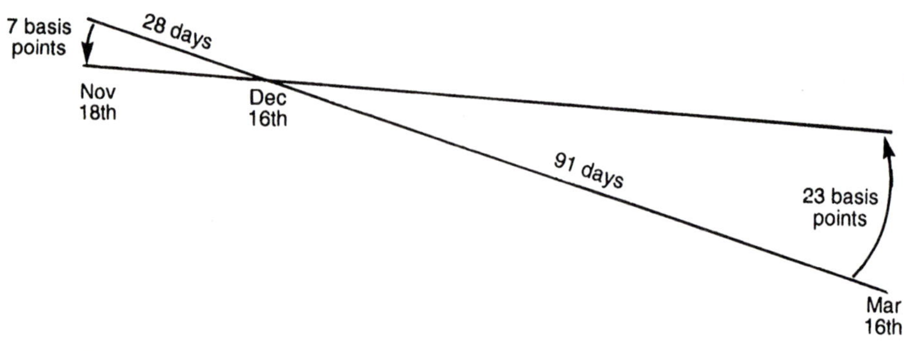

Figure 4.2

or

We can simply use the number of September contracts used in the interpolated hedge to determine the number of spreads required to hedge the basis risk of a spot hedge. This gives the hedge plus the basis risk hedge a structure of:

Sell 13 December futures

Buy 3 March futures

Interest Leverage Factor

One problem which should be considered is the effect of variation margin on a relatively long-term hedge. If variation margin is negative it must be financed but if variation margin is positive the proceeds can be re-invested. In both cases the interest payable or receivable exaggerates the impact of the cash flows of the futures hedges. Accordingly the number of contracts used in the hedge could be reduced by an appropriate amount. On short-term hedges or hedges using small numbers of futures contracts the effect will be minimal on the overall hedge design, but the impact of variation margin on a large long-term hedge can be significant.

An estimation of the effect of variation margin can be made by assuming that the margin will accrue regularly during the hedge period and will be constant for the duration of the hedged exposure.

Hedge period	Duration of hedged exposure
← $T1$ →	← $T2$ →

The interest leverage factor can thus be calculated as:

$$1 + R\left(\tfrac{1}{2}T1 + T2\right)/360$$

where R is the average short-term interest rate over the hedge period.

The Complete Futures Hedge?

To carry out a complex futures hedge on short-term interest exposure:

Number of contracts

= [Ratio of face values × ratio of maturities × regression coefficient × interest leverage factor]

+ basis risk hedge when appropriate

HEDGING WITH OPTIONS

It is more than coincidence that the price paid for an option is called a premium as is the price paid for an insurance policy. Basic hedging with options tends to be very much a question of the amount the hedger is prepared to pay for insurance on his actual, or potential, market exposure. Although an old market adage is 'hedge certainty with futures/FRAs, hedge uncertainty with options', it is often the case that an options hedge will give a more acceptable overall profit and loss profile than locking in to a rate with futures. Options can also be used as vehicles to enhance returns or to create aggressive market positions.

If one is considering the use of options to control short-term interest rate exposure it is prudent to first consider the types of options available. Exchange-traded options such as the Eurodollar, Euromark and Short Sterling are options on the underlying futures contract. As the futures are quoted as 100 – interest rate, to protect against rising interest rates put options would be purchased. Similarly, to protect against falling interest rates call options would be purchased. Many over-the-counter interest rate options are quoted on the actual interest rate. If this is the case, then calls are bought to cover exposure to rising interest rates and puts are bought to cover exposure to falling interest rates. It is somewhat imperative to ensure which is which.

Basic Hedge Examples

Buying Options against Cash Exposure

Buying options against cash exposure can be considered as the classic options hedge.

SCENARIO. In October a treasurer identifies a three-month sterling borrowing requirement in December. The current price for December Short Sterling futures is 89.00, implying a borrowing rate of 11.00 per cent for the delivery date in December, and the December Short Sterling 89.00 put option is priced at 30 basis points. Although the treasurer feels that UK rates will continue to fall he would like some protection against possible rises in rates as the UK economy is still weak. He accordingly buys the 89.00 put option which gives him the overall exposure shown in Figure 4.3. The worst rate he can achieve by this strategy is:

$$[100 - 89.00] + 30 \text{ basis points} = 11.30\%$$

and, at expiry, if cash rates are at 11.00 per cent or higher this is the rate he will achieve. However, if rates drop below 11.00 per cent then the treasurer will be able to borrow at this lower rate plus the option premium paid. Essentially for a cash outlay of 30 basis points he has protected against his interest rate risk. If rates move in his favour he can never perform as well as being unhedged but the ceiling on his overall borrowing cost may well give him a profit and loss profile which is appropriate to his degree of risk aversion.

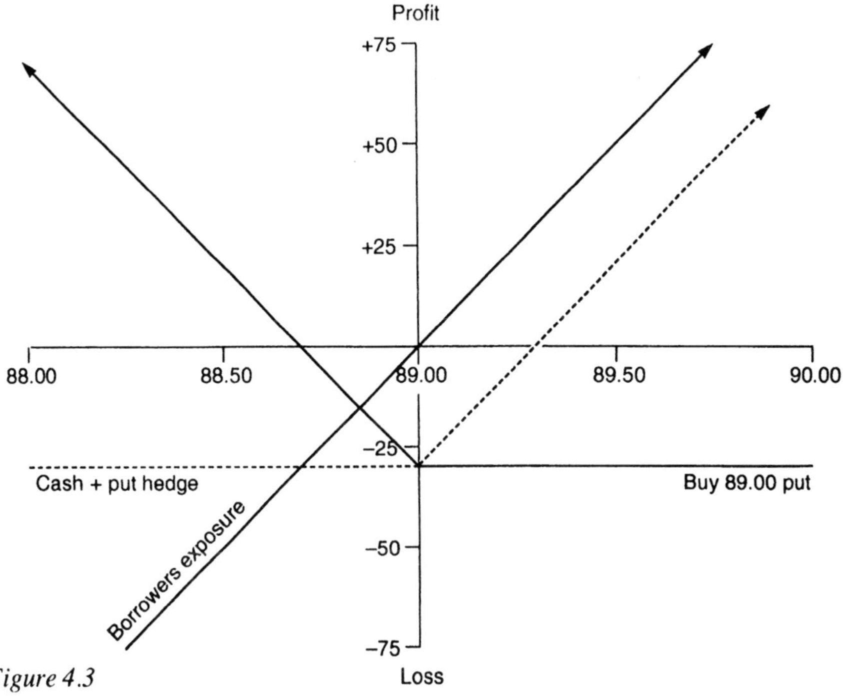

Figure 4.3

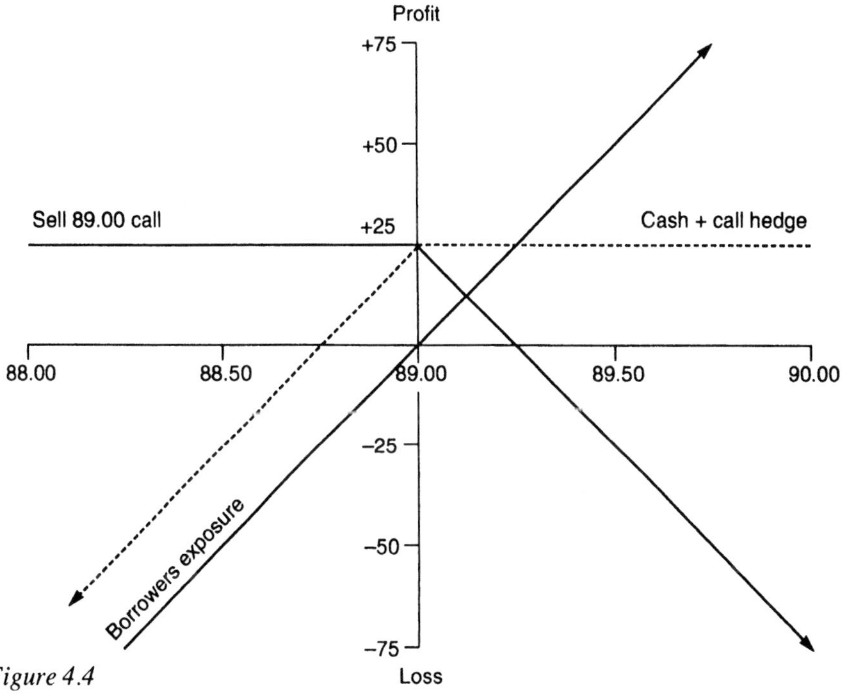

Figure 4.4

Note: By buying the put option against his cash exposure the treasurer has created a synthetic long call option position. A series of put options bought to cover differing exposure dates is equivalent to an interest rate cap.

Selling Options against Cash Exposure

An alternative approach the treasurer in the previous example could take is to sell the 89.00 call option, also priced at 30 basis points, against his cash exposure.

In Figure 4.4 the treasurer has no limit to his potential borrowing cost if rates rise more than the 30 basis points of premium he has received. However, this premium received can be regarded as a cushion against rising rates. In fact, if in December rates are between 10.70 per cent and 11.30 per cent this hedge will provide the best result for the treasurer. If rates are below 10.70 per cent, no hedge would provide the best result. If rates are above 11.30 per cent, buying the 89.00 put option provides the best result.

Note: Selling the call option against the cash exposure creates a synthetic short put position.

Cylinder Hedges

The simultaneous purchase and sale of different exercise price puts and calls can provide low (or zero) cost protection for an exposure. However the hedger has to forgo some potential gains to achieve this low cost hedge.

SCENARIO. Again the treasurer has a borrowing exposure in December. Current prices are:

December futures	88.95
December 88.75 put option	22 basis points
December 89.25 call option	18 basis points

The treasurer purchases the 88.75 put option and simultaneously sells the 89.25 call option. This gives him a net outlay of four basis points (22 bp – 18 bp).

As we can see (Figure 4.5) the treasurer has locked into a maximum borrowing rate of (100 – 88.75) + 4 bp = 11.29 per cent and will achieve this rate if in December cash rates are at 11.25 per cent or higher.

The minimum rate at which the treasurer will borrow is (100 – 89.25) + 4 bp = 10.79 per cent and this is the rate he will achieve if cash rates are at 10.75 per cent or lower in December.

With cash rates between the two exercise prices of the options the treasurer is,

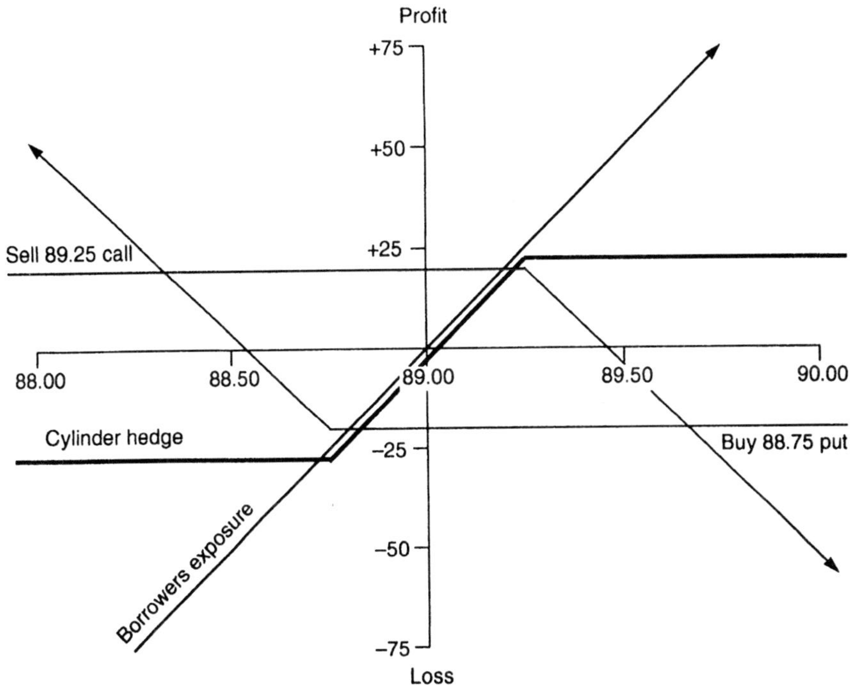

Figure 4.5

effectively, on a floating rate plus the net four basis points of premium paid out.

Note: A series of these cylinder hedges over different expiry dates is equivalent to an interest rate collar.

Buying a put option and selling a call option at the same exercise price creates a synthetic short futures position which may prove cheaper than the actual future available.

Lending Exposure

To hedge against an exposure to falling interest rates:

A. Buy calls
B. Sell puts
C. Buy calls and sell puts as a cylinder or synthetic future.

Note: In these examples we have assumed holding the options to expiry. If the hedge positions are lifted prior to expiry the options will have time value remaining as well as any intrinsic value.

Example
In the case of a borrowing exposure with a long put option:
A buyer of options is long of time value. A seller of options is short of time value.

Ratio Hedges

The basic option hedges we have looked at give good protection if positions are held to expiry. However, in the short term, movements in the underlying rates will not be fully reflected in the premiums of the options we have as protection. The plaintive cry of the options hedger 'Rates rose 20 basis points but my options only went up 5 basis points' is often heard.

The responsiveness of an option premium to small movements in the underlying asset is measured by the delta of the option. If a Short Sterling option has a delta of 0.40 and the Short Sterling future is at 90.00, a movement in the future price of five basis points to 90.05 would indicate a movement in the option price of 5 × 0.40 = two basis points.

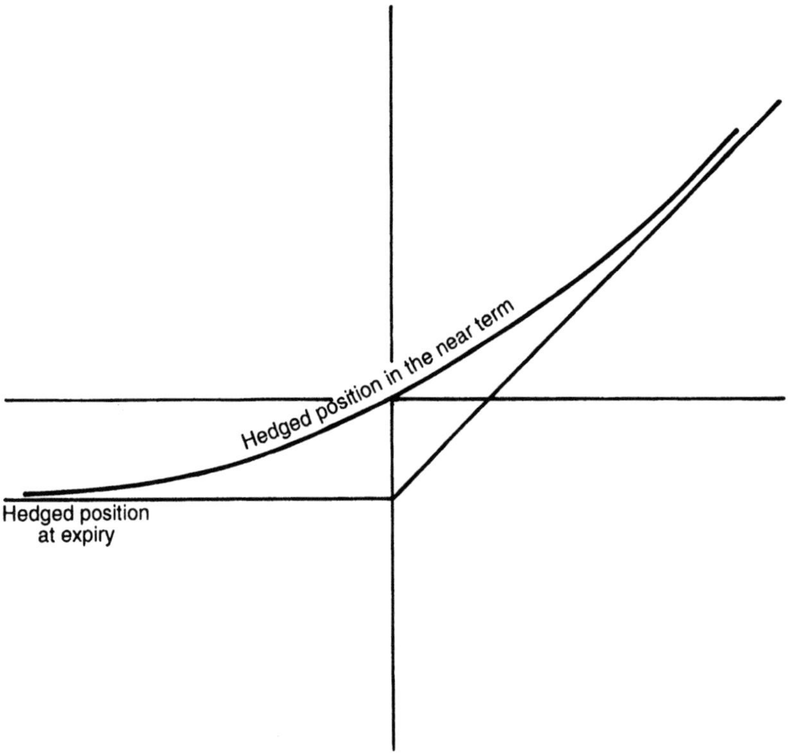

Figure 4.6

Delta can thus be taken into account when designing short-term hedges.
The hedge ratio formula to be used in a delta hedge is:

$$\text{Number of options} = \frac{\text{amount to be hedged}}{\text{option asset value}} \times \text{option delta}$$

Example
With a portfolio equivalent exposure of 50 futures contracts and options with a delta of 0.40

$$\text{Number of options} = \frac{\text{50 futures}}{\text{1 future}} \times 0.40 = 125 \text{ options}$$

This hedge will give full coverage for small movements in the price of the underlying asset. However, as the market moves so does the delta of the options. In order to maintain the delta neutrality of the exposure plus option hedge position the number of options used in the hedge must frequently be rebalanced. The hedger would consider the gamma of the options to identify the rate of change in the delta of the options.

Although ratio hedges are an essential tool for the arbitrageur they have several drawbacks for the hedger.

(1) The need for frequent rebalancing of the position. In practice this is not a great problem in liquid markets which are trending either up or down. The danger occurs in see-sawing markets when almost continuous rebalancing becomes necessary, incurring transaction costs and the loss of bid/offer spreads on each rebalancing. A trigger level for the rebalancing of the hedge is thus often used. This may well be of the order of a 2 per cent move in the delta of the hedge. If the underlying market is 'gapping' as well as oscillating the attendant costs of a ratio hedge can be large since the offsetting effects of the hedge are only approximate.
(2) The maximum possible loss on the position is usually more than that with a simple hedge and can not be precisely anticipated.
(3) A ratio hedge can only be deemed appropriate if the hedger will accept the risk profile at expiry at any stage of the hedge.

FUTURES CASE STUDY

20 May 1991
A bank identifies a 6-month borrowing exposure on $40 million which will be required on 22 August 1991. The bank's economic and technical experts are, for once, in agreement that there is a strong possibility that Eurodollar interest rates will rise substantially in the near future.

Current Market Rates

	Cash Rates	Maturity Date	Duration (days)
3 months	$6\frac{1}{8}$–$6\frac{1}{4}$	22/08/91	92
6 months	$6\frac{3}{8}$–$6\frac{1}{2}$	22/11/91	184
9 months	$6\frac{7}{16}$–$6\frac{9}{16}$	24/02/92	276

Eurodollar futures prices

		Delivery Date
June 1991	93.94	19/06/91
Sept. 1991	93.66	18/09/91
Dec. 1991	93.06	18/12/91
Mar. 1992	92.87	18/03/92

Exposure

The bank's exposure is to a rise in interest rates between 20 May and the actual borrowing date of 22 August when they will fix the rate at which the $40 million will be borrowed.

Potential Hedges

Forward/Forward Borrowing Rate

The bank can fix a forward/forward borrowing rate for 6-month money commencing on 22 August by using today's cash rates. They would borrow for 9 months at a rate of $6\frac{9}{16}$ per cent and simultaneously lend for 3 months at a rate of $6\frac{1}{8}$ per cent:

Forward/forward borrowing rate

$$= \left\{ \frac{[1 + (0.065625 \times 276/360)]}{[1 + (0.06125 \times 92/360)]} \right\} - 1 \times \frac{360}{184}$$

$$= 6.68\%$$

Thus the bank could lock in a borrowing rate of 6.68 per cent.

Note: We are assuming that the bank in question can borrow at money market rates. If an organisation normally borrows at a higher rate than LIBOR then this must be taken into consideration. The rates that can be locked into with both forward/forward and futures hedges are dependent on the credit status of the hedger.

Futures Implied Borrowing Rate

To assess the 6-month borrowing rate implied by the current futures prices for the exposure date of 22 August we would, initially, consider a simple hedge using September futures contracts only.

Anticipated Rate

To determine the implied 6-month borrowing rate from the futures we would, first of all, assess the implied 3-month borrowing rate for the 22 August date by using a straight line interpolation between the June and September futures prices.

June futures price of 93.94 implies a borrowing rate of 6.06 per cent on 19 June.

September futures price of 93.66 implies a borrowing rate of 6.34 per cent on 18 September.

To calculate the interpolated rate for 22 August we would initially draw the time line.

$$\text{19 June} \xrightarrow{\text{64 days}} \text{22 August} \xrightarrow{\text{27 days}} \text{18 Sept.}$$

We would then give the appropriate weighting to each implied rate to determine the interpolated rate.

$$(6.06\% \times 27/91) + (6.34\% \times 64/91) = 6.26\%$$

This interpolation could also be looked at in terms of the basis differential between the June and September contracts.

The differential basis is currently at 28 basis points

Implied basis at 22 August = 28 × 64/91 = 20 basis points

Therefore implied rate for 22 August would be the implied June rate plus the implied basis differential = 6.06% + 20 basis points

= 6.26%

Both of these approaches are equally valid.

22 August 3-month borrowing rate	= 6.26%
Plus 6 month–3 month spread (assumed constant)	$= 6\tfrac{1}{2}\% - 6\tfrac{1}{4}\% = 0.25\%$
22 August 6-month borrowing rate	= 6.51%

The major danger of using this approach is the assumption that the 6 month–3 month differential will remain constant between today and the actual exposure date. The other problem is the estimation of the basis level on the exposure date. Although there is much statistical evidence ('lies, damn lies and statistics') to support the theory of the linear convergence of basis it must be remembered that basis is dependent on the shape of the yield curve. If there are significant changes in the shape of the yield curve then the basis could prove to be very different at the exposure date to the previously interpolated level. Despite these drawbacks, the hedge using futures may well be preferred to the forward/forward hedge, not least because of the potentially more attractive borrowing rate which may be achieved.

Hedge Ratio

The hedge using only September contracts would be designed using the formula:

$$\frac{\text{Face value of exposure}}{\text{Face value of contract}} \times \frac{\text{Maturity of position}}{\text{Maturity of contract}} \times \text{Regression coefficient}$$
$$= \text{Number of contracts}$$

In using futures contracts to hedge a cash interest rate exposure it is important to look at the relationship between the actual exposure and the standardised futures contract. This relationship can be quantified by using regression techniques to determine a 'regression coefficient' between the two. For the sake of this example we have assumed a regression coefficient of 1. Any regression technique can only give how the relationship has worked in the past and may not be a reliable indicator as to the future movement of the relationship.

Thus our simple hedge would involve selling

$$\frac{\$40 \text{ million}}{\$1 \text{ million}} \times \frac{184 \text{ days}}{90 \text{ days}} \times 1.00 = 81.78 \text{ or } 82 \text{ contracts}$$

Rounding up the number of contracts to be used adds another small problem for the hedger. He has effectively gone short 0.22 of a futures contract by rounding and this may lead to a difference in the actual hedge result against the anticipated result dependent on the movement of rates over the hedge period.

This piled-up, or stack, hedge has possible limitations in terms of efficiency and as to how closely it can replicate the actual market exposure. However, before we consider a potentially more effective hedge, it is worth noting that in situations where there is relatively low liquidity in more distant futures contracts there may be a strong case for using a stack hedge. In practice it is never advisable to construct a hedge using illiquid contracts. The two main drawbacks are:

(1) It may not be possible to establish the hedge in the required size without moving the futures prices by an unwelcome amount.
(2) More dangerously, it may prove extremely difficult to unwind the hedge when required and/or without adversely moving the market price.

Let us now consider a potentially more effective hedge.

Strip Hedge

A strip of June, September and December futures should closely match the duration of the borrower's 6-month exposure. In addition September/December straddles could be used to control the basis risk of the hedge.

In this case it is perhaps more relevant to assess the projected 6-month borrowing rate by compounding two 3-month rates, one for 20 August and the other for 20 November, which correspond more closely to the strip of futures to be used.

To Calculate

20 August 3-month rate by interpolation as in stack hedged = 6.26%

20 November 3-month rate by interpolation between September and December futures

6.34% + [(6.94 – 6.34) 64/91 days] = 6.76%

20 August 6-month offer rate (by compounding 6.26% over 92 days and 6.76% over the next 92 days)

$$\{[1 + (0.0626 \times 92/360)] \times [1 + (0.0676 \times 92/360)]\} - 1 \times 360/184 = 6.56\%$$

In theory the exposure should be hedged by selling a combination of June, September and December contracts. To correspond to the August exposure we would use an appropriate weighting, in terms of days, to determine the ratio of June and September contracts to be used to hedge the 3-month borrowing exposure starting on 22 August. A similar computation would then be used to determine the number of September and December contracts to hedge the 3-month borrowing exposure starting on 22 November.

19 June	22 Aug.	18 Sept.	22 Nov.	18 Dec.
→ 64 days	→ 27 days	→ 65 days	→ 26 days	

To hedge the August date a ratio 27:64 June/September contracts should be used.

June contracts = 27/91 × 41 contracts = 12.16 contracts

September contracts = 64/91 × 41 contracts = 28.84 contracts

To hedge the November date a ratio of 26:65 September/December contracts should be used.

September contracts = 26/91 × 41 contracts = 11.71 contracts

December contracts = 65/91 × 41 contracts = 29.29 contracts

The total hedge would consist of selling 12.16 June contracts, 28.84 + 11.71 = 40.55 September contracts and 29.29 December contracts.

Note: The number of contracts used must be rounded to the nearest whole number.

Therefore the hedge would consist of selling 12 June, 41 September and 29 December contracts.

In practice there is only four weeks until the delivery of the June contract when the hedge would have to be adjusted. The uncertainty of adjusting the hedge would probably lead to the hedger immediately selling 12 extra September contracts in place of the 12 June contracts giving an actual initial hedge of selling 53 September and 29 December contracts. However, by using only the September and December contracts the hedger takes on an immediate exposure to basis risk.

Strip Hedge with Basis Risk Hedge

To hedge the basis risk attendant with the strip hedge the hedger would replace the missing June contracts with an equivalent amount of September/December straddles. Hence the hedger would sell 12 September/December straddles to control the basis risk.

This would lead to a final hedge structure of:

Sell 53 September contracts
Sell 29 December contracts
Sell 12 September/December straddles

or

Sell 65 September contracts
Sell 17 December contracts

Hedge Results

20 August 1991
Cash rates

3 months $7–7\frac{1}{8}\%$
6 months $7\frac{1}{8}–7\frac{1}{4}\%$
9 months $7\frac{7}{16}–7\frac{9}{16}\%$

Futures prices

September 1991 92.88
December 1991 92.72

As the bank's forecasts were correct and rates rose over the exposure period the bank were proved right in their decision to hedge their exposure. If no hedge had been put on the bank would have had to accept the current 6 months borrowing rate of 7.25 per cent as the cost of their borrowing. In fact the profit on each futures contract was:

	Sold 20 May	Bought 20 August	Profit
September 1991	93.66	92.88	78 ticks
December 1991	93.06	92.72	34 ticks

The overall profit on the futures position is dependent on the design of the hedge.

Stack Hedge

September 1991	82 contracts × 78 ticks = 6396 ticks profit

Strip Hedge without Basis Hedge

September 1991	53 contracts × 78 ticks = 4134 ticks profit
December 1991	29 contracts × 34 ticks = 986 ticks profit
	5120 ticks profit

Strip Hedge with Basis Hedge

September 1991	65 contracts × 78 ticks = 5070 ticks profit
December 1991	17 contracts × 34 ticks = 578 ticks profit
	5648 ticks profit

At first glance it appears that, as the stack hedge has made more than either of the strip hedges, it has proved to be the most successful hedge. However this is a somewhat naive view on the effectiveness of a hedge. In any specific scenario one type of hedge will perform better than the others. A successful hedge is one which comes close to achieving the target rate expected. Consistency of hedge performance is vital for the risk manager to perform effectively.

Hedge Performance Evaluation

To convert the profit on the hedge position into equivalent points on the borrowing rate for 6 months for \$40 million we would use the following formula.

$$\frac{\text{Number of ticks} \times \text{Tick value} \times 360/184 \text{ days}}{\$40{,}000{,}000} = \text{Interest rate points}$$

Hence net borrowing rates achieved against target rates are:

	Stack Hedge	Strip Hedge	
		No Basis Hedge	Basis Hedge
6-month borrowing rate	7.25%	7.25%	7.25%
Hedge result	–0.78%	–0.63%	–0.69%
Net 6-month borrowing rate	6.47%	6.62%	6.56%
Target rate	6.51%	6.56%	6.56%
Error	+0.04%	–0.06%	0

In fact, though all the hedges can be considered to have performed very well and have outperformed the 6.68 per cent which could have been locked in using the forward/forward rate, it is the strip hedge with the basis risk hedge which has achieved the expected result. It is prudent to note that although, in this instance, this hedge actually achieved the exact target rate this is the exception rather than the rule. Statistical evidence suggests that a strip hedge with basis risk hedge will usually provide the best performance but this cannot be guaranteed on any single hedge. A hedge result within five basis points of the target rate should be seen as a very successful hedge.

Although these figures are taken from an actual case it is probably relevant to consider an alternative scenario on 20 August.

Alternative Result

20 August prices are:

Cash rates
3 months $5\frac{5}{16}$–$5\frac{7}{16}$%
6 months $5\frac{5}{8}$ –$5\frac{3}{4}$%
9 months 6–$6\frac{1}{8}$%

Futures prices
September 1991 94.51
December 1991 93.46

In this instance rates have dropped substantially over the exposure period and again the yield curve shape has changed. As always when cash rates move in favour of the underlying exposure, the best result for the borrower would come from not hedging the position. This would give a borrowing rate of $5\frac{3}{4}$ per cent for the 6-month money.

The loss on each futures contract would be:

	Sold 20 May	**Bought 20 August**	**Loss**
September 1991	93.66	94.51	–85 ticks
December 1991	93.06	93.46	–40 ticks

Again the overall loss on the futures position is dependent on the hedge design.

Stack Hedge

September 1991	82 contracts × –85 ticks = 6970 ticks loss

Strip Hedge without Basis Hedge

September 1991	53 contracts × –85 ticks = 4505 ticks loss
December 1991	29 contracts × –40 ticks = 1160 ticks loss
	5665 ticks loss

Strip Hedge with Basis Risk Hedge

September 1991	65 contracts × –85 ticks = 5525 ticks loss
December 1991	17 contracts × –40 ticks = 680 ticks loss
	6205 ticks loss

In this instance the strip hedge without the basis hedge has given the best result in terms of rate achieved.

Hedge Performance Evaluation
Using the same principles as before:

	Stack Hedge	Strip Hedge	
		No Basis Hedge	Basis Hedge
6-month borrowing rate	5.75%	5.75%	5.75%
Hedge result	0.85%	0.69%	0.76%
Net 6-month borrowing rate	6.60%	6.44%	6.51%
Target rate	6.51%	6.56%	6.56%
Error	-0.09%	+0.12%	+0.05%

Again the strip hedge with the basis risk hedge has come closest to the target rate. Hedging with a high degree of certainty is an important weapon in the armoury of the risk manager.

A detailed analysis of the performance of each hedge would reveal that basis risk, changes in the shape of the yield curve and rounding the number of contracts are the causes of error in the hedges. By controlling these causes of uncertainty as much as possible we can achieve very accurate hedge results.

Note: In this case study no account has been taken of either transaction costs or the interest leverage factor. For most hedgers in the market, futures transaction costs are very low and will have only a minor impact on the overall hedge result. The interest leverage factor may have a larger impact but its effects are more difficult to assess. A more complex hedge structure may well take these factors into consideration.

FUTURES AND OPTIONS CASE STUDY

Scenario

18 September 1991
After successfully completing a takeover bid for a medium sized industrial company, a major German conglomerate, MUL, is looking to dispose of one section of the new acquisition which directly duplicates one of its own core businesses. Negotiations on the sale have reached an advanced stage. A price of DM 100 million has been agreed for the major manufacturing complex in Dusseldorf sale but further negotiations are taking place over two subsidiary factories in Essen. It has been agreed that the deadline date for the second part of the deal is 21 October 1991 and that the total purchase price will be paid to MUL on 14 November 1991. Although MUL have no immediate need of the cash for the sale they are holding secret talks towards another acquisition which should, if successful, take place in the middle of February 1992. MUL's chief economist is forecasting lower interest rates worldwide over the next few months and

believes the German market will be no exception to this. The company therefore believes that some form of hedge against falling interest rates between now and 12 November 1991 when they can fix a lending rate for 14 November is essential.

Potential Sale of Subsidiaries

The potential sale of the two subsidiary factories is being dealt with individually. MUL's negotiators believe that for each factory there is a 50 per cent chance of the sale going ahead. The non-negotiable asking prices are:

Factory A DM 20 million
Factory B DM 12 million

What is the exposure which MUL is faced with?

Exposure

MUL has a twofold exposure. Obviously, falling interest rates between today and 12 November is their actual market exposure. The trickier problem they have to face is the actual size of their market exposure. They know that on 14 November they will receive a minimum of DM 100 million from the already agreed sale of the complex in Dusseldorf but are uncertain of any amount over that figure. Accordingly they work out the probabilities of receiving amounts above DM 100 million. These are:

Amount		**Probability**
DM 0 million	no further sale	25%
DM 12 million	sale of factory B only	25%
DM 20 million	sale of factory A only	25%
DM 32 million	sale of both factories	25%

How should they approach this uncertainty?

Principle

In a scenario such as this a good rule of thumb is to hedge certainty with futures and to hedge uncertainty with options. Although a case could be made for hedging the mean expected amount (in this instance DM 116 million), if only the minimum possible amount (DM 100 million) was received and if interest rates actually rose over the exposure period, MUL would be over-hedged and thus subject to a potentially disastrous loss on the DM 16 million by which they had over-hedged. In fact, this would be the equivalent of a DM 16 million straight market position. The role of the hedger or risk manager in these situations is certainly not to assume additional exposure to the fluctuations of the interest rate markets.

Market Prices on 19 September 1991

Cash Rates

3 months $8\frac{3}{4}$–$8\frac{7}{8}$%
6 months $9\frac{1}{16}$–$9\frac{3}{16}$%
9 months $9\frac{1}{8}$–$9\frac{1}{4}$%

EuroDeutschmark (Euromark) Futures

December 1991	91.00
March 1992	90.60

EuroDeutschmark (Euromark) Options

	Exercise price	Premium (ticks)
December 1991 calls	90.50	65
	90.75	47
	91.00	28
	91.25	14
	91.50	7
	91.75	4
	92.00	1
March 1992 calls	90.00	76
	90.25	58
	90.50	40
	90.75	22
	91.00	13
	91.25	9
	91.50	5

Note: These options are on an underlying of a futures position. They are American style options and the premium is margined rather than paid upfront.

FUTURES HEDGE

Anticipated Rate

As MUL's exposure date lies between cash and the first available futures contract the anticipated rate would be determined by a straight line interpolation between today's 3-month cash rate and the implied lending rate from the December futures contract delivery date of 17 December 1991.

20 September —53 days→ 12 November —35 days→ 17 December

Today's cash 3-month lending rate is $8\frac{3}{4}$ per cent and the December futures price is 91.00. Remember that the futures price is based on a borrowing rate. To determine the implied lending rate from this borrowing rate we would deduct the $\frac{1}{8}$ per cent spread which is the norm between the borrowing and lending rates.

$$100 - \text{futures price} - \text{bid/offer spread} = \text{implied lending rate}$$

In this instance:

$$100 - 91.00 - 0.125 = 8.875\%$$

By interpolation the 3-month lending rate implied for 12 November would be

$$(8.75\% \times 35/88 \text{ days}) + (8.875\% \times 53/88 \text{ days}) = 8.83\%$$

and this is the rate MUL would hope to achieve on their guaranteed lending.

Futures Hedge Design

The first step will be to calculate the number of contracts to be used.

$$\frac{\text{Amount to be hedged}}{\text{Contract size}} \times \frac{\text{Duration of lending}}{\text{Duration of contract}}$$

$$= \text{Number of contracts}$$

In this case:

$$\frac{\text{DM 100 million}}{\text{DM 1 million}} \times \frac{92 \text{ days}}{91 \text{ days}} \times 101 \text{ contracts}$$

Buy 101 December 1991 Euromark futures contracts.

As we have seen previously a futures hedge with a basis risk hedge normally proves to be the most efficient.

To determine the number of straddles to buy to control the basis risk of the hedge we would use the same time line as before which shows that we have 35 days to basis risk. There is also 91 days between the delivery dates of the December and March futures contracts. Therefore the calculation for the number of straddles to be used is:

$$\frac{35 \text{ days}}{91 \text{ days}} \times 101 \text{ contracts} = 39 \text{ straddles}$$

Thus the futures hedge consists of:

Buy 101 December 1991 Euromark contracts
Buy 39 December/March straddles

Options Hedge

When hedging uncertainty the only 'perfect hedge' will be one done in retrospect. There are no absolute rules which must be followed. If a sensible view on probabilities is taken the hedge design will be dependent on the hedger's degree of risk aversion allied with the actual amount of 'insurance premium' they are prepared to pay.

In this example let us assume that all the available options are fairly priced. If they were not we would look to buy underpriced options and to sell overpriced options.

A logical approach to the problem would be to consider the average of MUL's potential excess over DM 100 million and to hedge that amount (DM 16 million) with at-the-money call options. These are the options with the highest time value and therefore potential. No premium is paid for intrinsic value (reducing the potential cost of the hedge) but adverse movements on the cash rates would lead to immediate intrinsic value gains on the option position. This first step of the options hedge can never be 'perfect' as the extra amount of DM 16 million may not be received.

There is also a potential DM 16 million which could be received if MUL sold both factories. Although the probability of receiving the full DM 132 million is only 25 per cent it may well prove to be prudent to place some form of hedge on the DM 16 million up to the full amount of DM 132 million. Doubtlessly, MUL would be delighted to complete the sale of both factories and receive the full amount of DM 132 million, though their joy may be tempered if interest rates dropped dramatically before they received the cash. A sensible approach would be to buy some low cost protection for the long shot. Buying relatively cheap out-of-the-money calls would seem to be the answer.

So a possible options hedge would be:

Buy 16 December 91.00 calls for a premium of 28 ticks.
Buy 16 December 91.50 calls for a premium of 7 ticks.

Giving an outlay of:

$$[(16 \times 28 \text{ ticks}) + (16 \times 7 \text{ ticks})] \times \text{DM } 25 = \text{DM } 14{,}000$$

Each option controls one futures contract. If exercised the buyer of a call option receives a long futures position at the exercise price of that option. If the options bought by MUL were exercised they would become futures positions and, as such, would therefore carry the same basis risk as futures. Although, in practice, on 21 October, when the exact amount to be hedged will be known, the call options bought will almost certainly have time value remaining as well as their intrinsic value. In this case the options would be sold back to the market to gain this time value. However, a cautious hedger may well decide to hedge the inherent basis risk in these options with option calendar spreads.

To calculate option calendar spreads:

Buy 16 × 35/91 December/March 91.00 call spreads = 6 spreads
Buy 16 × 35/91 December/March 91.50 call spreads = 6 spreads

This constitutes:

Buying 6 December 91.00 calls at 28 ticks
Selling 6 March 91.00 calls at 13 ticks

Buying 6 December 91.50 calls at 7 ticks
Selling 6 March 91.50 calls at 5 ticks

Giving an additional outlay of:

$$[(6 \times 28 \text{ ticks}) + (6 \times 7 \text{ ticks})] \times \text{DM } 25 = \text{DM } 5250$$

and premium receivable of

$$[(6 \times 13 \text{ ticks}) + (6 \times 5 \text{ ticks})] \times \text{DM } 25 = \text{DM } 2700$$

Full Hedge with Basis Risk Hedge

The full hedge would consist of:

Buying 140 December 1991 Euromark futures
Selling 39 March 1992 Euromark futures

Buying 22 December 1991 91.00 Euromark calls
Selling 6 March 1992 91.00 Euromark calls

Buying 22 December 1991 91.50 Euromark calls
Selling 6 March 1992 91.50 Euromark calls

This hedge has a net premium outlay of:

$$\text{DM } 14{,}000 + \text{DM } 5250 - \text{DM } 2700 = \text{DM } 16{,}550$$

Note: As premiums are only paid on exercise or at expiry no account need be taken of the financing cost of these premiums.

Anticipated Rate

If the final amount received by MUL was only the DM 100 million then in a worst case scenario it is possible that by November all the options would be so far out-of-the-money that they were worthless and the total premium paid would be lost. The effect of this on the overall anticipated rate would be:

$$\text{DM } 16{,}550 \times \frac{365/91}{\text{DM } 100 \text{ million}} = 7 \text{ basis points}$$

Therefore the minimum anticipated rate is:

$$8.83\% - 0.07\% = 8.76\%$$

21 October 1991

At the end of negotiations Factory A was sold for DM 20 million but the projected sale of Factory B proved abortive. Accordingly the hedge needs rebalancing for the remainder of the exposure period until the total proceeds on the sale of DM 120 million will be received.

Relevant Market Rates

Cash Rates

3 months $9\frac{1}{4}$–$8\frac{3}{8}$%
6 months $8\frac{11}{16}$–$8\frac{13}{16}$%
9 months 9%–$9\frac{1}{8}$%

Euromark Futures

December 1991	91.60
March 1992	91.05

Euromark Options

	Exercise Price	Premium
December 1991 calls	91.00	66 ticks
	91.50	28 ticks
March 1992 calls	91.00	38 ticks
	91.50	16 ticks

The 3-month lending rate has dropped by 50 basis points since the hedge was put on thus vindicating the decision to hedge.

Rebalancing Hedge

MUL has now only certainty to hedge. Accordingly they will now close their entire option position and replace with a suitable futures hedge.

Action
Sell 22 December 1991 calls at 66 ticks
Buy 6 March 1992 calls at 38 ticks

Sell 22 December 1991 calls at 28 ticks
Buy 6 March 1992 calls at 16 ticks

Giving the following profits/losses
91.00 December calls

$$22 \text{ contracts} \times (66 - 28 \text{ ticks}) \times \text{DM } 25 = \text{DM} + 20{,}900$$

91.00 March calls

$$6 \text{ contracts} \times (13 - 38 \text{ ticks}) \times \text{DM } 25 = \text{DM} - 3{,}750$$

91.50 December calls

$$22 \text{ contracts} \times (28 - 7 \text{ ticks}) \times \text{DM } 25 = \text{DM} + 11{,}550$$

91.50 March calls

$$6 \text{ contracts} \times (5 - 16 \text{ ticks}) \times \text{DM } 25 = \underline{\text{DM} - 1.650}$$

Net profit on options	DM 27,050

This realised profit can be placed on the money markets for 114 days until 14 February 1992 at $8\frac{7}{16}\%$ (current 114-day lending rate).

Replace with Futures

$$\text{Number of contracts} = \frac{\text{DM 20 million}}{\text{DM 1 million}} \times \frac{92 \text{ days}}{91 \text{ days}} = 20 \text{ contracts}$$

Buy 20 December 1991 futures at 91.60.
Add basis risk hedge as before

$$20 \text{ contracts} \times \frac{35 \text{ days}}{89 \text{ days}} = 8 \text{ straddles}$$

Buy 8 December/March straddles

So total futures for rebalancing

Buy 28 December 1991 futures at 91.60
Sell 8 March 1992 futures at 91.05
Plus original futures hedge

12 November 1991: Market Prices

Cash Rates

3 months 8%–8$\frac{1}{8}$%
6 months 8$\frac{9}{16}$–8$\frac{11}{16}$%
9 months 8$\frac{7}{8}$–9%

Euromark Futures

December 1991	91.88
March 1992	91.20

The DM 120 million is placed on 3 months deposit at the current 3-month rate of 8 per cent and the futures hedge is lifted. Any profits from the futures hedges can also be placed on the money markets at 8 per cent.

Futures Profits and Losses

	Purchase Price	Sale Price	Profit/Loss
140 December futures	91.00	91.88	88 ticks
39 March futures	91.20	90.60	-60 ticks
28 December futures	91.60	91.88	28 ticks
8 March futures	91.20	91.05	-15 ticks

So overall result on futures hedges:

140 contracts × 88 ticks × DM 25	= DM +308,000
39 contracts × -60 ticks × DM 25	= DM -58,500
28 contracts × 28 ticks × DM 25	= DM 19,600
8 contracts × -15 ticks × DM 25	= DM -3,000
Net futures profit	= DM 266,100

Lending Rate Achieved

If the DM 120 million plus the futures profit of DM 266,100 is placed on deposit at 8 per cent for 3 months.

DM 120,266,100 × [1 + (0.08 × 92/365)]	= DM 122,691,192
The options profit plus interest	
DM 27,050 × [1 + (0.084375 × 114/365)]	= DM 27,763
Total proceeds as at 14/2/1992	= DM 122,718,955

Overall lending rate achieved is calculated by:

$$\frac{\text{Total proceeds} - \text{initial investment}}{\text{Initial investment}} \times \text{Annualising factor}$$

$$= \text{Lending rate}$$

In this instance:

$$\frac{\text{DM } 122{,}718{,}955 - \text{DM } 120{,}000{,}000}{\text{DM } 120{,}000{,}000} \times \frac{365}{92} = 8.99\%$$

This has obviously proved to be a very successful hedge for MUL in terms of achieving a lending rate 99 basis points higher than the rate they would have received without any hedge. The hedge actually achieved a rate 16 basis points higher than the rate anticipated by interpolation. Remember that the 8.83 per cent that was interpolated was the rate on the certain DM 100 million that MUL would receive. A detailed analysis of the hedge would reveal:

(1) A windfall profit on the overhedging with options equivalent to 5 basis points on the lending rate.

(2) Interest on the futures and options profits equivalent to 2 basis points on the lending rate.

(3) The basis on 12 November was, in fact, zero when the anticipated level was 8 basis points. This would have lowered the effective lending rate by those 8 basis points if it were not for the cumulative effect of the basis risk hedges on both the futures and options position. The combined effect of these was to add the equivalent of 15 basis points to the lending rate on the DM 120 million. This gave, perhaps, a fortuitous, extra 7 basis points on the lending rate. It could be argued that this was a sign of inaccuracy in the basis hedge, though without this hedge the overall rate would have been 15 basis points lower.

Taking these factors into consideration I would regard this as a successful hedge in both performance and accuracy. Controlling the risk of a contingent exposure is rarely going to be a straightforward procedure but problems can be overcome with reasoned strategies which, when it comes to the crunch, achieve their objective for the hedger.

RISKS WHICH DERIVATIVES CAN CONTROL

The following checklists are not intended to be fully comprehensive but have two main aims:

(1) To demonstrate the scope of derivatives in controlling short-term risk.

(2) To aid the risk manager to identify potential problems which can be controlled by derivatives.

Long-term Borrowers

(1) Rise in interest rates before the Issuing House choice is finalised.
(2) Rise in interest rates, on syndicated loans, before Issuing House completes terms.
(3) Rise in interest rates, on floating debt, ahead of future coupon recalculations.
(4) Rising rates when a fixed borrowing has been swapped into a floating liability.
(5) Change in foreign exchange rates (where the proceeds of a loan are to be converted into another currency) before the loan is finalised and/or the proceeds received.
(6) Change in foreign exchange rates (where revenue will be in a different currency from loan) before future coupons fall due.

Issuing Houses

(1) Rise in interest rates before syndicated loan terms can be finalised for borrower.
(2) Rise in interest rates, on 'bought' deals, after terms have been finalised with borrower but before the issue can be brought to market.
(3) Rise in interest rates on floating rate debt ahead of future coupon calculations:
Advise client to cover his risk?
Undertake to cover risk for him?
(4) Change in foreign exchange rates (where the proceeds of a loan are to be converted into another currency) before the proceeds are available:
Advise client to cover his risk?
Undertake to cover risk for him?
(5) Change in foreign exchange rates (where revenue will be in a different currency from loan) before future coupons or loan repayment falls due:
Advise client to cover his risk?
Undertake to cover risk for him?

Underwriters

(1) Rise in interest rates between taking up a commitment and selling the unwanted part of final investors.
(2) Rise in interest rates between taking up a commitment and arranging to fund it.
(3) Fall in interest rates where funding is arranged in anticipation of taking up a commitment.
(4) Change in foreign exchange rates (where a commitment is not in the under-

writer's currency) in Risk 1.
(5) Change in foreign exchange rates, where commitment and funding are in different currencies, in Risk 2 and Risk 3.

Banks

Lending and Account Officers

(1) Advise client to cover his risk?
Undertake to cover it for him?
(2) Rise in interest rates against client before loan terms can be finalised.
(3) Rise in interest rates, ahead of future interest recalculations, in floating rate facilities.
(4) Change in foreign exchange rates before loan proceeds obtained if the borrower is converting them into another currency.
(5) Change in foreign exchange rates ahead of future interest payments or repayment of a loan where the borrower's revenues are in different currencies from the loan.

Treasury and Foreign Exchange Departments

(1) Rise in interest rates after loan terms are fixed with the client and prior to funding being completed.
(2) Fall in interest rates after funding has been completed and before loans are drawn down, e.g. employment of a C.D. issue.
(3) Adverse change in interest rates between rollovers on assets and liabilities which are fixed for different days, i.e. funding a gap in the book.
(4) Contractions in interest rate margins: for example, base rate floating rate loan over fixed term funding cost. Longer-term fixed rate loans over renewable short-term funding costs.
(5) Rise in interest rates prior to a short or long-term borrowing requirement.
(6) Matching (or deliberately mismatching) short-term assets and liabilities without inflation of balance sheet.
(7) Fixing a rate of return on assets ahead of receipt of funds anticipating a fall in rates.
(8) Establishing an aggressive market stance on interest rate direction without over-committing resources.
(9) Controlling potentially dangerous yield curve shifts without jeopardising overall position.
(10) Matching (or deliberating mismatching) foreign currency positions on the spot and forward markets.
(11) Arbitrage between cash and derivative markets.

Investment and Bond Trading Departments

(1) Fall in rates of return on bonds while awaiting receipt of funds.
(2) Covering cash exposure from market making activities until this can be reduced

in an orderly fashion.
(3) Adverse foreign exchange fluctuations in relation to foreign currency investments.
(4) Protecting profits or minimising losses on fixed interest portfolio investments.

Corporate Treasury Departments

(1) Fall in interest rates ahead of recipt of investable funds.
(2) Rise in rates prior to an anticipated borrowing (short or long, including variable rate debt).
(3) Protecting profit or minimising losses on fixed interest portfolio investment, e.g. anticipating a rise in rates when gains tax rules penalise sales of particular securities.
(4) Managing short-term asset and liability positions, e.g. adjusting their maturity profile (duration or convexity) using derivatives when modification of the underlying banking/money market positions would be complicated or onerous, or in relation to seasonal cash flow variations.
(5) Finer tuning short-term liability positions, e.g. expressing a view on interest rate trends between rollovers of a medium-term loan.
(6) Locking in to a rate of exchange for budgeted foreign currency inflows or outflows, especially when expectations might have to be modified during the year.
(7) Locking in to a rate of exchange for actual currency inflows or outflows when the derivatives markets offer lower costs than the banks.
(8) Arbitrage between the cash and derivatives markets.

Investment Managers

(1) Fall in interest rates ahead of an expected, or potential, inflow of cash.
(2) Protecting profits or minimising losses on fixed interest portfolio investments.
(3) Hedging the impact of foreign exchange fluctuations on overseas investments.
(4) Giving positive or negative leverage to a portfolio when interest rates are strongly expected to fall or rise.
(5) Arbitraging between the cash and derivatives markets.

5: Equity Portfolio Management

Patrick Thomas

1 INTRODUCTION

The use of equity related derivative instruments has grown rapidly over the past ten years with the appearance of many derivatives exchanges in most of the world's financial zones. Two principal products are traded:

- **Futures** – on underlying *equity indices*, e.g. FTSE-100 or S&P-500.
- **Options** – both on underlying *equity indices* or *equity index futures*, e.g. CAC-40 or S&P-100 and on *individual equities*, e.g. ICI.

Rivalling this growth in exchange-traded products has been a similar growth in over-the-counter (OTC) products, particularly in OTC options such as long-dated equity index options (often referred to warrants!). In this chapter we will concentrate on the use of exchange-traded products but it should be borne in mind that many of the arguments outlined in the following pages will apply equally well to OTC products.

Equity derivatives find widespread applications both as trading and as hedging instruments. In the sphere of risk management it is possible to identify the following classes of applications:

- **Hedging existing portfolios.** The fund manager has a *long* position and is seeking to protect the future *selling* price of his portfolio in order to lock-in his return.
- **Hedging anticipated portfolios.** The fund manager seeks to establish a new *long* position and until he has managed this is effectively *short* the new position. He will seek to protect the *purchase* price of the portfolio.
- **Effective risk diversification.** The fund manager seeks to minimise exposure to company-specific risk by creating portfolios which track a desired index in an efficient manner.
- **Arbitrage trading.** The fund manager seeks to improve the return on his portfolio whilst maintaining a hedged position.

Before we examine these applications in detail let us reiterate the features of futures and options positions which are most relevant to hedging:

- **Long futures.** Fixes forward *purchase* price.
- **Short futures.** Fixes forward *selling* price.
- **Long call option.** Fixes *maximum* forward *purchase* price.
- **Short call option.** Fixes *maximum* forward *selling* price.
- **Long put option.** Fixes *minimum* forward *selling* price.

- **Short put option.** Fixes *minimum* forward *purchase* price.

The reader should bear these points in mind when considering the appropriate strategy to hedge a long position or an anticipated long position. Note too that the use of futures and options gives considerable choice; which strategy is most *appropriate* will depend on the manager's view of market conditions but which strategy is most *effective* can only be assessed retrospectively.

2 KEY PRICING RELATIONSHIPS

In risk management we are usually more concerned with *relative price changes* than with *absolute* prices. The relative pricing relationships are usually determined by differentiating the absolute pricing equation. For equity-based portfolios there are three main pricing relationships of interest:

- Futures and underlying cash index.
- Options and underlying instrument.
- Cash stocks (or portfolios) and corresponding cash index

We list the principal results below and leave it to the more inquisitive reader to verify the formulae.

2.1 Futures and Underlying Cash Index

If F is the futures price, S is the value of the underlying index and B is the basis, then by definition

$$B = S - F$$

The basis is related to the *carry*, the difference between the dividend yield on the cash index and the cost of financing the cash position until futures expiry. For most equity indices, the dividend yield is less than the financing rate so that the carry is negative. As a consequence index futures generally trade at a premium to the corresponding cash index since, all other things being equal, there is an advantage in holding futures relative to cash.

We can transform the above equation to obtain our first important hedging equation:

$$\Delta F = \Delta S - \Delta B$$

One of the main decisions with futures hedging is what to do about the change in basis since it can be difficult to quantify. For short-term hedges the change in basis is usually ignored since it should be small. For hedges held until futures maturity we know exactly what the change in basis will be since basis must be zero at futures expiry. In between these two extreme cases we cannot predict basis with certainty.

We can also use the pricing relationships to determine the *fair value futures price*. Futures are priced relative to cash by means of arbitrage considerations based on the cash-and-carry transaction. In fact, arbitrage arguments result in an upper and lower price limit within which the futures price should be located and hence the definition of a fair value price is rather more tricky than many people realise. However, the *upper* bound can be considered to be the fair value price for investors who wish to *sell* futures since such investors will be interested in over priced futures whilst the *lower* bound (which may be difficult to calculate) can be considered to be the fair value price for those investors looking to *buy* futures. The upper bound for the fair value futures price is given approximately by:

$$F = S\left[1 + (R - D) \times \frac{N}{365}\right]$$

where R is the N-day money market offered rate, D is the dividend yield on the cash index and N is the number of days between settlement and futures expiry.

2.2 Options and the Underlying Instrument

With options hedges we need to distinguish between hedges held until expiry of the options or hedges held for shorter periods. For *long* options hedges held until expiry the key relationship is:

$$\Delta O = \text{Intrinsic value} - P$$

where ΔO is the change in value of the option and P is the option premium.

For *short* options hedges held until expiry the relationship is:

$$\Delta O = P - \text{Intrinsic value}$$

Since we do not know the intrinsic value of the option at expiry, option hedges held until expiry do not fix an exit price; they merely establish an upper or lower bound.

In the case of option hedges held for shorter periods we use the 'Greeks' usually determined from options pricing models. The most widely used pricing relationship (applicable for long or short positions) based on the 'delta' of the option is:

$$\Delta O = \Delta \times \Delta S$$

where ΔO is the change in option price, ΔS is the change in price of the underlying index or futures and Δ is the 'delta' of the option.

2.3 Cash Stocks and the Corresponding Index

Many hedgers will relate the price changes of cash stocks to the price changes of the corresponding index via the Capital Asset Pricing Model (CAPM). The hedging equation used is:

$$\Delta P \approx \beta \times \frac{P}{I} \times \Delta I$$

where P is the current value of the cash stock (or portfolio), I is the current value of the index and β is the 'beta' factor of the cash stock or portfolio.

There are many assumptions inherent in the use of this model, some of which stretch the imagination of even the most ardent admirer of finance theory. In addition bear in mind:

(1) that the CAPM-based model will only hedge the systematic risk of a stock or portfolio. It is likely to be most effective for large, well-diversified portfolios of blue-chip stocks,
(2) that beta factors estimated on past performance may not be good predictors of the future betas which strictly speaking should be used and
(3) that the beta of a portfolio may change during the lifetime of a hedge.

These points notwithstanding, a CAPM-based hedge may be the best hedge available and better than no hedge at all.

3 HEDGING EXISTING PORTFOLIOS

The main objective when hedging an existing long position is to use futures or options to establish some aspect of the forward *selling* price as described below.

3.1 Using Index Futures

Futures hedges effectively lock-in a forward price. In the absence of futures contracts on individual stocks, we must use index futures as described in Section 2.3 above. The important calculations when establishing the hedge are:

(1) How many index futures should you sell against the equity portfolio?
(2) What is the expected forward selling price?

To answer the first question, we use the CAPM formula to give us the *hedge ratio*:

$$\beta \times \frac{P}{I}$$

where β is the beta of the portfolio, P is the market value of the portfolio and I is the market value of the cash index.

The market value of the equity index is given by the level of the index multiplied by the value per point of the futures contract. In the case of the FTSE-100 futures, the value per point is £25. The beta of the portfolio shares is simply the weighted average of the individual shares' betas using the market values as weights. Thus the hedge ratio expresses our portfolio of shares as *index equivalents*.

Provided we maintain the hedge until futures expiry, the expected forward selling price for our share portfolio is given by the current 'value' of the futures price multiplied by the number of index equivalents divided by beta (see Example 5.1).

Example 5.1 Hedging a portfolio of UK shares with FTSE-100 index futures

Stock	**Price**	**Nominal Holding**	**Beta**	**Market Value**
ABC	£4.00	5,000,000	1.10	£20,000,000
DEF	£2.00	7,500,000	0.95	£15,000,000
GHI	£10.00	1,500,000	1.30	£15,000,000
FTSE-100	2500.00			£62,500
FTSE-100 FUTURES	2545.0			

Market value of portfolio (P) = £50,000,000

The market value weights of the three shares in the portfolio are then given by:

ABC	40%
DEF	30%
GHI	30%

Hence, the beta for the portfolio is given by:

$$\text{Portfolio beta} = 40\% \times 1.10 + 30\% \times 0.95 + 30\% \times 1.30$$
$$= 1.115$$

Thus, the number of FTSE-100 futures which will hedge the portfolio is given by

$$\text{Number of contracts} = \frac{50{,}000{,}000}{62{,}500} \times 1.115$$
$$= 892 \text{ contracts}$$

If the hedge is held until futures expiry and no dividends are received, the expected value of the portfolio is given approximately by:

$$\text{Expected value} = \left[\frac{m}{\beta} \times I + m \times (F - I)\right] \times £25$$

where m is the number of futures contracts in the hedge, F is the current futures price and I is the current level of cash index.

Hence

$$\text{Expected value} = [50{,}000{,}000 + 892 \times (2545 - 2500)] \times 25 = £51{,}003{,}500$$

3.2 Option Hedges Held until Expiry

3.2.1 Long Put Option Hedges

Whereas a futures hedge locks-in a forward selling price, a *long put* hedge establishes a minimum forward selling price and thus a minimum level of return on a portfolio or individual equity. Of course, the owner of the portfolio pays a premium for this benefit since he is able to profit from any movement of the market above this minimum price. The effective minimum forward selling price established by a long-term put option hedge is given by:

Minimum selling price = Exercise price of put – Option premium

If the portfolio is hedged with index put options the number of options which should be bought is determined using the CAPM in exactly the same way as described in Section 2. Note, however, that the value of an index point may be different in the options market. For example, the value of an index point for FTSE-100 options on LTOM is £10 as opposed to the value of an index point for the FTSE-100 futures contract of £25. Hence 2.5 times as many FTSE-100 options are required for every 1 FTSE-100 futures contract in a portfolio hedge.

Alternatively, since options are available on the principal shares in the index, the fund manager has the choice of hedging individual shares with the corresponding put option. This has the advantage of hedging the entire risk of the stock (as opposed to merely the systematic risk in the case of index derivatives) but may prove expensive in terms of transactions costs. When hedging with equity options, the hedge ratio is given by the number of shares being hedged divided by the number of shares per option. Equity options in the UK are options on 1000 shares and hence, for example, the number of ABC put options which would hedge a holding of 100,000 ABC shares would be 100.

Put option hedges are used primarily for two purposes:

(1) to lock-in a gain on a share or portfolio (usually with at-the-money options),

(2) to provide downside insurance (usually with out-of-the-money options)

In either case the effect of combining a put with a long position in the share or portfolio is to create a position (a 'synthetic call') which has the same profit profile as a call with the same exercise price as the put, i.e. the position has no sensitivity to downward movements below the exercise price but has 1:1 sensitivity to movements above the exercise price.

Example 5.2 illustrates the use of a put hedge to lock-in a trading gain. A fund manager has bought ABC shares for 260p against a current market price of 340p. He wishes to guarantee some or all of his gain. If he liquidates his holding he ensures a gain of 80p and is able to reinvest the proceeds of the sale until options expiry but will not participate in any further upward movement in the share price. On the other hand if he hedges with 340 puts which are priced at 20p he locks-in a minimum gain of 60p (80 – 20) and also will make further gains if ABC shares have moved above 340p by option expiry. The hedged position will be superior to the liquidated position if the share price exceeds about 370p at options expiry, taking transaction costs into consideration.

Note that Example 5.2 highlights a frequently overlooked complication. The commonly encountered profit profiles for options are usually profit profiles *at expiration*. Hence such profiles cannot be compared directly with payoffs which occur before

Figure 5.1 Long Put Hedge

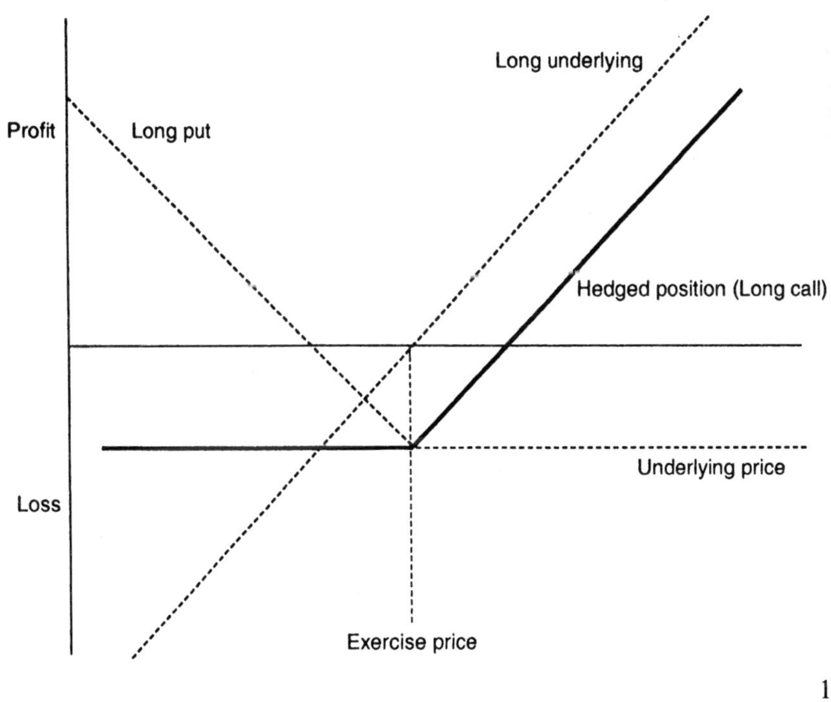

expiry (e.g. liquidating an equity position today). We must consider the impact of investing any surplus funds until options expiry and also the impact of any dividends received by the holder of shares in order to make valid comparisons.

There is a third possible strategy. The manager could liquidate his share holding and purchase ABC 340 calls. However, the calls are trading at 32p, 12p more expensive than the cost of the 340 put. At first glance this alternative strategy would appear to be 12p less efficient than creating the synthetic call. However, remember the put–call parity relationship and note that the difference between the cost of the 340 put and the 340 call allows for the fact that if you liquidate your ABC shares at 340p you can reinvest the proceeds but forgo any ABC dividends. On the other hand, if you create a synthetic call, you only receive dividends on ABC. Since money market rates are generally higher than dividend yields, calls will generally trade at a higher price than the corresponding puts.

The different strategies are illustrated in Figure 5.1 and Example 5.2. Note that the amount that you can guarantee by selling the ABC shares and investing the proceeds until option expiry is about 30p per share more than the minimum guaranteed by either of the option strategies. Hence the share price at expiry must be about 370p or greater for the option strategies to prove better *after the event.*

Example 5.2 Realising Profits: Liquidating Stock versus Creating or Buying Calls

Purchase price of ABC shares	=	260p
Current price of ABC shares	=	340p
Price of 6-month 340 call	=	28p
Price of 6-month 340 put	=	20p
6-month money market rate	=	10%
ABC dividend yield	=	5%

Strategy 1: Liquidate ABC holding and invest proceeds in money market until options expiry

$$\text{Terminal wealth per share} = 340 \times \left(\frac{1 + 10\%}{2}\right) = 357\text{p}$$

Strategy 2: Purchase ABC 340 puts

Minimum terminal wealth per share = Exercise price + Dividends − Option premium

$$= 340 + 340 \times \frac{5\%}{2} - 20 \times \left(1 + \frac{10\%}{2}\right)$$

$$= 327.5\text{p}$$

Strategy 3: Liquidate ABC holding and purchase ABC 340 calls. Invest balance in money market until options expiry

$$\text{Minimum terminal wealth per share} = (340 - 28) \times \left(1 + \frac{10\%}{2}\right)$$

$$= 327.6\text{p}$$

As an alternative to locking in profits, you could use a proportion of the profits to buy out-of-the-money puts to establish a floor for your portfolio value with the main purpose of insuring against a catastrophic collapse in share prices. For example, you buy a portfolio when the index is at 2400.00 and the index subsequently rises to 2500.00. Instead of locking-in your gains by buying 2500.0 index puts you spend less money and buy 2400.0 puts. This strategy is the simplest form of what is commonly called '*portfolio insurance*'.

3.2.2 90/10 and Related Strategies

We showed in the previous section that a portfolio whose value is protected by buying put options can be identical to a position which comprises call options with the balance of the cash invested in the money market until options expiry. The latter strategy is more versatile since the greatest part of the value of the portfolio is in cash rather than in equities and forms the basis of 90/10 and other related strategies including 'money-back' strategies.

In the 90/10 strategy, 90 per cent of the value of the portfolio is invested in cash and the remaining 10 per cent is used to buy call options, either on the underlying equity index or on individual equity options. Thus a minimum future value for the portfolio is fixed whilst participation in upward movements of the market is guaranteed. The strategy is a conservative strategy since it will always underperform in a bull market by the amount paid in option premia.

Closely related to the 90/10 strategy is the money-back strategy in which a sufficient amount is invested in discount securities to ensure that the original value of the fund is recovered at the maturity of the discount securities. The remainder of the fund is then invested in call options which mature at the same time as the discount securities. The money-back strategy is also a conservative strategy and will underperform a rising equity market and outperform a falling equity market.

Numerous other combinations of fixed income securities and call options may be used. Generally such strategies are conservative if the number of options purchased does not exceed the number of shares which would otherwise have been bought. If more options are bought than in the equivalent equity portfolio then the position is a geared position and is more aggressive than simply buying the underlying shares.

3.2.3 Short Call Hedges

Long put hedges establish a minimum selling price for a share or portfolio. Short call hedges establish the corresponding maximum selling price. At first sight this might seem a strange thing to do. The hedge basically restricts the upside potential in the position whilst leaving the position exposed to downside movements! However, a short call hedge enables the portfolio owner to:

(1) modify the risk-return profile of his portfolio by selling unwanted upside potential. The premium received affords some protection against downside movements and
(2) sell options when volatility seems uncharacteristically high in order to enhance the returns on the portfolio. The portfolio owner can rest happy in the knowledge that the written calls are always covered by stocks in his portfolio.

Example 5.3 illustrates the potential of a short call hedge for the ABC shares first encountered in Example 5.2. Suppose the holder of ABC stock which is currently priced at 340p believes that a maximum 6-month return of 22.30 per cent is a realistic target. He can achieve this by selling ABC 340 calls for 28p. Once this is done, this return is locked-in for any share price of 340p or higher at options expiry. Further if the share price is below 340p at options expiry he is cushioned from the loss by the amount of option premium taken in.

Figure 5.2 shows the profit potential for a short call hedge and indicates that the combined position of underlying shares plus short call option has the same profit profile as a written put of the same exercise price. An equivalent hedging stategy would therefore have been to have liquidated the ABC position, sold ABC puts and invested

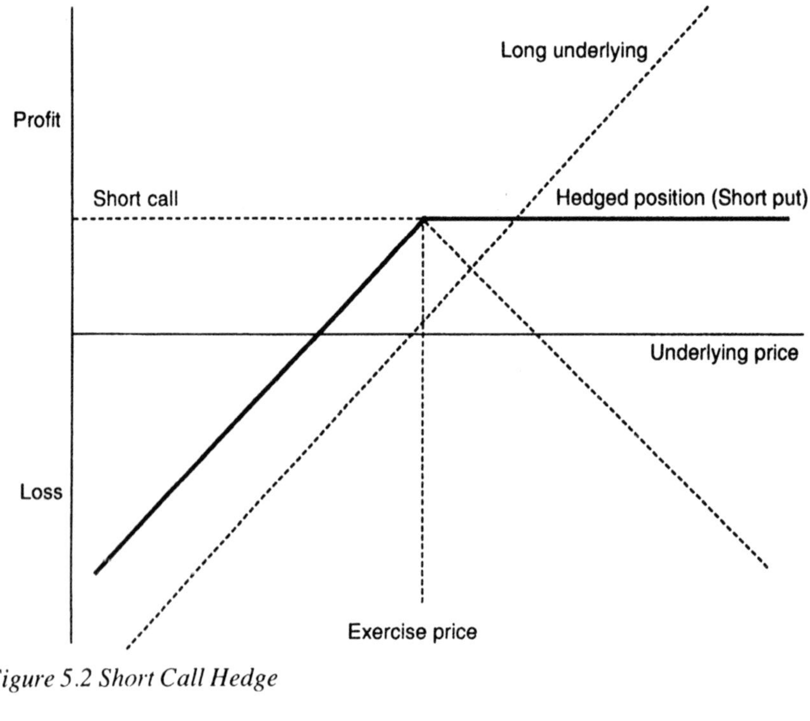

Figure 5.2 Short Call Hedge

the total sum realised in the money market until option expiry.

Example 5.3 Hedging by Restricting the Maximum Upside Gain

Current price of ABC shares	=	340p
Current price of 6-month ABC 340 calls	=	28p
Current price of 6-month ABC 340 puts	=	20p
6-month money market rate	=	10%
Dividend yield of ABC shares	=	5%

Strategy 1: Sell 340 calls against the ABC holding

$$\text{Maximum return} = \frac{\text{Exercise price} + \text{Dividends} + \text{Premium}}{\text{Current share price}}$$

$$= \left[\frac{340 + 340 \times \frac{5\%}{2} + 28\left(1 + \frac{10\%}{2}\right)}{340} - 1\right] \times 2$$

$$= 22.30\%$$

Strategy 2: Liquidate ABC holding and sell ABC 340 puts

$$\text{Maximum return} = \frac{(340 + 20)\left(1 + \frac{10\%}{2}\right)}{340}$$

$$= 22.30\%$$

3.2.4 Buy–write Strategies

Closely related to the short call hedge is the buy–write strategy in which an investor purchases a share and simultaneously sells a corresponding call option, preferably an option whose volatility is uncharacteristically high. The effect is to create a long position in the share at a lower entry price at the expense of limiting the upside potential of the position. The combined position is superior to a naked position in the share for all future share prices which imply a return less than the maximum return on the buy–write position as Example 5.4 shows.

Equivalent to the buy–write is the trade where the investor simply sells puts and invests the proceeds together with the money he would have spent on the shares in the money market.

Example 5.4 ABC buy–write

Current price of ABC shares	=	340p
Current price of 6-month ABC 340 calls	=	28p

Returns at option expiry (including 5 per cent dividend yield on ABC shares):

ABC Share Price	Long ABC Shares	Long ABC Shares Short ABC 340 Calls
400	40.3%	22.5%
380	28.5%	22.5%
369.4	22.5%	22.5%
360	16.8%	22.5%
340	0.0%	22.5%
320	–6.8%	10.5%
300	–18.5%	–1.24%
280	–30.3%	–13.0%

3.2.5 Synthetic Futures Hedges

It is possible to create positions which behave like futures from combinations of calls and puts of the same exercise price as follows:

Long call and short put at exercise price X	≡	Long synthetic futures at price X
Short call and long put at exercise price X	≡	Short synthetic futures at price X

Thus, to return to our ABC example, we could lock-in the price of ABC shares by selling an ABC 340 call and simultaneously buying an ABC 340 put to establish a short synthetic futures position at a price of 340. If we had originally bought the stock at 260 this trade would lock-in the return for the holding period since we know the purchase price and exit price. The total cash return would be augmented by the dividends received and also by the difference between the price of the call and the price of the put.

Creating a synthetic short futures position locks-in the forward selling price of the shares but suffers from the disadvantage of double transactions costs. In addition, if the options are American style, there is also the risk of early exercise against the short call part of the hedge.

3.2.6 Comparison of Short Futures, Long Put and Short Call Hedges

Figure 5.3 shows the comparison of the different hedges for the ABC example. With the benefit of hindsight, the following best and worst hedges emerge:

Market movement	Best hedge	Worst hedge
Large upward	No hedge	Short futures
Small upward or small downward	Short call	Long put
Large downward	Short futures	No hedge

Interestingly, the only hedge which costs money, the long put hedge, does not turn out to be the best hedge at all, whereas shorting calls, which often receive a bad press are never the worst thing to do since a short call hedge is better than no hedge at all in a falling market. So why are investors prepared to pay money for the long put hedge? The answer is that for large upward or large downward movements in the market, the long put hedge is the second best thing to do. This is clearly of considerable comfort to many different investors.

This discussion should bring home the message that you cannot divorce the hedging decision from your view on the market. There is no ideal hedge in all circumstances. In many ways you pay for what you get.

You should also remember that for each hedged position there is at least one equivalent synthetic position:

Hedged position	**Synthetic**
Long shares, short futures	Short cash
Long shares, long put	Short cash, long call
Long shares, short call	Short cash, short put

Some fund managers will not have the opportunity of liquidating their equity position. However, those managers who are able to do this should consider the different strategies carefully. By definition a synthetic position must have the same payoff profile as the equivalent underlying position *in the absence of transactions and other costs*. It is

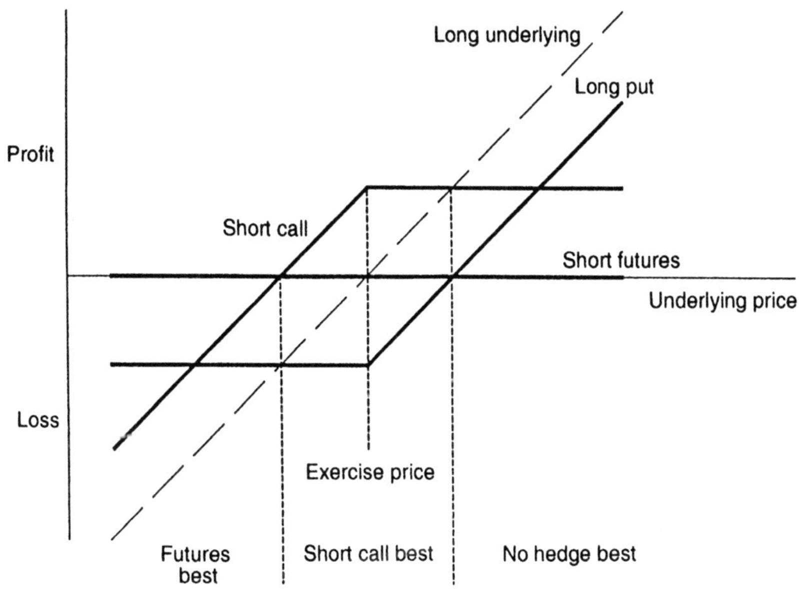

Figure 5.3 Comparison of Futures, Long Put and Short Call Hedges

these costs which will tip the balance in favour of one particular strategy. Note also that the synthetic position is more versatile with respect to cash. This may be important when considering overseas portfolios. With the hedged position the entire value of your portfolio is subject to currency risk. On the other hand the synthetic position allows you the freedom to invest the cash in the currency of your choice.

The simple options hedges can be extended with the addition of other options to produce hedges with more exotic profiles. For example, the long put hedge at exercise price X produces a synthetic call of exercise price X. We could sell a call of higher exercise price Y against this position and produce a synthetic vertical spread or collar. This hedge would insure against losses below X whilst foregoing any gains above Y. However, since we take in premium from the written call, the cost of the hedge is less than the simple long put hedge.

3.3 Dynamic Options Hedges

Section 2.2 discusses options hedges which are held to the maturity of the options contract. The hedge ratio is easy to calculate (1 option hedges the number of underlying shares in the option contract) and the hedge can be interpreted as fixing some aspect of the selling price of the portfolio *at options expiry*.

Often, however, you may wish to hedge for a shorter period. If futures or futures synthetics are used then the hedger will be subject to basis risk. In the case of options hedges the hedger will need to be more sophisticated in constructing his hedge to allow for the fact that the price of an option and the price of the underlying security do not change on a 1:1 basis. For short-term hedges, the hedger is usually interested in matching price changes in the portfolio with a corresponding price change in the hedge. He may be motivated to do this in order to neutralise his portfolio over a set of economic statistics or over a holiday period, for example. Thus he is trying to fix the future selling price at approximately today's level.

The simplest dynamic options hedge is based on the 'delta' of the option which measures the change in option price for a small change in the price of the underlying security (assuming that other factors which affect the option price remain constant):

$$\Delta O = \Delta \times \Delta S$$

where ΔO is the change in option price, ΔS is the corresponding change in the share price and Δ is the 'delta' of the option.

Since delta is a number which cannot be numerically greater than 1, the relationship above shows that option prices cannot change by more than the corresponding change in the underlying security. Thus the number of options required in a 'delta hedge' of the underlying is given by:

$$\text{Hedge ratio} = \frac{1}{\Delta}$$

i.e. the ratio of options to underlying is greater than 1:1.

We can delta hedge a share portfolio either by buying puts or by selling calls in the above hedge ratio. As for the option hedges described in Section 2.2. above we can choose between hedging with index options or hedging individual securities by the corresponding equity option. The basis for the choice is exactly the same as that for long-term options hedges. If you choose to use index options, you will only hedge the systematic risk of the portfolio but may well benefit in terms of lower transactions costs and possibly a more liquid market. Hedges of specific securities in the portfolio with the corresponding option are likely to be more accurate but may suffer from high transactions costs.

For options which are trading at-the-money, the delta is approximately 0.5 (calls) or –0.5 (puts) and the corresponding delta hedge is:

Long 2 puts per 1 share
Short 2 calls per 1 share

The profit profile of the two hedges is illustrated in Figure 5.4. The short-term profit profile is identical to that of an options straddle and hence *in the short term*

Delta ratioed put hedge ≡ Short cash, long straddle
Delta ratioed call hedge ≡ Short cash, short straddle

However, the figure also shows that if the ratioed hedge is held until expiry of the

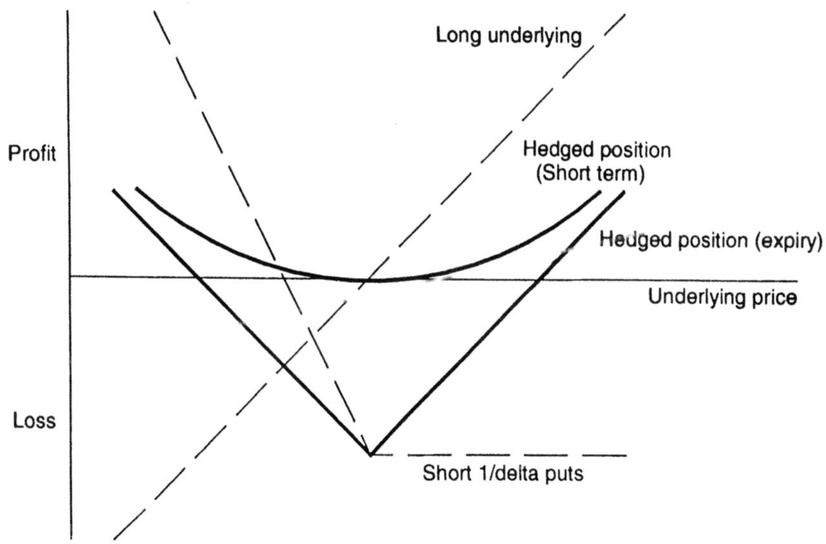

Figure 5.4 Dynamic Long Put Hedge

options contract, the position is overhedged and thus represents some sort of geared short position in the equity. Consequently in order to keep the hedge in balance, i.e. to preserve the delta neutrality of the hedge, constant rebalancing (buying or selling options) will be required.

Figure 5.4 appears to show that a ratioed put hedge is a one-way bet. No matter which way the market moves, the hedge always moves into profit. However, bear in mind that time value decay operates against the long hedger, over time the long hedger pays for the benefit of the convexity of his position in terms of the option premium. Similarly, a ratioed short call hedge is not necessarily a sophisticated method of losing money. The option writer will pick up time value as the hedge progresses.

3.4 Dynamic Hedges with Synthetic Options

In Section 2.2 we mentioned the use of out-of-the-money puts as a simple method of portfolio insurance. We can attempt to achieve similar results by creating synthetic option positions. Our objective may be to lock-in a minimum forward value for our portfolio whilst preserving our exposure to the upside potential. For example suppose the equity index is currently at 2500.00. We require an investment strategy which establishes a floor on the value of our portfolio at 2450.00 but enables us to participate in any upside movement over the next 6 months. Possible simple solutions would involve the buying of 2450 puts or liquidating the portfolio and buying 2450 calls.

The portfolio insurance technique can be redefined in a slightly different way. It is basically a form of domestic asset allocation. The uninsured position is an asset allocation with 100 per cent invested in equities whereas the insured position effectively has a small amount invested in equities and a near 100 per cent invested in cash.

There is a different method of achieving the same result. Recall that the payoff on a call option of exercise price X is

$$\text{Call payoff} = \max\{S - X, 0\}$$

where S is the asset value at option expiry.

Suppose our desired portfolio has a payoff which has a floor at X. In order to achieve this, we need to combine the calls with a discount security which has a value of X at options expiry. The present value of this discount security will be given by

$$\text{Value of discount security} = X \times e^{-rt}$$

where r is the rate of interest until options expiry and t is the time to options expiry.

Now consider, for simplicity, that the security does not pay dividends. The value of the call is given by the Black and Scholes pricing formula as:

$$C = SN(d_1) - Xe^{-rt}N(d_2)$$

where $N(d_1)$ and $N(d_2)$ are defined in the usual manner.

Hence the value of our portfolio which has the payoff:

$$\text{Portfolio payoff} = \max\{S, X\}$$

is given by:

$$\text{Portfolio} = SN(d_1) - [1 - N(d_2)]Xe^{-rt}$$

We can create our desired portfolio by buying shares and discount securities in the following amounts:

Shares:	$N(d_1)$
Discount securities	$[1 - N(d_2)]$

Since both $N(d_1)$ and $N(d_2)$ will vary as the share price or index changes, this strategy involves constant rebalancing of the ratio of shares to discount securities in order to achieve the correct payoff at the notional options expiry.

Thus rather than buying or owning shares worth S and puts of exercise price X worth P we own a fraction of these shares, $S \times N(d_1)$ and invest an amount X $[1 - N(d_1)]e^{-rt}$ in discount securities. The two positions must be equivalent with a payoff:

$$\text{Portfolio payoff} = \max\{S, X - P\}$$

The simple portfolio insurance policy involving buying puts and the creating a synthetic call position while a dynamic asset allocation policy gives the same payoff at option expiry, i.e. the cost of creating synthetic calls of exercise price X is equal to the value of a put of the same exercise price. (Can you see why? Remember that $N(d_1) > N(d_2)$.) What, therefore, is the point of a dynamic hedging policy which simply replicates what we can achieve with less fuss using the options markets?

The answer lies in several areas:

(1) The range of exercise prices available for traded options are limited. Hence a manager may often not be able to buy options which set a floor at his required value.
(2) The maturity of the traded options may not suit the investor's time horizon.
(3) The liquidity of the traded options may not be sufficiently high in all markets.

These and other factors may mitigate in favour of a dynamic options strategy. This then creates a further problem. The dynamic strategy requires constant rebalancing of the hedge. This can be extremely inefficient if the investor is constantly buying and selling equities in small quantities. Indeed, some fund managers may be restricted in their ability to sell the equities in their portfolios. The solution to this problem is to create the synthetic call by selling index futures against the equity portfolio. For example, if the synthetic call requires $n(d_1) \times S$ of shares then we need to sell $[1 - N(d_1)] \times S$ index futures against the portfolio to create the synthetic call.

Using futures for dynamic asset allocation in this way has a further advantage. The portfolio of shares will probably have been created by a detailed analysis of the merits of the individual equities. Using index futures for the portfolio insurance enables the investor to hedge against market movements whilst continuing to benefit from shrewd stock selection.

The principal problem with portfolio insurance involving dynamic asset allocation is that the synthetic call has no gamma and does not have the natural advantages of a long option position. In order to keep the hedge in balance, you are always selling late in a falling market and buying late in a rising market. In the event of a large discontinuous change in securities prices the portfolio will always be significantly underhedged.

4 HEDGING ANTICIPATED PORTFOLIOS – ASSET ALLOCATION

In section 3 we discussed the types of hedges which could be used to protect an existing portfolio. The common feature to all the hedges was that derivatives were used in various ways to short the market – either totally or partially – against the long position in the cash.

Now consider the general case of the asset allocation decision either domestic (equities versus bonds versus cash) or global. Once a decision has been reached to change the distribution of a portfolio you are:

(1) synthetically short of the securities into which you wish to move resources and
(2) synthetically long of the securities that you no longer deem appropriate to hold.

Until the asset allocation has been implemented you have unwanted exposure which may be hedged using the futures or options markets. Generally, the futures markets because of their liquidity and immediacy are used to hedge the synthetic positions:

> Hedge the synthetic shorts by buying the corresponding 3-month, bond or index futures.
> Hedge the synthetic longs by selling the corresponding 3-month, bond or index futures.

Once the desired market exposures have been approximately realised in this way, the securities analysts can then select the best bonds or shares to make up the desired portfolio. As cash securities are subsequently purchased, the futures hedges can be lifted.

The most liquid futures markets worldwide enable the investor to reallocate his investments in this way quickly and with little impact on the market. There are some disadvantages however. The first involves the classic hedger's dilemma. Futures rarely trade at a 'fair' price and so the hedger may often need to sell underpriced futures or buy overpriced futures. The problem is whether to take a small loss on the basis in order to profit from the expected benefits of the reallocation of assets. The second problem is that reallocation involving index futures creates a position in the index. This may not be the preferred position of the portfolio manager and hence the futures hedge may not be particularly efficient at hedging the synthetic positions.

These criticisms notwithstanding futures find widespread application in domestic and global asset allocation. An illustration of the use of futures in domestic asset allocation is given in Example 5.5.

Example 5.5 Domestic Asset Allocation using Futures

Current Portfolio		**Preferred Portfolio**	
Shares	70%	Shares	55%
Bonds	20%	Bonds	30%
Cash	10%	Cash	15%

Portfolio value = £1 bn

The fund manager can achieve the allocation in two ways:

1. In the spot markets:

   Sell 15 per cent of the funds value in equities
   Buy 10 per cent of the funds value in bonds
   Invest the remaining 5 per cent in cash
2. In the futures markets:
   First hedge the following synthetic positions in the corresponding futures markets:

-15%	equities	Sell FTSE-100 index futures
+10%	bonds	Buy Long Gilt futures
+5%	cash	Buy 3-month Sterling deposit futures or invest directly in cash

Then select the individual cash securities to buy or sell by your preferred method of analysis and gradually lift the futures hedges as the cash market positions are established.

Futures are particularly useful in global asset allocation since they allow an investor to create an index fund in several different currencies without the need to carry out extensive analysis of individual shares. However, global asset allocation strategies are more complex because of the currency exposures. It is no longer sufficient merely to hedge the underlying market exposures – you should hedge the corresponding currency exposures if it is your ultimate intention to purchase the underlying cash securities as shown in Example 5.6.

Example 5.6 Global Asset Allocation using Futures

Current Portfolio		Preferred Portfolio	
UK equities	30%	UK equities	20%
US equities	35%	US equities	25%
German equities	15%	German equities	30%
French equities	20%	French equities	25%
Portfolio value = £1 bn			

The synthetic positions are now:

Position	**Hedge**
Long 10% UK equities	Short FTSE-100 index futures
Long £100mn Sterling	Sell £ and buy DM or FF
Long 10% US equities	Short S&P-500 index futures
Long £100mn in US$	Sell $ and buy DM or FF
Short 15% German equities	Buy DAX index futures
Short £150mn in DM	Buy DM with $ or US$
Short 5% French equities	Buy CAC-40 futures
Short £50mn in FF	Buy FF with £ or US$

5 RISK DIVERSIFICATION USING INDEX FUTURES

All over the world, portfolio managers hedge the *specific* risk of their equities by not 'putting all their eggs in one basket'. After all the *raison d'être* of having a portfolio rather than simply a single equity is that you believe that it is best to mitigate some of the risk associated with individual equities through portfolio diversification.

Fund managers who are sufficiently confident in their equity analysts may attempt to outperform the market by judicious selection of individual equities. This inevitably involves some exposure to company specific risk. Other managers (less ambitious or more worldly-wise depending on your point of view) will seek to track the market by constructing cash portfolios which match an appropriate market index as closely as possible.

Index futures offer the fund manager an off-the-peg method of creating an index-based equity fund by creating a synthetic equity fund based on the identity:

$$\text{Long cash index} \equiv \text{Long index futures} + \text{short cash}$$

There are a number of benefits to creating an index-based fund in this way provided the *cash is managed appropriately*:

(1) The fund will track the index accurately whereas index funds based on sub-portfolios of the cash index will show some tracking error which will increase with time. This is of particular benefit to small funds.

(2) The only source of income to a cash based index fund are the dividends paid on the shares. A futures based fund can in principle derive revenue both from the interest earned on the cash and the variation margin on the futures position (should the futures price increase). In effect capital gains are realised immediately in cash (as indeed are capital losses).
(3) All fund managers like to buy cheap. Determining whether an equity index future is cheap is a matter of simple mathematics. Identifying underpriced equities is rather less straightforward.
(4) The index future based fund has more control over currency risk. Consider the case of a UK-based fund which wishes to purchase £100m of the S&P-500 equity index. If the fund buys shares, the entire £100m is invested in US$ and therefore subject to US$/£ currency risk. On the other hand, if a synthetic S&P-500 fund is established using index futures only the initial margin and variation margin are necessarily subject to currency risk. The balance of the cash can, if desired, be invested in the UK. Thus futures-based funds can be constructed such that the bulk of the currency risk is on the capital gains or losses. The principal (less the initial margin) need bear no currency risk.
(5) Transactions costs in establishing the futures-based fund will be low.

It would be surprising if futures-based funds were not without drawbacks and indeed this is the case.

(1) By opting for an index based fund you are ruling out the benefits from shrewd share selection.
(2) The initial margin required for equity indices is not insignificant (typically 1–5 per cent) and may be cash which is not earning interest or earning interest at an inferior rate. This point should not be overlooked when considering if the index future is cheap or expensive.
(3) Although initial transactions costs tend to favour the futures fund, the futures positions must be 'rolled-over' into the deferred future contract when the current contract expires. This causes additional transaction costs and also an additional pricing problem since rolling futures positions will be achieved by trading the near-deferred spread.

The criterion for deciding whether an index futures is cheap or expensive relative to the underlying cash index is whether the return made by holding your money as cash is greater than the dividend yield on the share portfolio plus the premium on the index futures contract, i.e. if:

$$S \times R \times \frac{N}{365} \geq S \times D \times \frac{N}{365} + F - S$$

i.e.

$$R \geq D + \frac{F - S}{S} \times \frac{365}{N}$$

where *R* is the money market lending rate until futures expiry, *D* is the dividend yield on the cash portfolio, *N* is the number of days until futures expiry, *S* is the value of the cash portfolio and *F* is the current futures price.

Note that this simple formula neglects the transactions costs (such as margin payments) which should be taken into account in a practical context.

We illustrate the choice between a cash index fund and a futures-based index fund in Example 5.7.

Example 5.7 Cash versus Synthetic Index Fund

Current price of FTSE-100 index	=	2450.00
Current price of FTSE-100 futures	=	2470.0
Time to futures expiry	=	90 days
90-day money market lending rate	=	10%
Dividend yield on FTSE-100 index	=	5%
Funds available for investment	=	£50m

First calculate the percentage annualised futures premium:

$$\text{Futures premium} = \frac{2470 - 2450}{2450} \times \frac{365}{90}$$

$$= 3.31\%$$

Thus the return I can achieve from investing by cash in the money market (10 per cent) is greater than the sum of the dividend yield (5 per cent) and the futures premium (3.31 per cent). Hence investing in the synthetic index position is beneficial on grounds of cheapness. (A yield pick up of about 1.69% is possible.)

The synthetic position would comprise:

Index futures:

$$\frac{50{,}000{,}000}{2450 \times 25} = 816 \text{ futures}$$

90-day government bills:

$$50{,}000{,}000 \times \left(1 + 10\% \times \frac{90}{365}\right) = 51{,}233{,}000 \text{ nominal}$$

To demonstrate the benefit of the synthetic position, choose any value for the cash index after 90 days, say 2500. By definition this must also be the futures EDSP.

The percentage change on the cash index is given by:

$$\frac{2500 - 2450}{2450} \times \frac{365}{90} + \text{Dividend yield} = 13.28\%$$

The percentage change on the synthetic position is given by:

Investment rate + Gain on futures position

$$= 10\% + \frac{816 \times (2500 - 2470) \times 25}{50{,}000{,}000} \times \frac{365}{90}$$

$$= 14.96\%$$

Thus the difference between the two investments is roughly in line with our expectations, the differences being caused by rounding errors.

Using equity index futures in this way is a specific application of using derivatives to establish synthetic equity positions. In principle, when seeking to purchase a share or portfolio of shares when there are corresponding derivative instruments, the investor should always consider whether there is an advantage in buying the cash security or in going long an equivalent futures or synthetic futures position (long call and short put at same exercise price, remember) and investing the spare cash in the money market until the expiry date of the derivative instrument.

6 HEDGING PRINCIPLES AND YIELD ENHANCEMENT

The hedging principles outlined above can often be developed to provide low-risk methods of yield enhancement. The basic idea is that the investor sets up a hedged position in which one of the components seems anomalously priced. The expectation is that the anomalous pricing will correct itself within a relatively short time when the hedge is lifted yielding additional gains to the portfolio. In any event, the investor has a hedged position for his portfolio and should the price correction not materialise quickly, he should not be substantially disadvantaged.

The following are some of the methods with which investors try to enhance the yields on their portfolios.

6.1 Basis Trading

As mentioned in Section 5.2, the 'basis' for an index futures contract is defined by:

$$\text{Basis} = \text{Cash index} - \text{futures price}$$

The basis is usually negative for index futures since the carry (dividend yield – financing cost) is usually negative, causing index futures to trade at a premium to cash under most conditions. At expiry, the basis is zero by definition since the futures price and the underlying index must have the same value. Thus the basis trends towards zero through the lifetime of the futures contract, a process known as 'convergence'.

The basis can be traded like a security given the following rules for the investor's position *in the basis*:

$$\text{Long cash, short futures} \Rightarrow \text{Long basis}$$

$$\text{Short cash, long futures} \Rightarrow \text{Short basis}$$

Thus a basis trader is taking a view on the convergence process.

One way of trading the basis is to purchase (sell) the index whilst simultaneously selling (buying) the index future. This method may incur large transactions costs on the cash leg of the trade.

An alternative for the fund manager is to sell futures contracts against his position as described in Section 3.1. Now, however the intention is not primarily to hedge (although this is a potentially beneficial consequence) but rather to pick-up yield from a swift increase in the basis. The best opportunities for such a trade will occur when the futures contract is towards the upper end of its fair price range. An example of a basis trade is given in Example 5.8.

Example 5.8 Basis Trade

Initial value of cash index	=	2500.00
Initial value of futures contract	=	2550.0
Days to futures expiry	=	90
Dividend yield on the cash index	=	5 per cent
90-day money market rate	=	10 per cent

The initial basis = 2500 – 2550 = –50 bp

First determine the value of the futures premium:

$$\text{Futures premium} = \frac{2550 - 2500}{2500} \times \frac{365}{90} = 8.11\%$$

Thus the futures are significantly over-valued and buying the basis seems reasonable. The minimum return on the position is (8.11 + 5) = 13.11 per cent if we are forced to maintain the position until futures expiry.

Two days later the new market conditions are:

Later value of cash index	=	2490
Later price of index futures	=	2525

Final basis = 2490 – 2525 = –35 bp

Gain from position in the basis = 15 bp

The gain from the basis position more than adequately compensates for the decline in the value of the cash position.

The worst case scenario for a basis trader is that the basis does not change within the required time scale and the position then behaves like a simple futures hedge giving a return equal to:

Return on futures hedge = Dividend yield + Futures premium

Whilst this return is not a disaster (it will usually be approximately equal to the money market rate) it may cause disappointment to investors in the event of a rising market.

6.2 Covered Call Writing

We have discussed the main features of writing calls against a long position in the underlying equities in Section 3.2.3. If the method is used for yield enhancement the investor's expectation is that he can pick up time value possibly from a sudden decrease in volatility of the option.

6.3 Relative Performance Trades

The modern portfolio theory approach to share price movements shows that the movement in share price can be analysed in terms of two main influences:

(1) the market in general (systematic risk)
(2) company specific factors (non-systematic risk)

These influences may operate on the share price in a reinforcing manner or, quite commonly may operate in opposite ways. For example, economic conditions may be poor for the market as a whole but you may believe that a certain company or market sector will outperform the market. The problem is that if you simply purchase the company's equity, the share may well outperform the market but the gains may be more than swamped by a general decline in the market. Remember, some shares outperformed the market during the 1987 crash but the owners of these shares still lost heavily.

However, the existence of index derivatives enables the investor to carry out a relative performance trade in which a long (short) position in the equity is hedged by a corresponding short (long) position in an index derivative. In this way we hedge the systematic risk of the share and hopefully profit from our exposure to the non-systematic risk. Consider the case of company XYZ which you believe will significantly outperform the market but you are worried about the impact of rising interest rates on the market as a whole. You can trade this view by buying call options on XYZ and simultaneously selling call options on the underlying market as illustrated in Example 5.9. Clearly this is not the only hedge we could apply. The rationale behind this particular trade is that we buy XYZ calls in order to go long XYZ in a cash efficient way and hedge with index calls both to recover some premium and also partially to hedge factors other than market direction which impact on the value of XYZ calls.

Example 5.9 Relative Performance Trade

Current value of cash index	=	2500.00
Current value of XYZ	=	350p
Delta of 2500 index call	=	0.48
Delta of 350 XYZ call	=	0.46
Beta factor for XYZ	=	0.95
Number of XYZ call options purchased	=	100

We intend to purchase 100 XYZ call options. We need to calculate the hedge involving index call options using the CAPM and delta ratioing as follows:

First express the position in the call options as equity equivalents in £:

$$\text{Equity equivalent} = \text{No. of options} \times 1000 \times \text{Share price} \times \text{Option } \Delta$$
$$= £161{,}000$$

To express the XYZ call option position in index equivalents multiply this number by the beta of XYZ

$$\text{Index equivalents of XYZ calls} = 161{,}000 \times 0.95 = £152{,}950$$

Now express the index call options as index equivalents bearing in mind that, at present, the value of UK index options is £10 per full index point:

$$\text{Index equivalents} = \text{Index level} \times £ \text{ per point} \times \text{Index option } \Delta$$
$$= £12{,}000$$

The number of index calls which should be written against the XYZ call option position is then given by the ratio of the two index equivalents:

$$\text{Hedge ratio} = \frac{152{,}950}{12{,}000} = 13 \text{ (rounded up)}$$

Thus the relative performance trade is:

Long 100 XYZ calls Short 13 index calls

We have illustrated a relative performance trade as a 'buy–write' involving call options. If you already own the stock the same principle can be applied – you might sell index options or index futures against the long position in the stock in order to protect the position against adverse movements in the market but to profit from any movement in the share price due to company-specific factors.

6.4 Synthetic Equity Positions

We have discussed the important aspects of synthetic equity positions above as a method of achieving risk reduction through efficient portfolio diversification. The other way of looking at the problem is from the point of view of yield enhancement. For example, if the index future is cheap relative to cash, provided you are seeking to invest in an index-tracking fund, it may be more beneficial to create a synthetic index fund rather than an equity based fund.

7 SUMMARY

The existence of the derivatives markets presents the equity investor with a wide range of additional techniques for improving portfolio performance and managing the risk of the position. The new techniques fall into the general categories of:

(1) hedging – establishing some aspects of the selling price of existing positions, the buying price of new positions or the mitigation of company-specific risk, and
(2) yield enhancement – developing the hedging principles to create low risk positions with superior return expectations to the underlying cash position.

Some of the techniques, whilst being possible by conventional means, are more efficient through the derivatives markets. Other techniques are unachievable by conventional means. The properties of options are particularly noteworthy since the unique payoff characteristics may be used to modify the expected return of a portfolio in a wide variety of ways to suit views on market direction and also option-specific properties such as volatility.

Not surprisingly, the existence of additional investment techniques requires closer attention to management:

(1) The investor must have a clear idea of his investment objectives. There is no 'correct' answer to how to use derivatives. However, it is inexcusable to use a derivatives strategy which is incompatible with the objectives.
(2) The investor must be flexible with respect to his objectives since the changing market environment will affect the suitability of the different strategies.
(3) The investor must become more knowledgeable and should fully understand the intricacies of the derivative instruments before he applies the techniques. On-the-job learning may not appeal to trustees.
(4) A systematic approach should be developed to analyse the opportunities pre-

sented by the different derivative instruments. A consideration of the number of derivative instruments available in the UK suggests that alone then the serious investor will require appropriate analytical systems. Such systems will probably involve real-time pricing and scenario analysis.

(5) Finally do not ignore the transactions costs when considering derivative strategies. Transactions costs are usually higher in the cash market but once you purchase an equity, it should last for ever (in principle!). Futures and options on the other hand have finite lifetimes and therefore if you want to continue to play the game you must periodically re-establish your positions and incur further transactions costs. One cost which should not be overlooked is the initial margin on futures position. In volatile markets this could amount to 5 per cent of the nominal value and may not necessarily earn interest.

6: Bond Futures as an Investment Tool

Daniel Corrigan

Fixed income fund managers have a range of bonds in which they may invest – from mortgage-backed securities, through inverse floating rate notes to plain vanilla corporate and government bonds and many more. There are, however, additional products investment managers are beginning to use – financial futures and option on bonds and bond futures. Recent history suggests futures are used mainly by traders and arbitrageurs. However, the appeal to investors of futures and options as investment products rather than hedging tools is widespread in the USA and is gaining acceptance in Europe.

Essentially investors may buy bond futures and options with the intention of taking delivery of the underlying security. This chapter is designed to provide an explanation of the value of a financial futures contract and how the value changes over the period to delivery. Should an investor wish to invest in a ten-year bond issued by a major government he may buy that bond outright in the usual manner or buy a number of bond futures contracts to reflect the desired investment level and take delivery of an underlying bond. Clearly this involves cheaper financing – the cost of running this position is limited to margins and brokerage charges rather than the full financing rate the alternative physical bond would require. Correspondingly income on the bond does not accrue to the investor until after the delivery date. Essentially the trades are similar but by buying bond futures contracts the investor defers settlement.

Clearly the investor has a choice to make – does he buy the underling bond or the bond futures contract? The choice will be heavily influenced by the relative value of the two instruments. If the bond is cheap to the bond futures contract he will probably buy the bond and vice versa. However, if he is happy with his position – be it long the bond or long the future – he may wish to hedge his market risk by selling an equal amount of bond futures contracts (or selling short bonds if he is long the futures contract). The resulting trade is known as a basis trade which enables the investor to lock in returns immediately up to three months prior to delivery. Clearly investors are unlikely to sell short bonds – in many cases it is prohibited by the authorities or by investor trust deeds – so the advantage to investors occurs when bonds are cheap to bond futures. In this case the investor will buy bonds, sell bond futures in a duration weighted amount – known as buying the basis.

Basis trading involves the purchase of a deliverable bond and simultaneous sale of a number of bond futures contracts or the reverse – the sale of a cash bond and simultaneous purchase of a number of bond futures contracts. It is a form of investment designed to extract risk-free profits by enforcing the delivery mechanism that underpins the bond futures contract. The contract seller has the right and obligation to deliver any bond which fulfils the relevant exchanges deliverability criteria and in return receives an amount of money according to a preset formula.

The party which is long the contract takes delivery either on a prescribed date or on one of a number in the delivery schedule. The price the seller receives is the EDSP (Exchange Delivery Settlement Price), the closing price for the futures contract on the last trading day multiplied by the price factor for the particular bond plus the accrued interest to that date.

The conversion factor or price factor as it is also known converts the yield on each bond to a notional coupon and maturity, e.g. 6 per cent ten-year bond. It is nothing other than the bond's price at the nominal contract yield divided by 100.

Price factors have the following characteristics. I would like to use by means of illustration the Bund future contract.

- Factors are unique to each bond. This is because no two bonds are identical, e.g. bonds deliverable into the June 1991 Bund contract range in coupon from $7\frac{1}{8}$ per cent to 9 per cent and in maturity from December 1999 to February 2001.
- Factors are unique to each contract but remain consistent throughout the delivery cycle.
- Factors are used to calculate the invoice price of bonds delivered to fulfil a short futures position.
- If the coupon is greater than 6 per cent (in the example above) the conversion factor is greater than one, if the coupon is less than 6 per cent the conversion factor is less than one.
- The conversion factor is the approximate number of futures contracts required to hedge a long or short position.

Deliverability Criteria

Delivery may be made of any bond which meets the exchanges criteria, e.g. for the Bund contract on LIFFE any Bund or German Unity Fund issue with $8\frac{1}{2}-10$ years remaining to maturity as at the tenth calendar day of the delivery month on a free-of-reallowance basis as listed by the relevant exchange. Delivery may be made via the Frankfurt Kassenverein, Euroclear or CEDEL.

Bonds issued after the contract has started to trade may or may not be deliverable into the current futures contract. Accordingly the investor should confirm for himself whether the bond is likely to be deliverable or not.

Bunds and Unity issues that fulfilled the deliverability criteria into the June 1991 Bund futures contract on LIFFE and DTB were the following:

Bund	$7\frac{1}{8}$%	20/12/99
Bund	$7\frac{1}{4}$%	20/01/00
Bund	$7\frac{3}{4}$%	21/02/00
Bund	$8\frac{3}{4}$%	22/05/00
Unity	$8\frac{3}{4}$%	20/07/00
Bund	$8\frac{1}{2}$%	21/08/00
Bund	9%	20/10/00
Bund	$8\frac{7}{8}$%	20/12/00
Bund	9%	22/01/01
Unity	$8\frac{1}{2}$%	20/02/01
Bund	$8\frac{3}{8}$%	21/05/91

THE CASH AND CARRY ARBITRAGE

The cash and carry arbitrage is a strategy where the trader buys a deliverable bond and sells an equal amount of futures contracts. If the positions are perfectly balanced the strategy involves no risk because the bond can be delivered into the contract on maturity of the future. Hence, the profit from this strategy is risk-free and should therefore not exceed the costs which are involved in the strategy. If, for example, the profit is higher than an equivalent short-term interest rate (the rate at which you borrow at in order to finance the bond purchase), then arbitrageurs will buy bonds and sell futures. In the case where the profit earned by the cash and carry trade is smaller than the risk-free market interest rate, arbitrageurs will sell the bonds and buy the futures and thus borrow money below the market interest rate. This kind of strategy is termed 'reverse cash and carry'. Both strategies, the cash and carry trade as well as the reverse cash and carry, assume that the positions involved can be held until maturity. For the cash and carry arbitrage the following cash flows occur:

Cost of Purchasing the Bund (Dem 250,000)

$$P + Ap = \left\{ 1 + (r \times \frac{d}{360}) \right\}$$

P is the clean price of the bond, Ap is the accrued interest (at purchase date), r is the rate of funding and d is the number of days from the opening until the closing of the position.

Earnings from the sale of *X* Futures (where *X* = *PF*)

$X(F - \text{EDSF})$ (which is equal to the variation margin accumulated over the holding period)

X is the number of futures contracts (= PF) and F is the initial futures price (at selling date).

Earnings from the delivery of the bond into the futures

$$(\text{EDSP} \times PF) + Ad$$

EDSP is the exchange delivery settlement price, PF is the price factor and Ad is the accrued interest (at delivery date).

If we combine these three formulae in an equation we can calculate the profit arising from the cash and carry trade.

$$\text{Profit} = PF \times (F - \text{EDSP}) + \left\{(\text{EDSP} \times PF) + Ad\right\} - (P + Ap) \times \left\{(1 + (r \times \frac{d}{360})\right\}$$

which simplifies to

$$\text{Profit} = PF \times F - (PF \times \text{EDSP}) + \left\{(\text{EDSP} \times PF) + Ad\right\} - (P + Ap) \times \left((1 + (r \times \frac{d}{360})\right)$$

$$\text{Profit} = PF \times F + Ad - (P + Ap) \times \left\{1 + (r\frac{d}{360})\right\}$$

In theory the profit of this strategy should be equal to zero because otherwise a risk-free profit can be earned. Assuming that we carry out the above strategy and use our own bonds, instead of funding them, we can solve the above equation for the funding rate (r) and obtain a rate of return which is called the 'implied repo rate'.

$$\text{Implied repo} - [(F + PF \times P) + (Ad - Ap)] \times 1/(P + Ap) \times 360/d$$

This rate, in theory should be equal to the funding rate. If this is not the case an arbitrage can be exercised. If the implied repo rate lies above the funding rate (r) it is profitable to exercise the cash and carry trade. If the implied rate is below r then the reverse cash and carry is profitable.

The bond with the highest repo rate is the cheapest to deliver (CTD). The idea behind it is that if the short-term risk-free interest rate is below the implied repo rate, the arbitrageur will carry out the cash and carry trade. The strategy will be most profitable when using the bond with the implied repo rate which shows the greatest difference to the financing rate (see below for an elaboration on the implied repo rate).

THE PRICING OF THE A BOND FUTURES CONTRACT

When talking about the futures price we must first distinguish between the 'fair value' and the 'relative value'. The fair value of a futures is the futures price which will lead to zero profits for the cash and carry arbitrage and is determined by the following equation:

$$\text{Futures Price} = \frac{\text{Price (CTD)} + \text{Cost of Carry (CTD)}}{\text{Price Factor (CTD)}} - \text{Income from CTD}$$

Cost of carry = Market value of bond × Interest rate × Holding period income from bond = AI on delivery day – AI on the transaction day (AI = Accrued Interest)

However, in the futures market the actual futures price is usually different from its fair value. The two main reasons for this are the delivery option and that there are legal obstacles for the reverse cash and carry arbitrage.

What is Basis Trading?

Gross basis is the difference between the market price of a bond and the current price implied by the futures contract. On 21 March 1991 a deliverable Bund $8\frac{7}{8}$ 20/12/00 was fixed in Frankfurt at 102.36 as the June Futures contract was trading 84.92. The conversion factor of this Bund into the June 1991 contract was 1.203046.

$$\begin{aligned}\text{Gross basis} &= 102.36 - (84.92 \times 1.203046)\\ &= 102.36 - 102.163\\ &= 0.197\end{aligned}$$

The other deliverable Bunds were fixed as follows:

Issue			Price	Factor basis	Gross
Bund	$7\frac{1}{8}$%	20/12/99	91.55	1.072719	0.455
Bund	$7\frac{1}{4}$%	20/01/00	92.30	1.081478	0.461
Bund	$7\frac{3}{4}$%	21/02/00	95.60	1.115144	0.902
Bund	$8\frac{3}{4}$%	22/05/00	101.50	1.185533	0.825
Unity	$8\frac{3}{4}$%	20/07/00	101.50	1.188164	0.601
Bund	$8\frac{1}{2}$%	21/08/00	100.26	1.172080	0.727
Bund	9%	20/10/00	103.15	1.209159	0.468
Bund	$8\frac{7}{8}$%	20/12/00	102.36	1.203046	0.197
Bund	9%	22/01/01	103.48	1.213305	0.446
Unity	$8\frac{1}{2}$%	20/02/01	100.30	1.178890	0.189

What does the data above tell us? First we know that if we are short a futures contract and do not wish to close it out prior to expiry we must deliver one of the eligible bonds. Correspondingly we know that if we are long a bond futures position and wish to run it until delivery we will be delivered one of the eligible bonds. Secondly we know that the short futures position holder has the option to identify which bonds he will deliver. Faced with the above we would expect the short seller to deliver that bond which minimises his loss or maximises his return, i.e. the cheapest bond to deliver.

The Cheapest to Deliver Bond

The determination of the CTD is fairly straightforward. All the seller has to do is to figure out the invoice amounts for the deliverable bonds included in the basket.

Example
Assume today is Monday 11 March 1991, the delivery day of the March-futures and only two Bunds can be delivered into the contract, the 7.75% and 8.5% Bund. The EDSP is 85.49.

	7.75% Bund 2000	**8.5% Bund 2001 (CTD)**
Price	96.163	101.144
Yield	8.374%	8.324%
Price factor	1.118319	1.183109
Coupon payable	20.02	20.02

The invoice amounts for the 7.75 per cent and the 8.5 per cent are respectively:

$$(85.49 \times 1.118319 \times 2.500 + 1{,}130) = \text{Dm}240{,}143$$
$$(85.49 \times 1.183109 \times 2.500 + 1{,}239) = \text{Dm}254{,}099$$

These are the amounts that the seller of the futures will receive for the delivery of the Bunds into the contract. The market prices for the two deliverable bonds are:

$$(96.163\% \times 250.000) + 1{,}130 = \text{Dm}241{,}538$$
$$(101.144\% \times 250.000) + 1{,}239 = \text{Dm}254{,}099$$

A comparison reveals that the seller will make a loss of Dm1,395 (Dm241,538 – Dm240,143) on the delivery of the 7.75% Bund whereas he incurs no loss on the delivery of the 8.5% Bund. Consequently the 8.5% Bund is the CTD.

If the prices above were to hold until delivery date, again ignoring funding, the following proceeds amounts (including accrued interest) would apply to each Bund.

Issue			Price	Factor basis	Gross	Proceeds
Bund	$7\frac{1}{8}$%	20/12/99	91.55	1.072719	0.455	88.7084
Bund	$7\frac{1}{4}$%	20/01/00	92.30	1.081478	0.461	88.1655
Bund	$7\frac{3}{4}$%	21/02/00	95.60	1.115144	0.902	88.0753
Bund	$8\frac{3}{4}$%	22/05/00	101.50	1.185533	0.825	90.0530
Unity	$8\frac{3}{4}$%	20/07/00	101.50	1.188164	0.601	93.2037
Bund	$8\frac{1}{2}$%	21/08/00	100.26	1.172080	0.727	92.3638
Bund	9%	20/10/00	103.15	1.209159	0.468	91.0572
Bund	$8\frac{7}{8}$%	20/12/00	102.36	1.203040	0.191	89.2750
Bund	9%	22/01/01	103.48	1.213305	0.446	88.7377
Unity	$8\frac{1}{2}$%	20/02/01	100.30	1.178890	0.189	87.6772

Clearly the Unity 8.5% 20/02/01 involves the lowest proceeds.

COST OF CARRY

Since cash and futures markets trade both the same underlying instrument, there should be no price difference on the expiration of the futures. Prior to expiration, however, the futures will either trade at a premium or at a discount relative to the cash. The seller of a futures will require a premium on the cash price, if the accrued interest on the bond will not fully cover the cost to carry the bond until the maturity of the futures. This premium, called 'negative carry', will emerge if a negative yield curve prevails in the market. If a market is characterised by a positive yield curve, i.e. that the interest earned on the bond exceeds the funding costs for the bond, then the futures will trade at a discount relative to the cash. This discount is referred to as 'positive carry'.

It is obvious that the premium or the discount will become smaller as the futures approaches maturity. This phenomenon, called 'convergence', is of highest importance to intermediaries who trade outright futures contracts. For a positive yield curve the convergence will result in profits/losses for the buyer/seller of futures assuming that there is no change in the interest rate. Conversely the buyer/seller will lose/earn the premium which is paid on the futures if the yield curve is negatively sloped.

To ignore funding costs is clearly an error. Accordingly we refine gross basis to take into account the cost of financing a position. Net basis as this is known is gross basis adjusted for net carry where net carry is coupon income (and re-investment if a coupon is paid in the interim) less borrowing expense. Net basis is the expected profit for a short cash/long futures trade. For example if the gross basis is 0.10 b.p. and the net basis 0.075 b.p. the expect loss is 0.075 b.p.

Using the same example as above and assuming a funding rate of 9 per cent for the

77 days to delivery for each of the Bunds we determine the following table of net basis. (The repo rates for each bond are unlikely to be consistent and many, especially the cheaper to deliver bonds, are often 'on special', i.e. trading at rates well under prevailing money market rates for like periods.)

Issue			Price	Factor	Gross Basis	Net Basis
Bund	$7\frac{1}{8}$%	20/12/99	91.55	1.072719	0.455	0.769
Bund	$7\frac{1}{4}$%	20/01/00	92.30	1.081478	0.461	0.752
Bund	$7\frac{3}{4}$%	21/02/00	95.60	1.115144	0.902	1.142
Bund	$8\frac{3}{4}$%	22/05/00	101.50	1.185533	0.825	1.056
Unity	$8\frac{3}{4}$%	20/07/00	101.50	1.188164	0.601	0.847
Bund	$8\frac{1}{2}$%	21/08/00	100.26	1.172080	0.727	0.983
Bund	9%	20/10/00	103.15	1.209159	0.468	0.653
Bund	$8\frac{7}{8}$%	20/12/00	102.36	1.203046	0.197	0.364
Bund	9%	22/01/01	103.48	1.213305	0.446	0.593
Unity	$8\frac{1}{2}$%	20/02/01	100.30	1.178890	0.189	0.365

In this case the cheapest to deliver is now $8\frac{7}{8}$% 20/12/00 with a net basis of 0.364 although the Unity $8\frac{1}{2}$% 20/02/01 is almost equally as cheap.

Implied Repo

An alternative way at looking at basis trading is to assess the implied repo rate from holding a position. The implied repo rate is the theoretical return to buying a bond, selling bond futures against it and delivering the bond.

$$\text{Implied repo rate} = [(\text{invoice price}/\text{purchase price} - 1)] \times 360/\text{no. of days}$$

If the implied repo rate is higher than the funding rate for the period the dealer should buy the basis, i.e. buy bonds, borrow funds (or enter into a repo agreement) and sell futures and deliver the bond. Alternatively, if the implied repo rate is lower than the borrowing costs the trader should sell the basis, i.e. sell the bond, invest the proceeds, buy bond futures and take delivery. (If the trader does not own the bond he may sell short and enter into a reverse repo to effect delivery.)

Concept of Cheapest to Deliver

The cheapest to deliver Bund is that which maximises return by buying the basis and delivering into the futures contract. This is the bond with the highest implied repo rate. As stated above the cheapest to deliver bond is that which has the lowest total proceeds. Predicting which bond will be cheapest to deliver over time is the main interest of basis traders as shifts in the CTD have many implications.

At yield levels higher than the notional contract yield, in the case of the Bund of 6 per cent, the CTD Bund will tend to be the higher duration Bunds, e.g. into the June 1991 contract Bund $8\frac{7}{8}$% 20/12/00 and Unity $8\frac{1}{2}$% 20/02/01. Intuitively this is the case – at higher yields the futures contract is below par and higher duration bonds fall faster in price than shorter duration bonds. Similarly, at lower yields the lower duration bonds rally in price at a much slower rate than other deliverables and become cheapest to deliver, e.g. Bund $7\frac{3}{4}$% 21/02/00 into the June 1991 contract.

Accordingly the futures contract tends to mirror the performance of the cheapest to deliver bond – essentially it takes on the characteristics of the underlying security. Below par the futures contract acts as a higher duration bond, above par it acts as a low duration bond. At par, dramatic change in duration implies high negative convexity.

Shifts in the CTD and the Grey Area

At certain futures levels a number of Bunds with differing characteristics vie to become CTD. It is in this area that there are sudden and abrupt shifts in the CTD as the futures contract attempts to mirror the underlying security. At certain future levels, it is readily apparent which Bund will be CTD. However, within certain price bands (usually a relatively small range), there exists a grey area and this indeterminancy of potential delivery makes the delivery option more valuable and causes the future to be further discounted.

A change of the CTD can also occur if there is a change in the relative yield spreads between the deliverable bonds. The yield spreads depend on the shape of the yield curve as well as on the individual characteristics of a bond, i.e. that it is traded at a premium or at a discount relative to the yield curve.

Option Adjusted Basis

Many bonds are available for delivery. The trader who is short the bond futures contract chooses which bond he will deliver to the Clearing House. This choice or option has a value as does any option. Accordingly we should attempt to place a value on these embedded options in order to assess the true basis of a bond. Clearly the futures contract in some way will reflect the value of the delivery option. How will this reflection occur?

In part the value of these options depends upon the volatility (and expected volatility of the futures market) and the time to maturity. By utilising the implied volatility from exchange listed options of the same issuer, simulating different interest rate paths to delivery and assigning a value to these options we may determine an option adjusted basis for each bond.

Assuming we are long the basis in a factor-weighted ratio we run this position to the last trading day. If the bond we are holding is no longer CTD we assume we will shift into the CTD and the value of this option is the gross basis differential on that day.

In the real world it is not always possible to state with certainty that one bond or another will be the cheapest to deliver on the last trading day. Different scenarios for the level of the market on delivery day, given prevailing yield differentials, lead to a different likelihood of one bond being CTD to another. We have seen the lower duration bonds lag in a rallying market and tend to CTD and vice versa. Accordingly given the market may rise or fall in the period to delivery, which bond is the CTD before expiration of the futures contract?

As it is usually the case that no one bond is clearly likely to be CTD at expiration accordingly we should replace the idea of one bond which is CTD with a concept of an expected distribution of CTDs according to the probability that each will be delivered. The probability assigned to each bond is determined first and foremost by the current level of the market and the yield differentials that prevail. By assuming the prevailing yield differentials held on the notice day and by simulating the level of the market by a range of increased and decreased interest rates (the range of which should be determined by the volatility of the market) we can determine which bond will be more likely to be delivered under the different scenarios. As a result probabilities may be assigned according to the likelihood of delivery. Clearly these probabilities will change with the level of the market and with changes in yield differentials.

As a result of the probabilistic approach to basis trading the trader should hold a basket of deliverables, the amount of each being determined by its respective probability of being CTD at delivery.

In this way the futures contract may be seen to be tracking a combination of bonds in which each bond carries a weight representative of its expected probability. Accordingly the duration of the futures contract is approximately equal to the weighted average of the durations of deliverable bonds. By entering into a basis trade using a basket of bonds according to their respective probabilities the trader will be opening a duration matched trade which will be less vulnerable to market shifts than a basis position involving one bond alone.

This development opens the way to basis trading in non-CTDs in the belief that the switch option into the CTD is very valuable.

The Delivery Mechanism

As the contract approaches its last trading day the basis trader may reverse his position or take delivery. However, the position has been risk weighted by using the price factor and accordingly the extra futures contracts are no longer required. This position, known as the tail should be bought back (or sold if delivery is to be taken) at the last moment to achieve a position in the ratio of 1:1.

Another problem with the pricing of the futures arises with the payment of margins. The above price equation for the futures assumes that there are no costs involved in the purchase of the futures. This is obviously not the case. The initial margin has to be provided although this can be done in the form of fixed income securities. The result of this is that only when the interest earned on the initial margin is equal to the financing cost for the bond, i.e. the margin can be provided at zero cost, the above equation holds. Dependent on whether there are net costs involved in the purchase of the futures it will trade at a premium or at a discount to its fair value.

HISTORY OF THE BASIS

Our analysis of the history of Bund basis trading begins with the June 1990 contract. The underlying bond remained expensive to the contract for most of the quarter as can be seen from Figure 6.1.

The chart of gross basis shows that at times it was possible to sell the basis on the cheapest to deliver and lock in returns of over DEM 5000 per million at delivery, before financing costs. On many occasions it proved possible to trade the channel from the short side and make attractive arbitrage profits. For example by selling DEM 10,000,000 of the CTD, DBR 7.25 20/12/00 and buying 44 of the June Bund contract at point A and reversing the trade at point B when the gross basis had tightened from 0.540 to 0.094 and the net basis had moved from 0.588 to 0.128.

As the contract neared expiry the basis converged in line with theory. However, by 25 May the basis was trading at zero and from then on until the last trading day of the contract the basis was positive. This risk-free trade enabled any market participant who has access to both cash and futures markets to buy the basis, i.e. buy the underlying bond and sell a duration weighted amount of futures contracts against it, run the

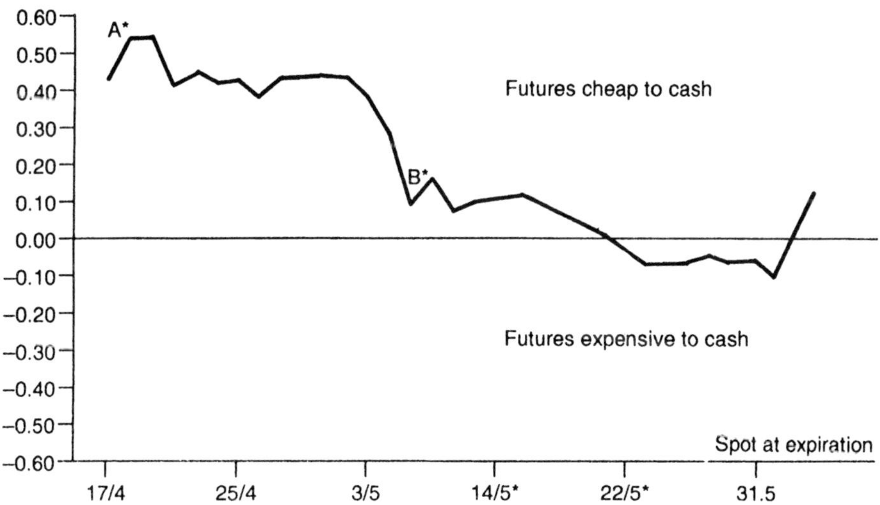

Figure 6.1 History of Gross Basis: CTD Bund – June 1990 Contract 17 April 1990 – 11 June 1990

position until expiry of the contract, and make delivery.

The delivery history is a very useful source of information. In June 1990 the volume of contracts taken to delivery was 4182 (incidentally an increase from 2904 in March 1990) representing DEM 1,200,000,000 nominal of Bunds. The range delivered was an extraordinary nine of the eleven permissible with the fifth cheapest to deliver, DBR 6.75 06/99 comprising the largest volume! This occurrence was by no means an irregularity. As we continue with the history of the basis the reader will see that the commonly held view that the cheapest to deliver bond will be delivered in the majority of cases is not consistent with the practice.

Delivery June 1990

A closer look at the cheapest to deliver analysis summary on 1 June 1990, one of the last trading days in which it was possible to comfortably engage in basis trading, reveals that it was profitable (before commissions and delivery costs) to buy eight of the eleven Bunds and deliver these into the contract. The reader will see that this was the exception and not the rule.

September 1990

This contract was full of thrills and spills not least of which was due to the Gulf crisis which added a great deal of uncertainty and volatility to LIFFE, DTB and to the Middle East. Those basis traders trading the channel were, on the whole, flat or long the basis as the contract had converged too quickly as may be determined from Figure 6.3.

For those traders long the basis (and implicitly long the delivery option) the increased volatility of the market enhanced their profile considerably. The period from early August to the last trading day of the September contract experienced wild swings in the basis as the underlying market was in turmoil. The second part of Figure 6.3 clarifies this.

The delivery schedule of the September contract was less diverse than for the June contract. Only 3589 contracts were delivered representing DEM 900 million nominal

Coupon	Maturity	Amount	CTD-Ranking on 1.6.90
6.375	21/12/1998	817	1
6.500	02/01/1999	600	6
6.750	20/01/1999	8	7
7.000	22/01/1999	64	10
6.750	21/06/1999	1588	5
7.000	20/09/1999	105	8
7.000	20/10/1999	680	4
7.125	20/12/1999	542	3
7.250	20/01/2000	378	2

Figure 6.2 June Delivery 1990

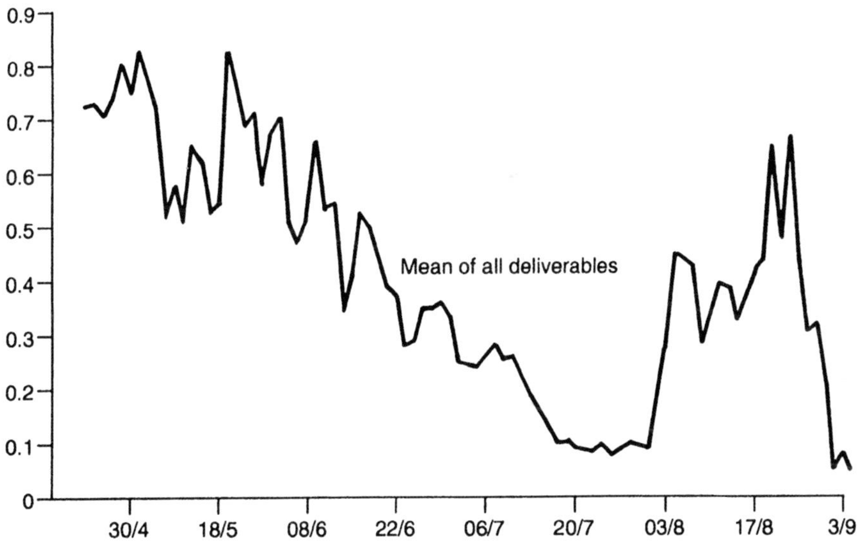

Figure 6.3 Basis Trading September 90 Future. Cheapest to Deliver. The basis was measured at the time of the Frankfurt SE fixing

of Bunds. The complete list is shown in Figure 6.4.

Clearly this distribution, heavily biased towards the CTD and second CTD records that theory and practice were one.

According to LIFFE the CTD changed 36 times during the contract's trading life (see Figure 6.5, page 148).

The use of open interest, i.e. contracts that remain open and are not yet offset, is a valuable tool in determining how many contracts will be delivered. Figure 6.6 shows how the open interest on three contracts changed over time. As may be seen a great number of participants do not wish to take or make delivery and accordingly switch into the deferred month as delivery approaches.

The path to delivery of individual Bunds is determined by the level of the overall market, the volatility of the market, the repo rate for each individual bond and the

Coupon	Maturity	Cheapest to Deliver	Ranking	Percentage Delivery
$7\frac{1}{8}$%	20 Dec 99	1,881	1	52%
$7\frac{1}{4}$%	20 Jan 00	1,012	2	28%
$7\frac{3}{4}$%	21 Feb 00	564	3	16%
7%	20 Oct 99	92	4	3%
7%	20 Sept 99	40	5	1%

Figure 6.4 Delivery Schedule: September 1990 Contract

Date	Security Number	Coupon	Maturity	Price	Value Basis	Fair Futures	Actual Futures
02-Jul-90	113473	7.000	20-Sep-99	89.26	0.49	83.84	83.38
03-Jul-90	113475	7.125	20-Dec-99	90.42	0.30	84.03	83.75
04-Jul-90	113474	7.000	20-Oct-99	89.99	0.33	84.39	84.08
05-Jul-90	113476	7.250	20-Jan-2000	91.14	0.33	83.96	83.66
06-Jul-90	113474	7.000	20-Oct-99	89.40	0.29	83.83	83.56
09-Jul-90	113473	7.000	20-Sep-99	89.03	0.24	83.51	83.29
10-Jul-90	113476	7.250	20-Jan-2000	90.56	0.29	83.44	83.17
11-Jul-90	113474	7.000	20-Oct-99	89.39	0.27	83.83	83.58
12-Jul-90	113476	7.250	20-Jan-2000	91.11	0.21	83.95	83.76
13-Jul-90	113475	7.125	20-Dec-99	90.95	0.22	84.51	84.31
16-Jul-90	113474	7.000	20-Oct-99	90.78	0.08	85.11	85.04
17-Jul-90	113475	7.125	20-Dec-99	91.30	0.20	84.86	84.67
18-Jul-90	113473	7.000	20-Sept-99	91.13	0.03	85.48	85.45
19-Jul-90	113472	6.750	21-Jun-99	89.20	0.15	85.10	84.96
20-Jul-90	113472	6.750	21-Jun-99	89.61	0.13	85.49	85.37
23-Jul-90	113477	7.750	21-Feb-2000	95.55	0.10	85.19	85.10
24-Jul-90	113472	6.750	21-Jun-99	88.68	0.16	84.58	84.43
25-Jul-90	113475	7.125	20-Dec-99	91.19	0.00	84.70	84.70
26-Jul-90	113472	6.750	21-Jun-99	88.80	0.14	84.68	84.55
27-Jul-90	113475	7.125	20-Dec-99	92.12	0.09	84.82	84.74
30-Jul-90	113474	7.000	20-Oct-99	90.54	0.19	84.85	84.67
31-Jul-90	113480	8.750	22-May-2000	99.95	0.05	84.50	84.46
01-Aug-90	113480	8.750	22-May-2000	99.45	0.14	84.08	83.96
02-Aug-90	113473	7.000	20-Sep-99	89.10	0.13	83.52	83.40
03-Aug-90	113475	7.125	20-Dec-99	89.25	0.17	82.89	82.73
06-Aug-90	113474	7.000	20-Oct-99	87.75	0.20	82.22	82.03
07-Aug-90	113475	7.125	20-Dec-99	89.02	0.06	82.67	82.61
08-Aug-90	113475	7.125	20-Dec-99	88.52	0.04	82.20	82.16
09-Aug-90	113475	7.125	20-Dec-99	89.18	0.37	82.81	82.47
10-Aug-90	113475	7.125	20-Dec-99	88.83	0.24	82.48	82.26
13-Aug-90	113476	7.250	20-Jan-2000	89.35	0.16	82.25	82.10
14-Aug-90	113476	7.250	20-Jan-2000	89.53	0.14	82.41	82.28
15-Aug-90	113474	7.000	20-Oct-99	88.24	0.09	82.65	82.57
16-Aug-90	113474	7.000	20-Oct-99	88.00	0.04	82.42	82.38
17-Aug-90	113476	7.250	20-Jan-2000	89.03	0.18	81.95	81.78
20-Aug-90	113474	7.000	20-Oct-99	87.23	0.31	81.69	81.40
21-Aug-90	113476	7.250	20-Jan-2000	88.50	0.17	81.46	81.30
22-Aug-90	113475	7.125	20-Dec-99	87.85	0.06	81.55	81.49
23-Aug-90	113476	7.250	20-Jan-2000	88.38	0.01	81.34	81.33
24-Aug-90	113475	7.125	20-Dec-99	87.82	0.07	81.51	81.45
28-Aug-90	113474	7.000	20-Oct-99	87.43	(0.02)	81.85	81.87
29-Aug-90	113476	7.250	20-Jan-2000	89.10	(0.03)	81.98	82.01
30-Aug-90	113476	7.250	20-Jan-2000	88.25	0.02	81.89	81.87
31-Aug-90	113476	7.250	20-Jan-2000	89.07	(0.08)	81.95	82.02
03-Sep-90	113475	7.125	20-Dec-99	87.90	0.06	81.57	81.51
04-Sep-90	113475	7.125	20-Dec-99	87.78	(0.27)	81.45	81.70

Figure 6.5 LIFFE September 90 German Government Bond Futures Contract Analysis of Cheapest to Deliver Bund

Note. These figures are closing prices and not Frankfurt fixings and accordingly need not be consistent with all other analyses in this chapter which are based on the latter.

yield differentials between the deliverables. The path to delivery of three of the deliverable bonds, all of which were delivered is shown in Figure 6.7.

As can be seen the paths diverge and spreads widen and narrow seemingly in an irregular pattern. Determining which bond will be delivered, given its prevailing ranking in the cheapest to deliver table is vital to basis traders and takes up a great deal of their working hours.

December 1990 delivery

The December 1990 contract offered basis traders a fairly predictable short basis arbitrage within a clearly defined channel for most of the trading period. This occurred as the underlying market rallied quite strongly. This in itself tends to tighten the basis as may be seen in Figure 6.8 which shows that in general terms as the market goes higher so the gross basis tightens.

Clearly the arbitrageur is hedged in terms of market risk but as the futures market tends to overshoot on the way up and on the way down, due mainly to the ease of access to traders, a bull market generally results in extraordinary profits for long basis traders.

The delivery schedule contained many surprises not least of which were found in the DTB deliveries (which began to trade on 23 November 1990).

Figures 6.9 and 6.10 are the deliveries for LIFFE and the DTB respectively – 11,655 contracts were taken to delivery on LIFFE and 1755 on DTB.

Figure 6.11 was the prevailing futures and cash bond prices at the Frankfurt fixings on 4 December, three days before the last trading day of the contract. DBR 9% 21/10/00 was the CTD and made up 66.65 per cent of deliveries into the LIFFE contract but only 3 per cent on the DTB. The second cheapest to deliver made up 22 per

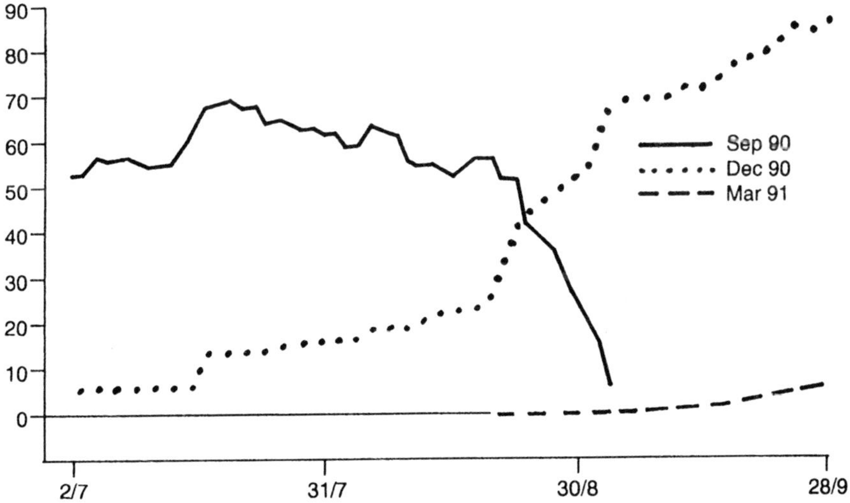

Figure 6.6 Bund Future Open Interest Roll-over. 2 July 1990 – 28 September 1990.

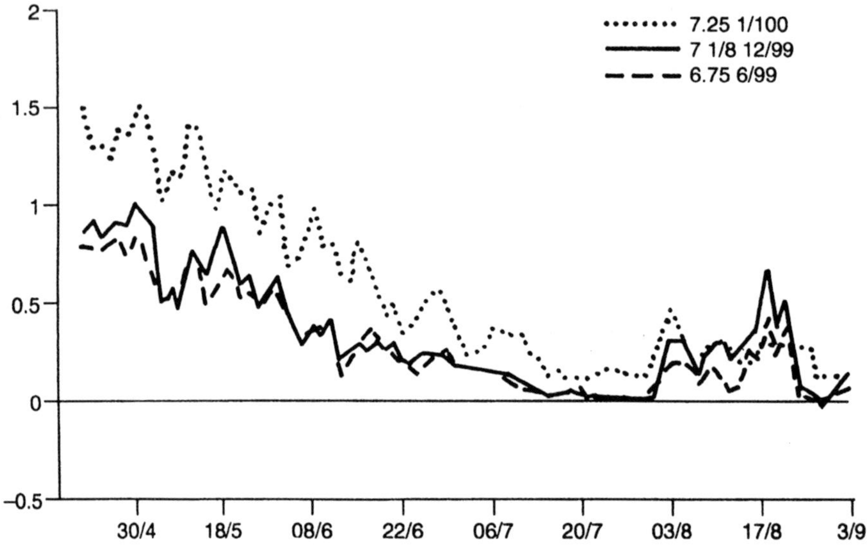

Figure 6.7 Basis Trading September 1990 Future: Cheapest to Deliver. The basis was measured at the time of the Frankfurt SE fixing.

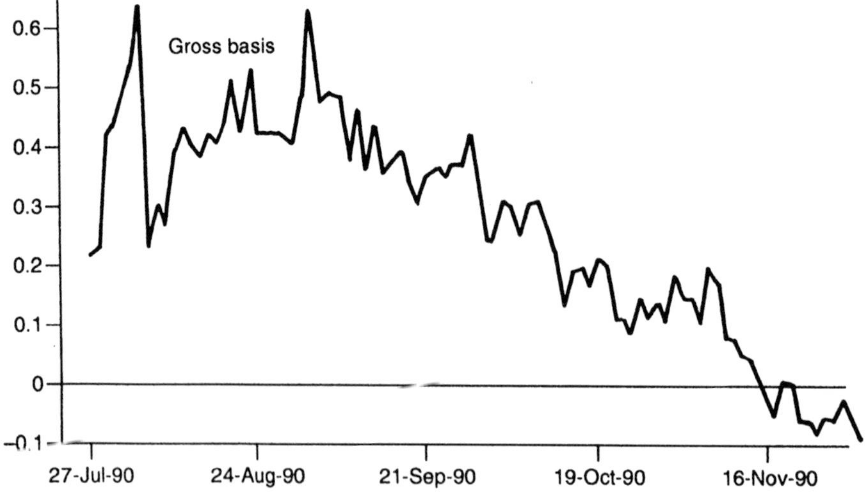

Figure 6.8 Gross Basis vs Future

THE LONDON INTERNATIONAL FINANCIAL FUTURES EXCHANGE
(ADMINISTRATION AND MANAGEMENT)

GERMAN GOVERNMENT BUND

DELIVERY MONTH – DECEMBER 1990

EXCHANGE DELIVERY SETTLEMENT PRICE (EDSP) 82.75

Delivery notice for a total of 11,655 lots were received the following Bunds will be delivered:

Bund	**Coupon**	**Maturity**	**Lots Delivered**
113472	6.750	21 June 1999	100
113473	7.000	20 Sep 1999	62
113474	7.000	20 Oct 1999	122
113475	7.125	20 Dec 1999	496
113476	7.250	20 Jan 2000	498
113477	7.750	21 Feb 2000	32
113480	8.500	21 Aug 2000	2,586
113481	9.000	20 Oct 2000	7,759
		TOTAL:	11,655

Market Supervision Department

Figure 6.9

cent of the deliveries on LIFFE but only 6 per cent on DTB. Therefore which Bunds comprised the majority of the deliveries on the DTB? Surprisingly the largest volumes were in the third, fifth and eighth CTD Bunds and at least one participant was fortunate to take delivery of 169 of the most expensive to deliver Bund, an unexpected windfall of DEM 4,000 per million!

March 1991

The March 1991 contract saw a steady convergence of the basis as outlined in Figures 6.12 and 6.13. The net basis tightened from 1.1 to –0.1 as the underlying market gradually improved and from the middle of December 1990 onwards it seemed to be correct to go long the basis, repo the Bund and lock in either a risk-free profit, if the implied repo was greater than the actual repo as was often the case, or obtain a free delivery option.

Figure 6.14 shows the relationship between the actual repo rate for general collateral during the period and the implied repo rate (the actual repo rate for individual Bunds varies greatly from issue to issue and from dealer to dealer and depending on the size and period of the trade. Accordingly an average is taken).

Product: **Bond Future**
Contract: **Bund Dec. 90**

Amt	Sec No.		Security Name	Maturity	Coupon		
140	103000	8.75%	BUND ANL 90/2000 F.D.E.	20.07.00	8.750	20.0	
169	113472	6.75%	BUND ANL 89/1999 II	21/06/99	6.750	21.0	9TH
80	113473	7.00%	BUND ANL 89/1999 III	20/09/99	7.000	20.0	7TH
50	113474	7.00%	BUND ANL 89/1999 IV	20/10/99	7.000	20.1	4TH
350	113475	7.125%	BUND ANL 89/1999	20/12/00	7.125	20.1	3RD
320	113476	7.25%	BUND ANL 90/2000	20/01/00	7.250	20.0	5TH
289	113477	7.75%	BUND ANL 90/2000	21/02/00	7.750	21.1	8TH
198	113479	8.75%	BUND ANL 90/2000	22/05/00	8.750	22.0	6TH
109	113480	8.50%	BUND ANL 90/2000	21/08/00	8.500	21.0	2ND
50	113481	9.00%	BUND ANL 90/2000	21/10/00	9.000	20.1	1ST

Figure 6.10

The LIFFE delivery schedule, Figure 6.15, suggests that theory and practice are beginning to converge with 91 per cent of the 11,460 made up of the two cheapest to deliver bonds.

This contract witnessed new issue risk as a new Unity bond, 8.5 02/01 was launched in early February and met all the delivery criteria. It was clearly the cheapest to deliver as it was the bond of longest maturity but few basis readers were caught unaware as they were on the whole long the basis.

Hedging a Portfolio with Futures

Armed with the knowledge we have gained from the previous chapter let us consider a classic bond portfolio hedge using futures. Although this case study is based on a Belgian bond portfolio the approach used is equally valid for all major currency bond portfolios.

N.B. The Belgian T-bond futures contract is based on a nominal BEF 2,500,000.

Bund		Price	Yield Change	Conv. Yield	C. Factor	Gross Basis	Implied Repo.	Actual Repo.	Net Basis
DBR 9	10/20/00	100.900	+0.13	8.853	1.217716	−0.097	20.28	8.50	−0.100
DBR $8\frac{1}{2}$	08/21/00	97.700	−0.19	8.851	1.178890	−0.077	17.72	8.50	−0.077
DBR $7\frac{1}{8}$	12/20/99	89.270	+0.04	8.901	1.076519	−0.16	9.47	8.50	−0.008
DBR 7	10/20/99	88.500	+0.05	8.925	1.066773	0.022	4.90	8.50	0.027
DBR $7\frac{1}{4}$	01/20/00	90.160	+0.04	8.863	1.085456	0.132	−8.93	8.50	0.140
DBR $8\frac{3}{4}$	05/22/00	99.200	−0.15	8.864	1.192933	0.258	−21.38	8.50	0.259
DBR 7	09/20/99	88.700	+0.01	8.899	1.066189	0.270	−28.20	8.50	0.276
DBR $7\frac{3}{4}$	02/01/00	93.250	+0.04	8.843	1.120382	0.326	−31.0	8.50	0.331
DBR $6\frac{3}{4}$	06/21/99	87.350	+0.01	8.916	1.048334	0.401	−45.76	8.50	0.409

Figure 6.11 Cheapest to Deliver Rankings on Last Trading Date: December 1990

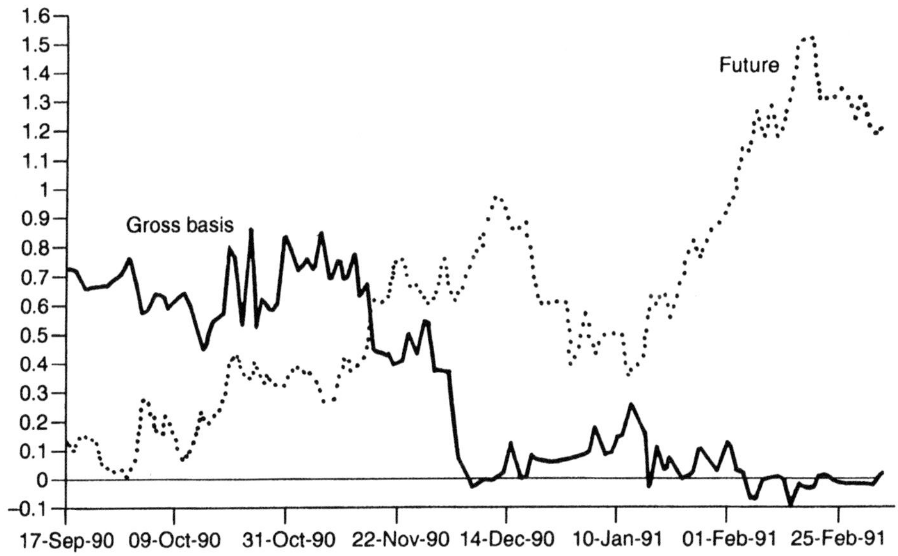

Figure 6.12 March 1991 Bund Contract. Gross Basis versus Future. 17 September 1990 – 5 March 1991

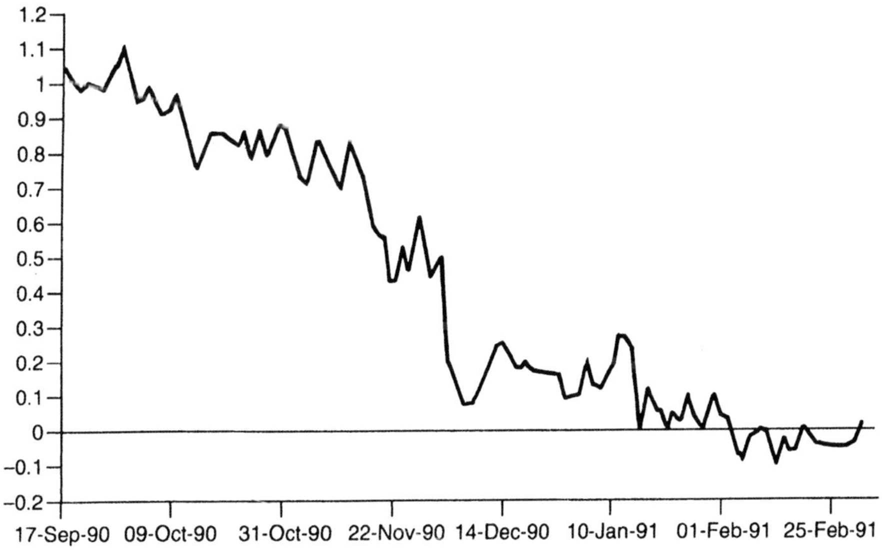

Figure 6.13 March 1991 Bund Contract. Net Basis. 17 September 1990 – 5 March 1991

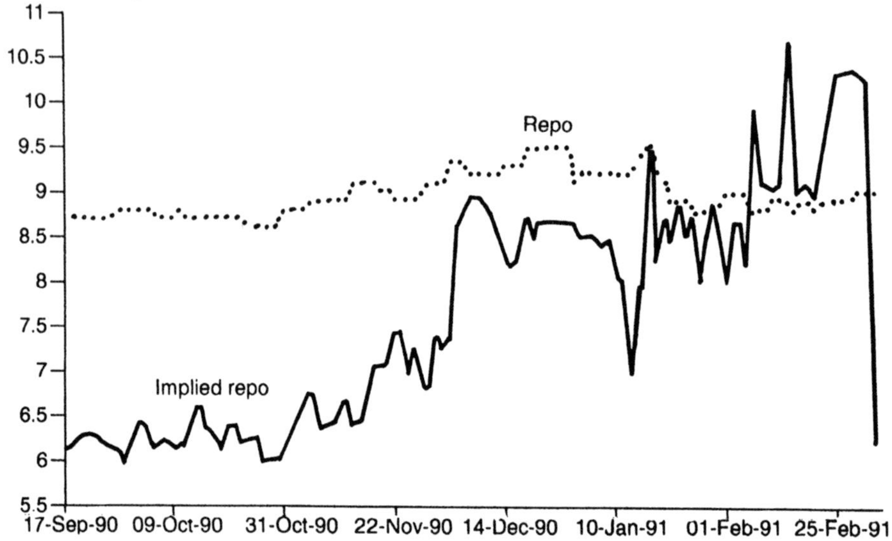

Figure 6.14 March 1991 Bund Contract. Implied repo versus repo. 17 September 1990 – 5 March 1991

APPENDIX: HEDGING A BOND PORTFOLIO WITH T-BOND FUTURES

CASE STUDY

SCENARIO: Assume the date is June 4th, 1991

The investment manager of a bank maintains a small bond portfolio. Its current components and value are shown in Table 1. During the last couple of months, the investment manager achieved significant profits to his bond portfolio, but he now believes all the signs are that rates will show a marked increase in the short-term. Table 2 indicates the month ahead forecast of long-term rates produced by the bank's economist. However, since the manager believes that any rise in rates will be a temporary phenomenon, he does not wish to liquidate his portfolio and incur substantial transactions costs. Hence the alternative of a bond futures hedge looks attractive. Thus the manager decides to explore the possibility of hedging the value of his portfolio with

TABLE 1 BANK BOND PORTFOLIO: AS AT JUNE 4TH 1991

Bond	Nominal Value	Clean Price	Redemption Yield	Market Value
8% 15/6/95	BEF 100mm	92.72	10.29%	BEF 92,720,000
8.25% 16/10/96	BEF 100mm	92.30	10.16%	BEF 92,300,000
10% 15/3/97	BEF 150mm	100.40	9.89%	BEF 150,600,000
9.50% 22/3/98	BEF 75mm	97.04	10.11%	BEF 72,780,000
8.25% 1/6/99	BEF 150mm	89.50	10.24%	BEF 134,250,000
Portfolio	BEF 575mm			BEF 542,650,000

bond futures. In particular he will wish to look at two questions:

- A. What prices can he hope to secure for his portfolio on his target date of July 4th.
- B. What precise futures hedge should be put on to achieve this.

Tables 3 to 6 give information on current bond futures prices, the impact of specific yield changes on the bond prices, and the duration figures for the individual bonds, and the current pattern of short-term rates.

Hedge Solution

A target value for the portfolio on 4th July can be found in two stages.

A. Find the price change implied for the cheapest deliverable bond by the current cash and futures prices.
B. Find the price change implied for the other bonds on their relative volatility with respect to the cheapest to deliver bond.

The cheapest deliverable bond for the September and December contracts is the 8.25% 1/6/99.

The implied price for the cheapest to deliver bond is found by multiplying the futures price by the price factor.

$$\text{Implied Price for 30 September} = 93.00 \times 0.9589 = 89.18$$
$$\text{Implied Price for 31 December} = 92.65 \times 0.9598 = 88.93$$

TABLE 2 INTEREST RATE FORECAST: AS AT JUNE 4TH FOR 1 MONTH AHEAD

Interest Rate Change	Probability
Negative	Zero
No Change	1%
+0.10%	2%
+0.20%	4%
+0.30%	10%
+0.40%	13%
+0.50%	20%
+0.60%	30%
+0.70%	10%
+0.80%	5%
+0.90%	3%
+1.0%	2%
more than +1.0%	Zero

Mean Expected Rate Exchange = 0.53%

TABLE 3 BOND FUTURES: AS AT 4TH JUNE

	September	December
Last Delivery Day	30th	31st
PRICE	93.00	92.65
OPEN INTEREST	23,200	3,100
VOLUME	18,600	2,250
PRICE FACTORS		
8% 15/6/95	0.9689	0.9705
8.25% 16/10/96	0.9705	0.9712
10% 15/3/97	1.0406	1.0395
9.5% 22/3/98	1.0227	1.0224
8.25% 1/6/99	0.9589	0.9598

(a) Note that the 8.25% 1/6/99 is the cheapest to deliver bond for both the September and December bond contracts.

(b) Note that not all the bonds in the portfolio are deliverable. Equivalent price factors are calculated for those that are not.

These prices can be combined with the cash price of 89.50 on the 4th June to obtain an implied price for the 4th July by interpolation.

$$\text{September Implied Price} \left[89.50 \times \frac{88}{118}\right] - \left[89.18 \times \frac{30}{118}\right] = 89.42$$

$$\text{December Implied Price} \left[89.50 \times \frac{180}{210}\right] - \left[89.18 \times \frac{30}{210}\right] = 89.42$$

TABLE 4 BANK BONDS
PERTURBATION ANALYSIS: AS AT 4TH JUNE
PRICE CHANGE

Change in Yield by 4 July	8% 15/6/95	8.25% 16/10/96	10% 15/3/97	9.5% 22/3/98	8.25% 1/6/99
+0.0%	+0.13	+0.90	−0.04	−0.01	+0.02
+0.1%	−0.17	−0.28	−0.46	−0.47	−0.46
+0.2%	−0.47	−0.65	−0.88	−0.93	−0.95
+0.3%	−0.76	−1.02	−1.29	−1.38	−1.42
+0.4%	−1.05	−1.39	−1.71	−1.83	−1.90
+0.5%	−1.34	−1.75	−2.12	−2.28	−2.37
+0.6%	−1.63	−2.12	−2.53	−2.73	−2.84
+0.7%	−1.92	−2.48	−2.94	−3.17	−3.31
+0.8%	−2.21	−2.84	−3.34	−3.62	−3.77
+0.9%	−2.49	−3.20	−3.75	−4.05	−4.23
+1.0%	−2.78	−3.55	−4.15	−4.49	−4.68

TABLE 5 BANK BONDS – DURATION ANALYSIS AS AT 4TH JUNE

Bond	Duration (Years)
8% 15/6/95	3.58
8.25% 16/10/96	4.52
10% 15/3/97	4.67
9.5% 22/3/98	5.29
8.25% 1/6/99	6.04

Since the price implied by the December contract is the same and basis risk will be greater using this contract for hedging, all further calculations are carried out using the September contract.

With the September contract, therefore, the price change implied for the cheapest deliverable bond is:

89.50 minus 89.42 = 0.08

To ascertain the equivalent price changes for the other bonds in the portfolio, their relative volatilities are estimated using the duration numbers given in Table 5.

$$\text{Relative Volatility} = \frac{\text{Duration of Bond}}{\text{Duration of Cheapest to Deliver}} \times \frac{\text{Price of Bond}}{\text{Price of Cheapest to Deliver}} \times \frac{\text{Cheapest to Deliver } 1 + \text{Redemption Yield}}{1 + \text{Bond Redemption Yield}}$$

8% 15/6/95 $\quad \dfrac{3.58}{6.04} \times \dfrac{92.72}{89.50} \times \dfrac{1.1024}{1.1029} = 0.614$

8.25% 16/10/96 $\quad \dfrac{4.52}{6.04} \times \dfrac{92.30}{89.50} \times \dfrac{1.1024}{1.1016} = 0.772$

10% 15/3/97 $\quad \dfrac{4.67}{6.04} \times \dfrac{100.40}{98.50} \times \dfrac{1.1024}{1.0989} = 0.870$

TABLE 6 SHORT-TERM INTEREST RATES

7-DAY	$9\frac{7}{8}$ – 10
1-MONTH	$9\frac{7}{8}$ – 10
3-MONTH	$9\frac{7}{8}$ – 10
6-MONTH	$9\frac{7}{8}$ – 10
1-YEAR	$9\frac{7}{8}$ – 10

9.5% 22/3/98 $\dfrac{5.29}{6.04} \times \dfrac{97.04}{89.50} \times \dfrac{1.1024}{1.1011} = 0.951$

Now the expected price changes for the other bonds can be easily estimated.

8% 15/6/95	0.08 × 0.614 = 0.05
8.25% 16/10/96	0.08 × 0.772 = 0.06
10% 15/3/97	0.08 × 0.870 = 0.07
9.5% 22/3/98	0.08 × 0.951 = 0.08

Hence the portfolio manager expects to achieve the following bond prices on July 4th (*).

Bond	**Expected Price**	**Market Value**
8% 15/6/95	92.67	92,670,000
8.25% 16/10/96	92.24	92,240,000
10% 15/3/97	100.33	150,495,000
9.5% 22/3/98	96.96	72,720,000
8.25% 1/6/99	89.42	134,130,000
		542,255,000

Thus by hedging the bond portfolio with bond futures, the bond manager is expecting to lock in a portfolio of BEF 542,255,000 on 4th July. Although this is some BEF 395,000 less than the current value of the portfolio, it is significantly higher than would be the value of the portfolio if the mean expected interest rate rise of 0.53% occurs.

(*) Similar expected prices could be obtained from the perturbation analysis of Table 4 on the basis of relative volatilities with the mean expected rate change of 0.53%. The interested reader is left to calculate these numbers.

In order to achieve these anticipated prices, the bond manager must sell futures contracts. To hedge the cheapest to deliver bond, he simply sells:

$$\frac{\text{Nominal Amount Held}}{\text{Face Value of Futures Contracts}} \times \frac{\text{Price}}{\text{Factor}}$$

$$\frac{150{,}000{,}000}{2{,}500{,}000} \times 0.9589 = 57.53 \text{ Contracts}$$

To hedge the other bonds, the manager sells as a hedge against each bond:

$$\frac{\text{Nominal Amount}}{\text{Face Value of}} \times \text{Relative Volatility} \times \text{Price Factor of Cheapest to Deliver}$$

Hence the final hedge will consist of:

8% 15/6/95	$\frac{100,000,000}{2,500,000} \times 0.614 \times 0.9589 =$	23.55
8.25% 16/10/96	$\frac{100,000,000}{2,500,000} \times 0.772 \times 0.9589 =$	29.61
10% 15/3/97	$\frac{150,000,000}{2,500,000} \times 0.870 \times 0.9589 =$	50.06
9.5% 22/3/98	$\frac{75,000,000}{2,500,000} \times 0.951 \times 0.9589 =$	27.36
8.25% 1/6/99	$\frac{150,000,000}{2,500,000} \times 0.9589 =$	57.53
	Number of Contracts	188.11

So the total hedge will consist of selling 188 bond futures contracts.

SELL 188 FUTURES AT 93.00

(*) Note that duration has been used to weight the hedge. Two alternative strategies are often used in designing bond hedges. First, relative volatilities could be calculated from the perturbation numbers given in Table 4, and assuming all the redemption yields will change by the 0.53% predicted by the economist. However, as can be seen, the relative volatility and appropriate numbers of contracts for the hedge are almost identical with the duration approach.

Bond	Relative Volatility	Number of Contracts
8% 15/6/95	0.568	21.78
8.25% 16/10/96	0.741	28.42
10% 15/3/97	0.893	51.38
9.5% 22/3/98	0.962	27.67
8.25% 1/6/99	1.000	57.53
		186.78

The difference in the suggested hedge is only 1 contract

An even simpler method is simply to multiply each bond's nominal value by its own conversion factor to determine the right number of contracts for a hedge. This method is generally not as accurate as perturbation or duration analysis.

Note that for the sake of simplicity here, we have simply used the nearby contract and ignored the question of adding straddles to hedge basis risk. If basis risk hedging is required, then the calculation of the number of straddles would be carried out in the usual manner.

4D ←→ 88D ←→ 92D ←→

JUNE 30 JULY 4 SEPTEMBER 30 DECEMBER 31

$$\text{NUMBER OF STRADDLES} = 188\left[\frac{88}{92}\right] = 180$$

That is in addition to the sale of 188 September contracts, a further 180 September–December straddles would be sold giving a total hedge of:

SHORT	368	SEPTEMBER
LONG	180	DECEMBER

Result Analysis

Now let's move ahead to July 4th, and have a look at the results. We assume the investment manager believes rates have risen about as far as is likely, and decides to take his profit on the futures hedge.

The important questions are:

(1) What effective price has been achieved for each stock?
(2) Why did these prices differ from the target prices set on June 4th?
(3) How is the performance of the hedge rated?

Tables 7 and 8 give the futures prices and bond portfolio information as of July 4th.

The hedger can calculate effective prices for each bond by working out

- gain on futures to hedge the bond
- value of bond on 4th July

By July 4th the September bond contracts are showing a gain of 155 ticks each (93.00 minus 91.45).

$$\text{TOTAL PROFIT} = 188 \text{ CONTRACTS} \times 250 \times 155 \text{ TICKS}$$
$$\underline{\text{BEF } 7{,}285{,}000}$$

The total market value of the portfolio on July 4th is BEF 533,810,000. Adding to this the futures profit, the effective market value is BEF 541,095,000. There is a difference of BEF 1,160,000 between this and the expected value of BEF 542,255,000.

The profits can be allocated to individual bonds in proportion to the size of the individual hedges.

Bond	Futures Profit	Contracts	Market Value	Effective Price	Target Price
8% 15/6/95	930,000	(24)	91,960,000	92.89	92.67
8.25% 16/10/96	1,162,500	(30)	91,210,000	92.37	92.24
10% 15/3/97	1,937,500	(50)	146,925,000	99.24	100.33
9.5% 22/3/98	1,046,250	(27)	71,745,000	97.06	96.96
8.25% 1/6/99	2,208,750	(57)	131,970,000	89.45	89.42

In all cases, the effective price exceeds the cash market price since the futures position has shown a profit. The hedge has not, of course, locked in the cash prices obtaining back on June 4th. However, the hedge has not exactly locked in the target prices implied by the futures market, althought results were very close for four of the bonds.

The result of the hedge was an effective difference of BEF 1,160,000 between the expected value of the portfolio and the realised sum of the cash value on July 4th and the futures profit. It is useful to analyse this difference.

Basis Risk

One of the main reasons a futures hedge may not work perfectly is unexpected movements in the basis, that is, the relationship between the futures price and the cash price of the cheapest to deliver bond did not move exactly in line with the price factor.

EXPECTED CHEAPEST TO DELIVER PRICE 4TH JULY		=	89.42
EQUIVALENT FUTURES PRICE	= 89.42/0.9589	=	93.25
EXPECTED BASIS WITH SEPTEMBER FUTURES =	93.25 – 93.00	=	0.25
CHEAPEST TO DELIVER PRICE 4TH JULY		=	87.98
EQUIVALENT FUTURES PRICE	= 87.98/0.9589	=	91.75
ACTUAL BASIS FOR SEPTEMBER FUTURE	91.75 – 91.45	=	0.30

This increase in basis has favourably affected the short hedger.

TOTAL GAIN = 5 × 250 × 188 = 235,000

BASIC CHANGE = BEF 235,000

In addition, the futures profit will be slightly different to what it should be, because the bond manager was forced to hedge with a round number of contracts rather than the exact amount of 188.11.

TOTAL LOSS = 0.11 × 250 × 155 = 4,262.50

ROUNDING ERROR = BEF 4,262.50

The remaining discrepancies in hedge performance will be accounted for by two causes. First duration may not be totally accurate in assessing the relative change in the price of the individual bond for a given change in the yield of the cheapest to deliver, and second the yield of the individual bond may not have altered by exactly the same as that of the cheapest to deliver.

As can be seen the major problem with the hedge has been the large differences between different bonds in changes in redemption yield. The worst offender was the 10% 15/3/97, where the redemption yield rose by 0.58% compared with a change in the cheapest to deliver of only 0.32%. Yield curve shifts are one of the primary risks in hedging with bond futures. Nonetheless the hedge result compares favourably with the potential cash market loss of nearly BEF 8,840,000.

Bond	**Actual Value Change**	**Expected Value (*) Change**	**Actual Change For 0.32% Change (CTD)**	**Change Due to Differential Yield Change**
	1	**2**	**3**	**4 (1–3)**
8% 15/6/95	–760,000	–933,280	–817,436	+56,436
8.25% 16/10/96	–1,090,000	–1,173,440	–1,094,826	+4,826
10% 15/3/97	–3,675,000	–1,983,600	–2,064,986	–1,610,014
9.5% 22/3/98	–1,035,000	–1,084,140	–1,104,223	+69,223
	–6,560,000	–5,174,460	–5,081,471	–1,478,529

Error due to Inexact Duration = +92,989

Error due to Yield Curve Changes = –1,478,529

(*) $$\text{Price Change of Cheapest to Deliver} \times \text{Relative Volatility} \times \frac{\text{Face Value of Bond}}{100}$$

8% 15/6/95 $$1.52 \times 0.614 \times \frac{100{,}000{,}000}{100} = 933.280$$

8.25% 16/10/96 $$1.52 \times 0.772 \times \frac{100{,}000{,}000}{100} = 1{,}173{,}440$$

10% 15/3/97 $$1.52 \times 0.870 \times \frac{150{,}000{,}000}{100} = 1{,}983{,}600$$

TABLE 7 BANK PORTFOLIO: AS AT 4TH JULY

8% 15/6/95	BEF 100mm	91.96	10.59	+0.30	91,960,000
8.25% 16/10/96	BEF 100mm	91.21	10.48	+0.32	91,210,000
10% 15/3/97	BEF 150mm	97.95	10.47	+0.58	146,925,000
9.5% 22/3/98	BEF 75mm	95.66	10.41	+0.30	71,745,000
8.25% 1/6/99	BEF 150mm	87.98	10.56	+0.32	131,970,000
PORTFOLIO	BEF 575mm				533,810,000

9.5% 22/3/98 $$1.52 \times 0.951 \times \frac{75{,}000{,}000}{100} = 1{,}084{,}140$$

Hedge Efficiency

EXPECTED VALUE OF PORTFOLIO = 542,255,000
ACTUAL VALUE + FUTURES PROFIT = 541,095,000
DIFFERENCE TO BE ACCOUNTED FOR = 1,160,000

A. BASIS CHANGE = +235,000
B. ROUNDING ERROR = −4,262.5
C. DURATION ERROR = −1,478,529
D. YIELD CURVE CHANGES = +92,989

TOTAL EXPLAINED ERROR = −1,154,802.50

The remaining unexplained error of BEF 5,197.50 is due to rounding errors in the calculations.

Finally, it is worth mentioning what the result would be if we looked at the basis risk hedge.

TOTAL FUTURES PROFIT = 368 × 250 × 155 TICKS
minus
180 × 250 × 160 TICKS
= BEF +7,060,000

In this case the result for the hedger is actually worse than the case where basis risk

TABLE 8 BOND FUTURES: AS AT 4TH JULY

Delivery Month	Price	Open Interest	Volume
September	91.45	42,000	21,250
December	91.05	5,620	4,120

was not hedged. This is simply because the favourable basis move which helped the hedge result was more than offset by the unfavourable movement in the September–December futures spread from an original level of 35 ticks to 40 ticks on July 4th. This is a valuable lesson that though in general basis risk hedging should improve hedge effectiveness, there are occasions like this when it works in the opposite direction. Even so the net loss is small relative to the overall hedge result.

PART 4

RISK MANAGEMENT SYSTEMS

7: Establishing a Risk Management System

John Wisbey

For any risk management system to be effective, its basic assumptions and methods must be 'in tune' with the way of thinking of the organisation or individual using it. Just as the best of orchestras cannot play effectively if their score sheet is different from that of their conductor, a system that produces reports that shows risk where management does not acknowledge there to be any risk will simply not be used to best effect – or, worse, will only be used after a major loss and a change of personnel.

Whether through lack of systems or through lack of proper analysis of risk the fact is that many companies have gone out of business or have lost their independence, with thousands of job losses in either case, owing to their not managing risk properly – and often this risk has been in the interest rate or currency markets rather than in the company's basic business.

The main financial risks that need to be managed by any organisation are the following.

- *Interest rate and currency risk.* Management of interest rate and currency risk is the main subject dealt with in this chapter. It is also the risk that best lends itself to use of an advanced computer system, since most human beings cannot intuitively evaluate the risk of a very large and complicated portfolio of financial instruments.
- *Credit risk.* Credit risk is a developing subject with increased use of netting arrangements and an accounting standard (FASB 105) that now addresses these.
- *Liquidity risk.* This is in many ways the most important risk of all. Few companies fail because of an excess of liabilities over assets, but far more fail owing to an inability to meet their bills at the right time.

  Generally speaking, a complicated computer system is less necessary for managing this kind of risk, although in the 1990s it would be surprising to find major companies doing this kind of analysis manually.

No computer-based risk management system can manage any better than a manual one could, but it can do so very much more quickly and completely accurately – which in the financial markets is normally essential. There is still no substitute for common sense however, nor any exception to the first law of computing – Garbage in, Garbage out! How many banks have lost hundreds of thousands of dollars through an interest rate swap being input the wrong way round into a computer system? In the inquest that invariably follows such a clerical error, someone is bound to ask the question 'How come nobody noticed', but by then it is normally too late. Because relatively few senior managers in the world yet understand derivative risk the other question that should be asked much more often is 'How come we didn't analyse that risk properly'. Everyone understands a Profit and Loss number; the goal of a good risk management system must be to present clearly today's risks that will generate tomorrow's profit and loss.

In the first paragraph of this chapter I mentioned the importance of a risk management system being 'in tune' with the thought process of the organisation or of the individual using it. How do we reconcile this with clear presentation of today's risks that generate tomorrow's profit and loss – or is even this question an assumption about using a mark-to-market methodology? There are in fact probably two main ways of looking at risk – these are as follows:

(1) *Bank trader*. A bank trader generally does not need to have a position. He or she trades either to service customers or (far more often) to take advantage of trading opportunities or a view of market direction. Profit and loss depends almost entirely on a combination of positioning ability and on the level of deal flow. While the level of deal flow cannot be managed any more easily than, say, the level of car sales can by Ford, there are enough systems in the market that there is little reason for a trader not to know what his or her position is. It is easier to manage risk than to guarantee profit and loss – as any US derivatives trader whose customers used to be leveraged buyouts and real estate companies can confirm. The point here is that, as in manufacturing industry, P&L is a function of trading volume and not only of good control of risk or costs.

(2) *Non-bank*. A treasurer almost never starts with no position – his company may be an electricity utility with massive borrowings, or it may be a life insurance company with premiums to invest over the next forty years before payout. There is therefore an inherent interest rate or currency risk from the underlying business; this risk may sometimes be much larger than management anticipated in relation to the firm's underlying profitability – ask any S&L about the importance of interest rate risk or any European car manufacturer about the importance of currency movements.

The key to effective interest rate or currency risk management for a company of this kind is the ability to: (i) model likely debt (or asset) profiles, (ii) scenario analysis of interest and currency rates before hedging, (iii) scenario analysis of interest and currency rates after hedging.

In choosing a risk management system it is likely that the selection criteria used will be different for bank traders and for corporate treasurers on the lines discussed.

CHOOSING A RISK MANAGEMENT SYSTEM

There are so many types of derivatives, including exchange traded futures and options, FRAs, interest rate swaps, interest rate caps, currency options and equity derivatives that the reality is that most financial organisations will employ several different groups or at least several different traders to do the job. Their requirements from trading systems can be appreciably different – for example a futures trader needs instant access to exchange prices but is probably relatively indifferent to the structure of the LIBOR curve beyond five years, whereas a swap trader specialising in the far end of the yield curve is likely to be far more concerned about yield curve construction and the algorithms for calculating hedge equivalents. Both will of course be insistent on being able to get a print-out of trades done, P&L, and a position report.

The first decision to be made is whether to build a system in-house, to buy an external system from a software company or to commission a software company to build a 'bespoke' system. The pros and cons of each course of action are as follows.

In-house System

Advantages

- Get exactly what you want (although probably not *when* you want)
- Can set own priorities
- Proprietary

Disadvantages

- Likely to take much longer and therefore cost much more than estimated. Assume 200–300 per cent over-run on time estimates from a programmer not used to programs of more than 10,000 lines length.
- Much of the work involved (e.g. programming of date handling and date conventions) is completely essential but carries no value added compared to acquiring external software.
- Proper planning, specification and testing are very time-consuming; practitioners have to be heavily involved for this to be effective.
- Consequent opportunity losses.
- No feedback from a customer base.

Other factors

- If there is a small project team, there could be vulnerability to key staff departures.
- Who will maintain the software, and at what cost?
- Auditability.

External System

Advantages

- Known initial cost.

- Available immediately.
- Real cost likely to be appreciably cheaper than equivalent in-house alternative.
- Software development likely to be done more professionally than in-house.
- No need to 're-invent the wheel' or to get involved in managing a software project.
- Any problems in software likely to be detected more quickly than in an in-house system owing to more testing, beta sites and a larger customer base.
- Software company is likely to upgrade its product to keep pace with changes in technology.
- Maintenance cost likely to be appreciably lower than the cost of employing a team of programmers.
- Auditability.

Disadvantages

- Time needs to be spent in evaluating different systems.
- Software company's development priorities may be different from your own.
- Requested enhancements may not be agreed to owing to conflicts with other customers' requirements.
- Version control may mean a long wait for what appears to be (and often is) a minor enhancement.
- Not proprietary.
- Some software companies have a bad reputation for fielding support staff who have little idea about the workings of their system – and then charging for their time!

Other factors

- Who will you actually be dealing with?
- What do other customers think of the system?
- Still need to address issues in interfacing with existing in-house systems.

External Bespoke Software

Advantages

- Get exactly what you want (although probably not *when* you want)
- Can set own priorities
- Software development likely to be done more professionally than in-house.
- No need to get involved in managing a software project.

Disadvantages

- Much more expensive than buying an external system.

- Software company's project management skills are unlikely to be matched by depth of knowledge among its personnel of risk management techniques; as for an in-house system a large amount of practitioner time has to be spent to make the project effective, with consequent opportunity loss.
- Cost over-runs likely to be for your account, not that of the software company.
- Lack of careful specification will be used as excuse for substantial time and cost over-runs.
- Software company likely to retain copyright to the software.
- Later enhancements are likely to add appreciably to the original cost, yet they will be essential in order to protect the initial investment.

The answer to which of the above solutions works best for an institution will depend on the likely size of the business, the range of instruments traded, and the timescale envisaged. Popular thought as at mid-1992 can probably be summarised as follows:

(1) It makes sense initially to buy external systems, since the opportunity cost of waiting for a system to be developed is far too great.
(2) There is currently no system which meets all requirements, and those systems that claim to do so are mostly very much a lowest common denominator if the claim is valid at all.
(3) Longer term, it would be highly desirable to have one system that does everything, whether an in-house system or an external one. Shorter term this is not practical so that it is currently necessary to use a variety of systems.
(4) This process can be taken significantly further by only using systems that can interface with other programs through well laid out download files; advanced users can then use the services of a systems integrator (a company specialising in making systems interact with each other) to extract maximum value out of a variety of systems.

The factors likely to be relevant in choosing a system are the following:

(1) How established is the system?
(2) Does the methodology tie in with a user's way of looking at risk?
(3) What do other users think about the system and the customer support?
(4) How knowledgeable about the market are the people responsible for developing the product? Are they accessible? Are they responsive to requests for enhancement?
(5) Is the system (a) user-friendly? (b) accurate? (c) reliable?
(6) Is the valuation methodology (a) consistent between front and back office? (b) consistent with the methodology used for hedging?

    If the answer to (a) is no there is likely to be a certain amount of on-going frustration in reconciling valuations; if the answer to (b) is no there is probably cause for concern if the system is to be used for risk management.
(7) Cost of (a) licence fee, (b) maintenance, (c) training.

    It is relevant to ask existing users what the real costs of using a system are: in other words a product developed by a company that charges for every meeting will cost significantly more than one developed by a company that is generous with its time.

(8) Demonstration – is it possible to have or use a demonstration copy of the system prior to using it? Every system has its good and bad points, and a quick demonstration by a software vendor is unlikely to concentrate on the bad points. This is quite an important point to bear in mind when comparing a system one has seen a lot of with one that looked good on a vendor's machine.

A further factor which needs to be addressed as honestly as possible is that of what relationship a user actually wants to have with a software company.

Some users genuinely want to have involvement in the on-going development of the system they use to trade, and are prepared to spend time on it although they probably have no wish to manage a software development. For them it is key that they respect or at least can relate to the people they deal with at the software company. A small or medium-sized company which is likely to be more flexible is probably of greater interest to such users than a company with a very large customer base that may have less room for manoeuvre.

Other users just want a system that works and regard software companies as a necessary evil – probably not quite as bad as the in-house Information Technology Department, but nevertheless definitely not something they want to have a close relationship with. This is a perfectly reasonable attitude – after all how many of us have met the developers of Lotus 1-2-3? Such users will tend to focus on who else is using a system, its reliability, how good the support is, how comprehensive the user manual is, and so on. A user of this kind will tend to err on the side of caution and will probably not take the risk of using a very new software company – even though the first impression of the product may be favourable.

INSTALLING A RISK MANAGEMENT SYSTEM

Having been through the initial phase of deciding on a risk management system, the time will come actually to install and start using it. Like the transition between courtship and marriage this can sometimes be a little painful. The first step is presumably to enter counterparty details, all trade details, set up adequate reporting structures and so on. Obviously it is also necessary to update yield curves and other risk parameters like volatility. The various frustrations that may well be encountered in this phase can include all of the following:

(1) The system seemed very fast on the vendor's 50 MHz 486 machine, but now that 1000 trades have been entered it is not at all fast on the user's 16 MHz 386SX machine – but unfortunately there is no budget left to upgrade one PC, let alone every PC on which the system will be used.

(2) Inability to enter some trades of an unusual kind; in every large book there will

always be some 'specials' which seemed good trades at the time but which are in reality very costly to administer – these will invariably be long-dated deals that remain on the books long after the trader who did them has moved on to other things. How to get these trades into the system?

(3) Some aspects of the system are incomprehensibly undeveloped when it would only take four hours to do the job better on a spreadsheet.
(4) The interface that has to be built with the in-house system may take longer to build than anticipated.
(5) The senior executive in the software company that one enjoyed dealing with before the sale was made is never available, and the support staff do not have enough experience or knowledge of the market.
(6) Now that the system is in place there is increased demand from senior management for regular reports – this, together with having to become really familiar with the system, is an extra demand on time that could previously be spent on other things.
(7) The financial markets are still just as difficult to read as they were before the system arrived.

Hopefully these frustrations are all more than outweighed by having a really useful trading tool in place; if the system works well, credit can be taken for a good decision and enhanced trading performance. On the other hand, on the same basis that a workman likes to blame his tools, a system is a magnificent excuse for many things from the serious to the trivial – after all 'system down' sounds a more plausible reason for a trader in a large bank not to make a price to an important customer in a fast market than the traditional 'dealer at lunch'!

If a system has been acquired as a prelude to trading, then intensive use of it before live trading is advisable. This may reveal not only quirks of the system, but also aspects of trading and market practice of which the trader was not aware.

If a system is being used to replace another system or to move away from, for example, internal spreadsheets, a period of at least a month of parallel running must be advisable. There are any number of reasons for this, not least the lack of familiarity with the new system, but it is generally a matter of basic prudence. The system is probably being used to manage risks that will make or lose the user far more than the cost of the software licence fee, so it is better to be safe than sorry.

PITFALLS

There are many pitfalls in using a risk management system, some of which are common sense on the part of the user, some of which relate to shortcomings of the software, and some of which are less obvious. Among the more obvious are the following:

(1) *Blind belief*. The written word often carries more weight than the spoken word, and similarly a well laid-out printed report looks very final. Like any piece of

work, however, it needs careful checking for input errors, for plausibility etc.

An extreme example of blind belief in a system was that of a bank trader who quoted a cap price off a demonstration copy of OBERON immediately after it had been installed and without even checking his volatility tables. Our chief programmer was horrified.

(2) *Accuracy of input.* If there is not extremely careful control of trade input and ongoing maintenance of close-outs, rate fixings and other settlements, risk management reports are dangerous pieces of paper. The example given earlier of a US$100 million swap being entered the wrong way round is an extreme example, but it is equally clear that a much smaller input error could render a hedge equivalent report useless since decisions would be made using the wrong facts.

(3) *Failure to take back-ups.* One of the more frustrating experiences of running a software company is having to help out a customer who has failed to make back-up copies of the vital records generated by a system that his bank or company is using for P&L purposes. Reality is that hard disks do fail and that data corruption can occur; failure to take back-ups is therefore a very basic failure in internal control. The software company is very definitely not responsible for this!

(4) *Preparation and training.* A good and well-developed risk management system is likely to have well over ten man years of programming effort in it, and is therefore likely to require appreciable preparation to become familiar with. It is not reasonable or sensible to expect even the most talented of back office or middle office staff to become familiar with a system in the course of inputting the first 50 live trades.

COVER

When we take out house insurance, it is not because we expect or wish to see the building burnt down or the contents stolen, but rather as a precaution in case this should happen. Similar contingency planning is at the very least prudent for a risk management system. Already mentioned above is the need to take regular back-ups of data, but there are numerous other issues which need to be carefully addressed. Careful planning of this kind invariably takes time but it could save a great deal of time and money later. Much of this is a matter of common sense and contingency planning in case equipment breaks down. The following is an initial check-list of what could go wrong, with a possible solution in each case:

(1) *Hard disk failure.* As discussed above it is vital to take regular back-ups of important data.

(2) *Network failure.* If all the risk management software is on a network and there is a network problem, then no-one will be able to use it. If a back-up copy of the software has been kept on a local drive, then at least the system can be used – even if only on a stand-alone PC.

(3) *Off-site back-up.* However diligently a back-up procedure is followed, this would

be useless in the case of fire or theft; the back-up should therefore be stored in a fireproof location – ideally away from the computer from which the back-up was made.

(4) *Software problem with risk management system.* It is a reality of life that a very big system is unlikely to be completely perfect or bug-free – given the speed at which the financial markets evolve and the timeframe in which a product has to be developed. However much testing goes into a software release, some bugs will still slip through the net – unless timescales for delivery are substantially extended which is normally unacceptable to users. While developing OBERON this author has heard major complaints about every one of the other leading systems in the market – including all of those that stress quality control and reliability in their advertising! Quality control, together with accurate estimation of time to complete a task, are the two hardest parts of software development – and the easiest for amateurs to under-estimate.

There are a number of ways in which software may cause problems, and it is worth analysing these. They divide into four main categories namely:

- Methodology.
- Bugs (errors in coding).
- Limitations (e.g. memory or database problems with a long trade or with too many trades).
- Implementation of new versions.

(1) *Methodology.* One of the first things to do when evaluating a software system is to check that the methodology used for pricing, valuation and hedging is acceptable. If it is different from that used internally then a commercial decision has to be taken as to whether those differences matter. Obviously the existence of a difference does not necessarily imply a defect in the software; sometimes the system may be an improvement on current internal methodology. Usually, however, such differences have profit and loss implications which have to be explained to a number of colleagues.

If the methodology is slightly different, there are really only three options, namely:

- Live with the new methodology.
- Persuade the software company to change it.
- Pay the software company to adapt it.

If the methodology is simply wrong, then the software company can usually be expected to change it – but a user's idea of the time it should take to do this may often be a considerable under-estimate.

(2) *Bugs.* Bugs (which are basically errors in a programmer's logic) can be graded on a scale of 1 to 10 in terms of seriousness. Some bugs (usually the minority) will prevent use of the system altogether while others are more like a typing mistake in a letter – annoying but usually not critical. The former type of bug can be

expected to get a software company's immediate attention while the latter will probably be recorded and rectified in a later release.

A large number of bugs can be 'got round' by an experienced user of a system, and a good customer support manager in a software company can be invaluable in giving this kind of hint. Other bugs can only be rectified by changing the source code, and a helpful software company will endeavour to send the new program as quickly as possible. It is then a matter of internal policy whether or not to accept the upgrade.

Bugs are a fact of life in software development – however much we try to minimise their incidence, no software company will give a warranty that its software is bug free. My advice to a user of a large software system wanting maximum support from a software company would be as follows:

- Report all bugs as soon as possible after they arise, whether major or minor.
- Try and report bugs by fax; hard copy is more likely to be copied to all the relevant people.
- Give as much detailed information as possible about how a problem arose and attach supporting evidence if possible; if the software company cannot replicate the problem it may not be able to help.
- Ask for confirmation of whether the software company agrees that this is a bug rather than a user error.
- Keep a central record of bugs reported; check whether they have been fixed in future releases of the software.

(3) *Limitations.* All systems have limitations – the question is whether a user is likely to find these a problem in practice. Some limitations are self-imposed, while others are more fundamental. As an example of the former, we decided arbitrarily while building OBERON that no user was likely to run more than 200 different trading books (in practice most banks would not run more than 10–20 different books in a derivative trading area). Over a year after releasing the software we found to our surprise that one of our customers needed to maintain more than 250 books owing to the way in which he was maintaining client accounts. This was quite easy to change, and OBERON's maximum number of books is now 500. As an example of more fundamental limitations in systems, the architecture of a computer or of a database can impose constraints that it is difficult or impossible to get around. For example any program written in a DOS environment came up against major problems with the 640 KB memory constraint until more ways became available of using the full memory of a 386 machine. Some databases may have a maximum number of records or a maximum record length – these are not really problems that a user wants to know about, but if they are causing a software developer problems this will soon show up in limited functionality or in delays in software releases.

(4) *Implementation of new versions.* Production of a new software release will often have involved several man years' work on the part of the software developer, and

there will often have been considerable change to the code. Usually a new release will have new functionality and various bugs will have been fixed.

Because of the modular construction of source code one change in a central library routine (for example to do with date handling) can have knock-on effects in the whole of a system. The disturbing effect of this in software development is that features that have worked reliably for a long time and which from a 'menu' point of view appear not to have changed at all may suddenly no longer work properly. This is one of the less exciting aspects of testing software but it is very important – it is notably foolish only to test new features without going back over the ones that worked before. A staggering article that this author read recently stated that only around 60 per cent of program changes to large software systems worked correctly first time because of the knock-on effects of program changes causing changes in unforeseen places. Of course the vast majority of errors are detected internally and never released to users, but it is worth reflecting that if it is really true that 40 per cent of changes cause errors then mathematically it follows that even after four complete cycles of testing there will still be bugs in 2.56 per cent of all changes made. It certainly pays a user to be aware of the problem in terms of how willingly to install a new release of software.

It can probably be safely assumed that all software companies perform extensive testing of new releases – after all their credibility depends on this long term. It cannot, however, be assumed that this testing will remove all bugs, and a statistical case can be made for stating that this is in fact highly unlikely. If time permits, the user's solution must therefore be to submit a new software release to a period of parallel running against the former release. All too often users are unwilling to find time to do this or may lack the memory on their computers to store both releases at the same time. If it is possible to find the time, however, it is definitely a prudent step to take, and the user running a trading desk should absolutely insist on this.

Lastly it is worth reflecting on what one would do if the risk management system were inoperable for several days – for whatever reason. The answer probably depends on the scale of business being managed on the system. If a bank regularly runs 2000 futures lot equivalent open positions in derivatives, then a 5 tick move in futures will make or lose US$250,000. Having a second risk management system in place as a back-up (whether an internal or external system) could well be cheap compared with the risk of not knowing one's position for several hours let alone days.

CONTROL

Most well-run trading operations are quite tightly controlled, even if traders are able to take big risks. Traders operate within established counterparty and position limits. In most banks in London or New York, even a senior trader would not be allowed to sign a counterparty confirmation nor to settle his own trade. Similarly, on the systems front, there are several basic controls that it is usual and prudent to put into place. Many would apply just as much if a manual system were used. These controls include the following:

- Separation of front and back office functions. With a system this can either be achieved with two independent databases or with different levels of security access in a network environment.
- Restriction of individuals' ability to perform various functions; e.g. if a system is used in a bank's front office by the marketing desk, the traders are unlikely to want the marketing team to be able to update their market price and volatility data.
- Daily checks on details of all trades entered and other events such as fixings or expiries.
- Investigation of reasons for any amendments to trade details or deletions of trades.
- Daily print-out of all market prices and volatility data used in arriving at P&L.
- Verifying that market data input into the system is consistent with market prices. For instance most treasury managers have little intuitive feel for volatility levels; relying on a trader's assessment of volatility can allow bad positions to be run for much longer than stop-loss limits would allow. Random monitoring of market prices calculated from volatility input is an important check that a trader is not falsifying his option P&L.
- Reconciliation of P&L and main risk parameters between one release of software and the next, and a full explanation of any differences.
- Daily trade by trade reconciliation of P&L and main risk parameters against previous day's figures.
- Daily back-up (as mentioned above).
- Check confirmation generated and sent for every trade, fixing or other event.
- Daily diaries of forthcoming fixings, option expiries etc. Missing an option expiry which is in the money is one of the worst mistakes that can be made in the option business if the option is not settled automatically according to a reference rate.
- Daily limit excess reports.

8: The Future of Risk Management

Martyn Holmes and Chris Painter

The London Clearing House Ltd (LCH) acts as central futures and options counterparty to the Clearing Members of London's derivatives exchanges. The responsibility and complexity of this role have made LCH closely examine the nature of the risks it faces. They have concluded that statistical techniques do not adequately encompass the complexity of the risk management problem. This has led to a search for alternative risk management techniques. These investigations have proved justified and resulted in the development of a prototype risk management system using logical techniques. The system was developed by Enigma Systems for LCH and has been fully incorporated into clearing house risk management operations. LCH has now committed itself to the development of a system extension.

The purpose of this chapter is to describe observations made in the course of the project regarding the nature of risk, the adequacy of existing risk management techniques and how existing risk management limitations can be more fully addressed with the use of logical techniques. The second part of the chapter provides an insight into the technology behind these new techniques, the tools and benefits they provide and the future impact this will have. Logical techniques will remain an important area of research and look set to create a new direction for risk management.

In analysing the nature of risk we need to recognise that risk is an inherent part of our environment. We live in an uncertain world where future events cannot be predicted. This applies as much to weather prediction as to the future direction of financial markets or the long-term creditworthiness of counterparties. Quite simply, there are no magic formulae or perfect answers. This non-predictability applies whether we are referring to earthquakes, civil wars or football matches. The notion that the future can be predicted with certainty, as assumed in the log-normal distributions of option pricing modelling, is misleading. In the real world, we are forced to judge the future based on our present knowledge even if this is far from perfect.

Risk assessment focuses on identifying potential pitfalls and assessing their seriousness. It is a qualitative judgment, without a perfect answer. Judging market liquidity prior to executing an arbitrage trade involves using one's market experience together with an assessment of current market conditions to judge whether an order can be executed at the desired price. The final decision is qualitative. Numbers are important in the risk assessment process, but at a relatively low level. For example, balance sheet ratios are used in credit analysis to assess the financial quality of a company, but are combined at a higher level with other qualitative judgements, such as quality of management, off-balance sheet risks and political risk, to produce an overall assessment of credit quality.

Risk is more about the possible than the probable. Risk assessment requires an ability to view the entire spectrum of possible outcomes from a given situation. It is frequently the more obscure risks which cause the greatest problems, simply because most people remain unaware of them. The Polly Peck share suspension highlighted an options liquidity risk that was not obvious at first sight, but which proved critical for those locked into positions. Similarly, the surprise timing of the UK government's decision to join ERM upset money markets and LIFFE's Short Sterling Contract, leading to a period of high interest rate volatility. This reiterates the point that an ability to take a lateral view is critical in risk assessment. This was shown particularly clearly in the case of Eagle Trust, where an acquisition during 1989 at an initial cost of only £86,000 resulted in costs of £33 million from an off-balance sheet exposure and the bankruptcy of the company.

Financial risk managers have considerable economic responsibility and need to understand more about the risks they face. Not only must financiers achieve adequate returns on the capital they employ, but must ensure that the quality of the financial system is maintained. The value of good risk assessment is particularly high, as has been shown by the UK secondary banking crisis in 1974, the Third World banking crisis in the early eighties and the large corporate loan write-offs during the 1990/1991 recession.

Risk tends to emanate from sources of uncertainty and impact related bodies. This can be described as a causal chain. For example, the warming in East–West relations could signal an economic downturn for the defence industry, or alternatively, a failure of General Agreement on Tariffs and Trade (GATT) talks could lead to a slump in profits for multinational trading companies. Investigating the nature of these linkages is an important step towards more fully understanding risk. We intuitively know that the set of parameters driving risk varies over time as shown by the temporary impact of the Gulf War, speculation over the timing of the election and the impact of German Reunification.

Existing statistical risk management techniques, such as option pricing modelling, fail to capture the qualitative complexity of risk. These numerical techniques were introduced in the infancy of options markets, when market conditions were relatively stable, few related instruments existed and trading volumes were considerably lower. Statistical techniques provided a rudimentary means of understanding the option pricing relationships in this new world, including the impact of changes in underlying price, volatility and time to expiry. This lack of flexibility forced unrealistic assumptions to be made and the validity of statistical techniques to be limited. Option pricing assumptions include that markets should be perfectly efficient and are therefore without transaction costs, options can be priced solely with reference to the underlying security and the future returns distribution for the underlying instrument is stochastic. These assumptions are not valid in the real world. Traders intuitively know that pricing models must be viewed with scepticism, particularly during volatile market conditions. This was demonstrated during the period immediately prior to the takeover bid for Consolidated Goldfields plc by Minorco, when takeover bid speculation (and therefore the prospect of an upward jump in share price) led to out-of-the-money call options trading at extremely high premiums. Assumptions of market continuity and zero rehedging costs were incorrect, meaning that options provided a unique non-replicable form of convexity, making their limited loss, unlimited profit characteristics particularly attractive.

Statistical techniques miss the point. The notion of the perfect option price is not valid, the world is simply neither stable nor predictable and the search for the perfect pricing model is a fruitless one. Statistical techniques show symptoms, they do not explain the underlying causal relationships behind the risks we face. They are advanced score-keeping techniques and do not address the underlying risk relationships that drive the symptoms. An example of this was the dismissal of Mr George Walker from his position as Chief Executive of Brent Walker plc. The 7p rise in the Brent Walker share price to 32p, following Mr Walker's dismissal was a symptom of management change, but failed to address the underlying reasons resulting in his dismissal. An informed expert is needed to identify and evaluate the qualitative patterns driving risk. In Brent Walker's case this meant assessing the impact of the change in management on the company's future strategy and the implications of greater control being passed to bankers. Hence, statistical techniques do not help us to understand the nature of risks and are far from ideal in terms of assessing and managing risk.

The usefulness of statistical risk management techniques will continue to decrease. The nature of risk faced within derivatives markets has changed considerably with the evolution of the industry over the past two decades. Deregulation and globalisation have produced an explosion in the range of derivative products available, both in terms of their individual complexity and the number of synthetic risk engineering alternatives they create. Derivatives exchanges have fuelled this product growth by introducing new products, accompanied by over-the-counter products intended to fill the gaps between the standardised exchange instruments. Globalisation has enabled firms to expand internationally and has magnified the range of counterparties available in any given market. This enhances the risk of a global domino effect, making it possible for a problem in Japan to lead to a default in Europe and a subsequent collapse in the US.

Risk managers and regulators have struggled to cope with this rapid increase in complexity, as demonstrated by the BCCI case. The statistical techniques they use have proved to be increasingly costly to operate, as information costs have grown exponentially with the geographical growth of the industry. As a result, statistical techniques have lacked the flexibility to cope with the more complex nature of risk. Their costs have increased rapidly and the validity of their output has continued to fall. An example of the failure of statistical techniques is the inability of national economic models to consistently produce accurate forecasts, despite considerable resources being made available.

New risk management techniques are required. As risks become more complex, the performance of statistical risk management techniques will continue to deteriorate. Regular losses of increasing magnitude will confirm to risk managers the need for a more innovative approach. The Crash of October 1987 highlighted to many investors and traders, the limitations of their existing approach. Portfolio insurers based their investment strategies on the assumption that markets are liquid and continuous, enabling investment portfolios to be continually rehedged as market movements occur. This, theoretically, enables synthetic call options to be constructed from a continually delta adjusted number of futures contracts, together with a money market deposit. These invalid assumptions of continuity and liquidity have been implicitly assumed in option pricing theory and were only exposed as inadequate after the Crash of 1987. The height of the Crash brought major problems as stock market, and then futures market liquidity contracted, with dislocations occurring between the cash and futures markets. This previously unforeseen liquidity risk resulted in heavy losses for portfolio insurers. October 1987 also highlighted the inadequacy of risk management procedures within certain areas of the derivatives industry, including a £3 million default by a private client writing FT-SE stock index puts on the London Traded Options Market (LTOM). This default highlighted the importance of market robustness and the need for a central counterparty with genuine risk management expertise, such as the London Clearing House Ltd. Robustness promotes investor confidence and aids the development of market liquidity, particularly where credit quality is seen as a constraining factor to the market's development. A similar central role would aid the development of liquidity in UK money markets, OTC derivatives markets and government bond repurchase markets.

Many practitioners are aware of the limitations of statistical techniques, but are unaware of the existence of alternative techniques. The world of option pricing theory is mathematically complex, with few traders possessing the technical skills to challenge its theoretical proponents, who often possess a strong self-interest in the continued usage of these techniques. This has resulted in extensive statistical research which has focused on the modification of existing models rather than seeking valid alternatives to existing statistical techniques.

Alternative techniques must enable risk to be understood more fully. In searching for alternative techniques, it is important to think carefully about the risk management benefits required. Risk can be conceptualised as a complex and dynamic domino effect with causal chains linking sources of uncertainty to bodies impacted by these uncertainties, which may themselves drive risk elsewhere. This can be illustrated by the announcement of a forthcoming privatisation which attracts funds away from building societies, thereby delaying mortgage rate cuts, with a consequent knock-on effect on the property market. The previous example of a complex global web of credit risk resulting from the globalisation of derivative markets communicates the concept of real world risk as being highly inter-related in nature. We need to understand more about the nature of these causal chains and identify which factors drive the risk. These factors are not exact or permanent in nature and vary over a period of time. For example, the Gulf War had a strong short-term impact on risk, which rapidly subsided with the onset of peace. We need to more systematically understand the qualitative patterns that drive risk. This will inevitably force us to formalise more of our own expertise and closely analyse our own perception of risk.

The complex qualitative nature of risk, together with the increasingly limited validity of statistical techniques make it clear that current approaches need to be reviewed. The future of risk management is likely to be driven by techniques more closely linked to the true nature of risk. The implementation of such techniques will ensure that the risk manager comprehends the causal relationships underlying risk, leaving him less vulnerable to the unforeseen and more able to identify and control areas of risk in the future.

Appendix: Credit Implications for Firms That Use Derivatives

The boom in risk management products known as derivatives is becoming one of the most significant financial market developments of the 1990s. As Moody's reported in another Special Comment earlier this year ('Securities Derivatives: Risk and Opportunities' of 16 January 1991) business strategies involving derivative products have important implications for the credit quality of providers. This comment explores the potential consequences – some negative and some positive – for the credit health of users of derivatives – including banks, securities firms, and non-financial companies globally.

WHAT ARE DERIVATIVES?

Derivatives refer to a widening assortment of options and futures, and instruments that have option- and/or future-like characteristics. Examples include warrants, swaps, swaptions, forward-rate agreements (FRAs), collars, caps and floors. Derivatives can be stand-alone (such as an option on a basket of stocks) or imbedded in another instrument (such as a callable bond, or a bond whose redemption value changes depending on fluctuations in foreign exchange rates).

Derivatives tend to fall into four families:

(1) Interest rate.
(2) Equity.
(3) Foreign exchange.
(4) Commodities.

In addition, derivatives markets exist on real estate, freight areas, and a host of other underlying items. However, there is much mixing and matching, and a particular position could comprise several types of derivatives on more than one underlying instrument. An example of this would be a 'swaption' (an option on a swap) on a so-called CIRCUS swap (a combined interest-rate and currency swap). It is this flexibility that helps to make derivatives so useful to risk managers.

RISK AND OPPORTUNITIES OF DERIVATIVES FOR PROVIDERS AND INTERMEDIARIES

On the positive side, derivatives are key products for providers and intermediaries (which are mainly securities firms and banks) not only because they are often highly profitable in and of themselves, but also because they are in heavy demand from clients, and they are vital to these firms' core underwriting, trading, asset management, and asset/liability management activities.

On the negative side, there are several points to consider for providers and intermediaries:

- The increasing number of derivatives market participants, and the maturation of some products, are squeezing margins.
- The complexity of derivatives makes their analysis and management difficult.
- The substantial market risks inherent in many derivatives can lead to large, sudden losses – particularly if management controls are weak.
- Credit risks are expanding. This reflects two facts: that more and more derivatives these participants write and trade are long-term in nature – often not maturing for many years – and that counterparties tend to be other corporations, not just clearing units of securities exchanges. Such corporations can have weak and fluctuating credit standings.
- Principal activities in derivatives are a use of a firm's credit capacity. This use can affect a firm's ability to place its debt, potentially resulting in greater funding risks.
- The legal aspects of derivatives are often not well defined, reflective of the rapid growth and development of derivatives.
- Regulation is still in an early stage. New or altered regulations could adversely affect previously existing derivatives positions.
- The liquidity of many derivatives is not particularly good, thus decreasing participants' overall liquidity. Also, illiquidity makes marking-to-market – a key component of risk management – more difficult and judgmental.

The following examples demonstrate the risk of derivatives for such participants:

Merrill Lynch: Complex Derivative-Linked Securities

During 1987, Merrill Lynch & Co., Inc., the US securities broker/dealer, incurred gross trading losses of $377 million on certain principal-only (PO) mortgage-backed security positions and related hedges. The losses were caused by unauthorised trading activity and market volatility. The problems were related to fears of slower prepayments of POs caused by rising interest rates, which significantly reduced the market value of the POs. The lack of appropriate hedges against the PO positions exacerbated these losses. Subsequent to this event, Merrill's trading risk controls were reviewed and tightened.

Bank of New England: Foreign Exchange and Interest-Rate Derivatives

In early 1990, as Bank of New England (BNE) was sliding to insolvency due to asset quality problems, the bank was faced with managing – and ultimately unwinding – about $30 billion in foreign exchange and interest-rate derivatives. Doing so, however, became extremely difficult because counterparties, worried about BNE's sometime problems, often did not want to do business with the bank, thus impairing its ability to take offsetting positions. Also, unwinding certain positions sometimes created interest-rate or foreign exchange exposures that became hard to control, again because of counterparty hesitancy. Furthermore, use of futures exchanges to hedge these exposures was problematic: the sizes of trades BNE sometimes needed were so large that there was often inadequate liquidity, which caused prices to move. BNE eventually unwound most of its book, and even earned a small profit due to favourable market movements.

Risks and Opportunities of Derivatives for Ultimate Users

For many of the same reasons, derivatives products also present substantial opportunities and potential risks to firms that use them. Among the major users of derivatives are financial institutions themselves – for example, banks and securities firms that use them to hedge their portfolios of securities held to meet client needs, or to manage interest-rate risks in loan portfolios. Major institutional investors, such as insurance companies and pension funds, are increasingly using derivatives products (such as stock-index or interest-rate options) to improve investment returns, to diversify investment opportunities, and as hedging devices in sophisticated portfolio management techniques. This financial institutions sector includes a large portion of derivatives users. Such institutions often have a sophisticated understanding of the products they are using, and are prudent in their use and management of derivatives products. However, risks remain, as the examples below show.

Société des Bourses Françaises: Financial Futures

In the aftermath of the stock market crash in 1987, the Société des Bourses Françaises (SBF) lost over FF600 million due to speculative financial futures trading on the Matif with the assets of the SBF's reserve fund. The loss reduced the SBF's reserve fund by about one third. The reserve fund's role is to support member securities firms which incur unexpected and heavy losses. The future losses occurred as SBF sold contracts short while the market fell. The SBF was then caught when prices turned sharply higher. The SBF subsequently obtained a FF650 million injection to replenish its reserve fund.

US Thrifts: Risk-Controlled Arbitrage

Many US thrifts were active users of derivatives in so-called risk-controlled arbitrage during the 1980s. In general, risk-controlled arbitrage entailed buying complex mortgage-backed or other securities, and trying to lock in funding costs by hedging interest-rate risks by using derivatives like caps and swaps. The bulk of these risk-controlled arbitrages failed to work – sometimes spectacularly – because of poor analysis, weak management, gyrating markets, and other factors. Many thrifts were driven to insolvency because of their activities in this area. Although the final reckoning has not yet been made, most likely billions of dollars in losses will eventually be incurred from these ill-fated derivatives-linked ventures.

Non-financial firms, such as industrial companies, service firms, mining concerns, utilities and municipal authorities are also increasingly active users of derivatives, as these examples demonstrate:

- A car maker planning to build an assembly plant buys interest-rate options to help lock in its financing costs prior to the actual borrowing.
- A utility issues floating-rate foreign currency bonds because of attractive market conditions, and enters into a CIRCUS (combined interest-rate and currency) swap to lock in its financing costs.
- A mining company sells gold (or copper, or lead, or palladium) forward to take advantage of today's attractive forward prices, thus helping it to manage its revenues.
- An airline buys long-dated, out-of-the-money options or petroleum to help it guard against a spike in jet fuel prices.
- A consulting firm with global operations enters into diverse foreign exchange forward, futures, and/or options contracts to help it avoid fluctuations in exchange rates that would adversely affect its revenues and costs as denominated in its base currency.

As is clear from these examples, derivatives are potentially powerful tools to help firms manage financial and business risks. In so far as firms are able to utilise them prudently and effectively for these purposes, derivatives can contribute to users' financial stability – a positive factor for their credit quality.

However, poor controls, inadequate analysis, and weak counterparty creditworthiness – to name but a few problems – can not only eliminate the benefits of derivatives, but can also create difficulties that did not exist before. The following case histories demonstrate this risk.

Allied-Lyons: Foreign Exchange

During fiscal 1991, Allied-Lyons Plc, a British drinks and food group, incurred losses of £147 million trading in foreign exchange derivatives. In mid-1989, Allied-Lyons's treasury unit expanded its foreign exchange hedging activities, including the writing of foreign currency options. During 1990, the scale of options trading grew substantially beyond the company's foreign currency cash flows. These developments occurred without the knowledge or authorisation of Allied-Lyons's board. In March 1991, during the annual audit, the chairman of Allied-Lyons instructed National Westminster Bank to close out the positions in order to prevent even more losses.

Local Authorities in the United Kingdom: Interest-Rate Swaps

About 130 local authorities in the United Kingdom entered into interest-rate swaps throughout the 1980s to manage their borrowing costs. As interest rates rose towards the end of the decade, one such authority – Hammersmith and Fulham – incurred substantial losses on its swap transactions. Hammersmith and Fulham's exposure to swaps went well beyond its own debt levels, suggesting speculation or poor controls. On 24 January 1991, the House of Lords, Great Britain's highest court of appeal, ruled that the use of swaps by local authorities was *ultra vires*, and that all such transactions were null and void. This ruling left the local authorities' counterparties with potential losses on their swap transactions of around £600 million.

Klöckner & Co.: Commodities

During 1988, Klöckner & Co. KGaA, a German commodities trading company, lost almost DM700 million in international crude oil trading. Klöckner was a party to several crude oil forward contracts with Gatoil Overseas Inc., which had been concluded without the knowledge of senior management. Klöckner was responsible for the settlement of the forward contracts in its own name – at the risk of Gatoil Overseas against payment of a commission – as a result of these unauthorised transactions. When faced with falling oil prices, Gatoil Overseas refused to fulfil its end of the agreements. Klöckner thus found itself in a situation where it was the sole counterparty in the transactions, without any opportunity for recourse. The loss represented more than half of Klöckner's subscribed capital. Klöckner subsequently obtained an equity injection from Deutsche Bank in order to replenish its capital and provide liquidity.

Tateho Chemical Industries: Zaitech

During 1987 Tateho Chemical Industries Co. Ltd, a medium-sized Japanese firm, incurred a loss of about Y20 billion due to speculative investments in futures on Japanese Government bonds. The loss represented the bulk of the company's book equity. Tateho employees apparently speculated in bonds via futures in anticipation of a market upswing, without the approval of the senior management. The losses occurred mainly between May and August of 1987 because of a sharp drop in Japanese Government bond prices.

Japanese Industrial Firms: Option-linked Bonds

Many Japanese industrial firms issued billions of dollars of bonds in the Euromarkets with put options, attached equity warrants, or convertible into company stock. Changing financial circumstances, including the fall in Japanese equity prices, have often resulted in these bonds being put back on the issuing firms, maturing without the warrants being exercised, or maturing without being converted. Such conversion or exercise was supposed to have paid off the bonds. Because of these events, many firms are facing substantial refinancing challenges.

Therefore, the implications for users from employing derivatives must be understood in order to gauge properly users' creditworthiness. The main issues are as follows:

- Derivatives sometimes contain substantial market, management, legal, regulatory, liquidity, and credit risks that can result in significant losses to users.
- Derivatives can increase the 'surprise' factor in users' profits. As shown, losses can be sudden and substantial.
- Derivatives generally decrease the transparency of users' financial statements. Current accounting rules do a poor job of capturing the real risks of derivatives.
- Users' risk profiles can be enormously shifted in minutes. Thus, even an accurate analysis of a user's risk profile may have a short lifespan.
- Derivatives can be used as speculative gambles despite public assertions that they are risk-reducing hedges.
- Derivatives can also cause managements to take greater risks because of the perceived ability of derivatives to control the risk. Thus, if a derivatives position goes bad, the problem it exposes could be bigger than it might have otherwise been.

ACCOUNTING RULES FOR DERIVATIVES

United States

In response to the rapidly increasing use and development of derivative instruments and the lack of disclosure with respect to the risks involved in such instruments, the Financial Accounting Standards Board recently issued Statement of Financial Accounting Standards (SFAS) No. 106, 'Disclosure of Information about Financial Instruments with Off-Balance-Sheet Risk and Financial Instruments with Concentrations of Credit Risk'. SFAS No. 105 requires companies to disclose in their financial statements the following information about financial instruments with off-balance sheet risk:

- the face, contract or notional principal amount:
- the nature and terms of the instruments, including a discussion of credit and market risks, the related accounting policy, and the cash requirements;
- the amount of accounting loss that would be incurred if any party to the financial instrument failed completely to perform according to the terms of the contract and if all collateral proved to be worthless;
- collateral policies.

Although SFAS No. 105 improves disclosure of derivative and other off-balance-sheet risks somewhat, these risks are disclosed only annually. Also, many important risks are not covered, such as risks stemming from poor controls.

Europe

Disclosure requirements in major European countries are vague. Disclosure of risks associated with derivative instruments is mostly voluntary. For example, while provisions for derivative-based losses can be made, disclosure is mandatory only where losses are material and reasonably certain. This situation leaves much ambiguity with respect to the actual risk profile of a company's derivatives activities, particularly where those activities form an important part of the company's risk management. In practice, few firms disclose much about their derivatives activity, and what is said is often not very useful.

Japan

In May 1990, the Financial Accounting Deliberation Council issued an opinion recommending that companies disclose unrealised gains or losses from investment securities, options and futures in their financial statements (such as the *yuka shoken hokokusho*). Other relevant bodies have also issued directives on derivatives disclosure. Although such disclosure is helpful, it still falls short of providing timely and relevant analysis of the full range of risks of derivatives.

KEY RISKS OF DERIVATIVES

Market Risk

Derivatives' values are often highly sensitive to changes in the values of the underlying instrument, such as petroleum prices or interest rates. This characteristic means that firms that use – and especially firms that write – derivatives are vulnerable to market price swings. For example, a firm that writes foreign exchange options to hedge

foreign exchange risks technically has an unlimited market risk exposure on the derivative. Also, if a derivative is used to hedge a potential risk that does not eventually occur, the derivative position could have to be closed out at a large loss because of unusual price movements.
One specific problem that can arise is the so-called 'fallacy of composition'. For example, a complex risk management situation, such as a sterling-based mining firm trying to hedge future price movements in US dollar-denominated gold being mined in Canada, is generally hedged by breaking it down into its component parts, and then hedging all of the parts. However, this strategy may not work because the presumption of additivity – that the total is the sum of its parts – may not hold. The risk situation, in total, could perform differently from the individual performances of its components because of interactions among the component parts.
Another market risk issue is the valuation of derivatives, which is often a difficult process because of derivatives' arcane and customised nature. One cannot simply look up most derivatives' prices in the newspaper. Because of this situation, many prices of derivatives are interpolated using a price grid (for example, of the dealer quotes on five- and seven-year interest-rate swaps, the middle value is used to price the six-year swap being entered into), or by computing the price as determined by financial theory. This presumes that the theory is correct, and that all of the necessary components of the derivative being priced have been identified and factored in. To the extent that derivatives are mispriced, a firm's financial statements and risk-management policies may be wrong.

Management Risk

The complexity of derivatives makes it challenging for managers to understand and to keep track of what is going on. Thus, there is a premium on risk management. Most of the big losses – and near misses – in the derivatives markets have been at least partially caused by failures in management oversight. Not only are derivatives' risks difficult to figure out from a purely conceptual viewpoint, but monitoring the activity can be cumbersome. For example, analytical systems may not be integrated so that a manager can easily understand the aggregate risks of a position. Furthermore, particularly for leading-edge derivative products, there may be no formal analytical or tracking systems at all, records may be *ad hoc*, and the manager or auditor may be at a loss about what is going on.

Furthermore, the complexity of derivatives, in and of itself, can make risk management more difficult, even if everything is properly specified, priced, and analysed. One reason for this is that, for example, hedging a particular risk situation may require the use of several cash-market instruments and/or derivatives because of the situation's complexity. Should the hedge not be put on all at once, the ability of the user to get all of the pieces of the hedge in place later on, at the prices hoped, may be frustrated. Also, putting a few (but not all) of the parts of the hedge in place could make the aggregate position even riskier than the position would have been without any hedge at all. In the case just described, prudently controlling the position's market risk may mean hedging the hedge itself until all of the components of the hedge are in place, which can also be difficult.

Credit Risk

Many counterparties are other firms – especially securities firms and banks – and not just the clearing corporations of exchanges, as was true a number of years ago. Thus, users are faced with greater credit risks. Also, the credit quality of these counterparties can deteriorate. Losses stemming from counterparty failure can vary widely. For example, a counterparty that fails to honour a deep-in-the-money option may generate a large loss for the user, but if it were a deep-out-of-the-money option, the loss could be small. The market volatility of derivative also means that credit exposures can swing widely in a short period of time, making credit risk management difficult.

Legal Risk

In some cases, the development of derivatives has outpaced the evolution of laws regarding how the derivatives will be treated if the counterparty defaults, although things are clearer than they were a few years ago. Also, firms may find out after the fact that some of their counterparties were not legally permitted to enter into certain transactions, as the case of swaps with British local authorities showed. Given the likelihood of continued derivative-product development, this legal risk will probably continue for some time. Prudent firms control this risk by careful documentation that specifies the rights and obligations of all parties, as well as the jurisdiction under which disputes will be settled. Legal opinions on the legal, valid, and binding nature of the contract can also be helpful.

Furthermore, the ranking of derivatives in the event of a counterparty's insolvency can vary depending on the kind of derivative it is, the nationality and type of the counterparty, and other factors. Derivatives are often classified as executory contracts, which can be treated as subordinated claims.

Regulatory Risk

Some issuers of derivatives are regulated: others are not. To the extent that an issue is regulated, the user may take some comfort that the entity's overall creditworthiness could be supported. However, regulators can turn certain derivatives into junior claims in some cases. In addition, regulators around the world are becoming more interested in derivatives, and they could eventually alter or impose new regulations, which could adversely affect counterparties' performance capacities in the derivative markets.

Liquidity Risk

The secondary market liquidity of derivatives varies, depending on the type and tenor of the derivative. As a general statement, the more arcane, customised and long-term the derivative, the less liquid it is. This frequent lack of deep, liquid secondary markets for many derivatives can decrease users' overall liquidity, thus boosting risk levels by making it more difficult to get out of the derivative. To the extent that the derivatives business becomes concentrated in a few major counterparties, liquidity could be reduced further. Illiquid derivatives positions are also harder to value accurately. Prudent firms partially address this liquidity issue by taking conservative marks.

ANALYTICAL CHECKLIST

The following checklist is a sample of the questions Moody's analysts pose in order to assess the risks stemming from companies' expanding use of derivatives.

(1) *What is your overall management philosophy regarding derivatives? Can you provide any examples?*
This question is designed to determine the firm's broad views. To the extent that no examples, or examples that are inconsistent with the stated philosophy, are given, it can be a warning of inadequate oversight and controls.

(2) *What derivatives do you use? In what capacity? For how long?*
The purpose of this question is to gauge the activity level and scope of a user.

(3) *How do you analyse, monitor and control the risks of derivatives?*
- market
- management
- legal
- regulatory
- liquidity
- credit

This broad question helps Moody's to understand whether the firm has thought about these issues at all, and if so, the diligence, sophistication and conservatism with which it has addressed them.

(4) *Have any losses been incurred from your derivatives activity? Can you describe them?*
The answer to this question can provide valuable insights into a firm's control, audit and analytical competence, as well as its risk appetite.

(5) *What is the role of your internal and external auditors?*
This helps Moody's determine whether there are independent checks on the firm's derivatives activity.

(6) *How do you separate duties – e.g., dealing, analysis, confirmation, settlement and monitoring?*
Here we are trying to determine whether there are fundamental cross-checks and controls inherent in the derivatives effort.

(7) *What is the firm's performance management system? How does it work?*
This is a key question. Derivatives are used because they are supposed to do something. A good performance measurement system can determine whether, in fact, the derivatives are performing as planned. If they are not, it is a signal for management to investigate why.

(8) *What is the role of your board of directors?*
Here we are trying to find out if the ultimate stewards of the firm have approved of and are monitoring what is going on.

(9) *Is the treasury area a profit centre?*
Corporations' treasury areas, in which derivatives are generally managed, are often profit centres. As such, there could be incentives to take undue risks, or to enter into trades outside of policy guidelines in order to generate returns.

(10) *What training does the staff have in the analysis and use of derivatives?*
Here the goal is to determine the skills and competence of front-line personnel.

(11) *Who is authorised to execute trades?*
This question is meant to determine the seniority of people who actually commit the firm's capital.

(12) *What are the rating standards for derivatives' counterparties?*
The answer to this question helps Moody's to determine the firm's credit risk exposures.

(13) *How does the firm's 'back office' handle derivatives?*
Derivatives are complex, and a strong back office is needed to maintain control.

(14) *What is the process for approving a new derivative?*
Going through this process can provide a good overview of a firm's analytical and risk control methods.

Index

The following titles in the *Finance and Capital Markets* Series are also published by Macmillan:

Options Explained ISBN 0-333-56911-3

A hands-on guide to options, concentrating on theoretical concepts essential to applying options on a wide variety of assets. Coverage includes pricing and alternative formulae together with an analysis of put-call parity and how the investor can manage risk most effectively.

December 1991 £75

Bund Options ISBN 0-333-56910-5

A comprehensive and practical introduction to these new and active markets, offering an analysis of basics, pricing, trading, hedging and risk management.

December 1991 £75

Off Balance Sheet Finance ISBN 0-333-56041-8

Written in the light of the Accounting Standards Board, this book discusses the various financing practices which have grown up over recent years and explains how they will be affected by the new accounting standard being developed by the ASB. It will provide an expert analysis of the accounting rules which will govern the treatment of off balance sheet finance when the standard comes into force.

January 1993 £95